SEAPORTS OF INDIA AND CEYLON

Allister Macmillan

SEAPORTS OF INDIA AND CEYLON

BY

ALLISTER MACMILLAN

GYAN

Published by

Gyan Publishing House
5, Ansari Road
Daryaganj, New Delhi-110002
Phone: 011-47034999, 9811692060
E-mail: books@gyanbooks.com

Distribution Network
gyanbooks.com
India, USA, Canada, UK, Australia, France

ISBN : 978-81-212-3985-1 (PB)
First Published, 1928, London

2nd Impression 2020

Printed at: Gyan Press, Delhi.

Seaports
of
India & Ceylon

Reader, let this little taste that I have given thee of the Summer Ilands satisfie thee for the present: ere it be long thou shalt have a larger relation thereof. Hastie ocasione of business doth make mee write somewhat hastilie, and leave out many things which were fitte to be spoken of: wherefore against my will I am forced to leave my worke, which I have begunne, before I come into the middest of it: but I hope it will suffice you that are my friends to passe it over in the best manner you can, for there is much broken English of it and badly penned: regard I pray you the matter not the manner, the truth of the storie not the stile.

Jourdan, 1613.

SEAPORTS OF INDIA & CEYLON

HISTORICAL AND DESCRIPTIVE
COMMERCIAL AND INDUSTRIAL
FACTS, FIGURES, & RESOURCES

COMPILED AND EDITED BY ALLISTER MACMILLAN, F.R.G.S.

1928.

W. H. & L. COLLINGRIDGE, 148 & 149, ALDERSGATE STREET,
LONDON, E.C.1.

PREFACE

THE bibliography of the Indian Empire is vast and comprehensive, in keeping with the great history, absorbing interest, and paramount importance of that territory of 1,805,352 square miles and its remarkable medley of 320 millions of people, speaking something like 150 different languages, whose perplexing diversities in caste and creed, in condition and outlook, create problems and potentialities far beyond the demarcations of ordinary appraisement and the orthodox standards of Western comparison.

Many, too, are the books that have been written about Ceylon, the exquisitely beautiful and fertile island Crown Colony of 25,363 square miles and a population of about 5,000,000, so closely related by history and blood to the peninsula from which it is separated by only thirty-two miles of sea.

In this volume there is no attempt to deal with the political difficulties and social aspirations of the inhabitants of these wonderful portions of the British Empire. A conscientious effort has been made, however, to convey useful and interesting information regarding the seaports with which it is concerned, more especially their commercial and industrial activities. The work is the latest addition to a series of similar publications compiled by me on various parts of the world; and the appreciation with which these have been received, as well as the success they have attained, is a gratifying indication that they are of proved attraction and utility.

The time and labour necessary for a book of this description are considerable. In the compilation of the various historical and descriptive sections I am greatly indebted to the kind and capable assistance of the following gentlemen: Mr. T. E. Harris, the well-known artist, who has resided for upwards of thirty years at Calcutta; Mr. R. P. Masani, the brilliant Parsi writer and Managing Director of the Central Bank, Bombay; Mr. T. E. Grady, Sub-editor of the *Madras Mail*, Madras; Mr. Gordon M. Dyce-Keele, Editor of the *Daily Gazette*, Karachi; Mr. J. J. Nolan, F.R.G.S., formerly Editor of the *Rangoon Times*; Mr. L. A. Arndt, the gifted Burgher litterateur, late of St. Thomas's College, Colombo; and Mr. S. E. Hancox, B.A., retired from the Government Service of Ceylon. The articles on the business houses are the result of my own personal investigation and observation, rendered possible only by the courtesy and kindness of the principals of the firms detailed, to whom I desire to convey my heartiest thanks and appreciation. Similar expressions are likewise due to the photographers whose names appear under the various reproductions of photos supplied or taken specially by them for this volume, which, whatever its merits or demerits, can only be estimated properly by those familiar with the peculiar difficulties inseparable from the specialised character of the undertaking.

Allister Macmillan

PREFACE

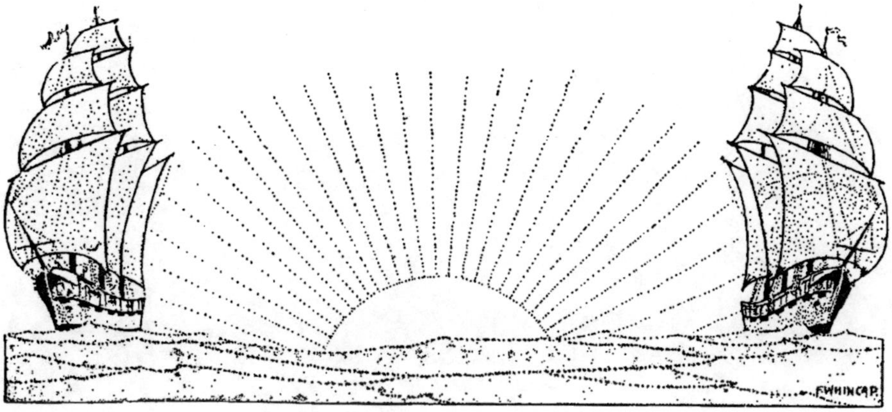

LETTERPRESS CONTENTS

HISTORICAL AND DESCRIPTIVE

COMMERCIAL AND INDUSTRIAL

CEYLON.

"Where every Prospect Pleases."

Be not afeard; the isle is full of noises,
Sounds and sweet airs that give delight and hurt
 not.
Sometimes a thousand twangling instruments
Will hum about mine ears, and sometimes voices
That, if I then had waked after long sleep,
Will make me sleep again; and then, in dreaming,
The clouds methought would open and show
 riches
Ready to drop upon me, that, when I waked,
I cried to dream again.

—Shakespeare: *The Tempest.*

"Lanka, the Resplendent."

LANDFALL is now an out-worn thrill, but there is promise of romance in the first far-off glimpse of Ceylon, when the voyager sees Adam's Peak emerge out of the ocean, like the spiked boss of a mighty shield, to lift up a roseate dawn. Let season and hour conspire that the approach to this beautiful island may be a worthy prelude to the delights in store. Dawn and the month of January are the most favourable combination, affording clear skies and softened tones. The watcher on deck, faring from the North, would for many a night have observed, on the straight run from Aden, the increased declination of the Pole Star and the circling Bear; with the drop of the horizon the famous constellation of the Southern Cross would have climbed into view. As the steamer ploughed eastward he would have seen the western star-groups set more swiftly and the eastern arise ahead of time. That, at any rate, if he were so minded, would be the witness of his eyes to the nearness of lat. 7 N., long. 80 E., which is the unromantic cartographical indication of Colombo's place on the planet. And it were well thus to have an eye for the celestial guide-marks of the old-time voyagers, for, as we shall see, the newest lover of Ceylon is but the latest in a long and varied line. Many are the lands and many the tongues, from the dim past to the present day, in which her praises have been sung.

It is not the dawn silhouette of the central mountain mass alone that makes the first sight of Ceylon memorable. Eye-weary from the desert landscapes lately passed, as we approach up the coast from the south we find relief (and a revelation) in the gladdening verdure that clothes the land from mountain to plain, to ring the gleaming shore with a continuous girdle of coconut-palms; in the glimpses of green and silver coves; blue seas that match the immaculate vault above; or, in the season of the south-west monsoon, great breakers that dash themselves on shore or sea-wall and veil the land in a scudding drift of foam.

That impression of a shining, verdant isle we shall bear away with us. It will endure when we have forgotten that Ceylon is the land of the ruby, the sapphire, and the pearl, the land of the elephant and the peacock, the land of tea; or when perhaps we have forgotten, what we shall learn, that it is the land of a people with an ancient culture eagerly embracing a new, an understanding and friendly people that has already plucked the fruits of a century of friendship with British missionary, ruler, and colonist. For, as we now enter Colombo's fine harbour, which is entirely the work of human enterprise wresting a safe anchorage out of a wave-torn beach, with all the evidence of a clamorous trade around, we are aware of the green battalions pressing to the brink so as to give jetty and pier and other apparatus of human activity the appearance of an intrusion into Nature's domain with the precarious purchase of a bare foothold on its margin. Red roof and stark chimney, storage tank and hotel facade lie submerged in verdure; church spire and dome and tower stand breast-deep in the green flood.

That is how "Lanka the Resplendent" is first seen. As the twin arms of the bay close around us, we mark the belt of palms fading into the horizon's glare to northward, while in the south Mount Lavinia Head, with its hotel shining in the sun, bars from view, but does not break, the wondrous cincture.

Believed by some to have been the Tarshish of the Bible, whence her ships carried wood for the building of Solomon's temple, and peacocks and ivory for trade; reported to Alexander the Great by his admirals as having a 500-mile coastline and abounding in sea-monsters; swept by hordes of continental invaders; conquered and brought to a high pitch of development by the dynasty of one such, a royal scion; converted to Buddhism, a faith to foster which was extolled as the highest kingly virtue and the glories of which, as sung in the ancient chronicle (itself a unique boast among Indian countries), were one with the glories of her kings; drawn into the main stream of history by embassies to Rome, whose chronicler, Pliny, has recorded one, and Marcellinus another; mapped by Ptolemy, the geographer, upon information elicited from Phœnician and Arab merchants; visited by the much-travelled Chinese monk, Fa Hien, for the purpose of consulting the sacred books; busied in the ways of commerce while no town in northern Europe had yet received its charter; scene of an Arabian Night's tale, in which Sinbad the Sailor figures as the type of the men who have praised the hospitality of her people; visited by Marco Polo, who tells how Kublai Khan coveted the king's ruby and obtained a dish of green porphyry, a relic of Adam; closed to European traffic by the Arab mastery of the Indian seas; linked with Venice in the heyday of her prosperity by a trade agreement; accidentally re-discovered by Portuguese seamen and thus once more drawn into the main current of European affairs, until after centuries of vicissitudes, in which statecraft saved her from one invader to throw her into the hands of another, the chances of the Napoleonic wars and the balance of parties brought England here as the successor of the Dutch, to carry on the enterprise they had barely begun, Ceylon has in the last hundred years and more been firmly set on the broad highway of peaceful progress and development, worthy of her fair repute in literature.

[Photo: Plâté, Ltd.

SHADOW OF ADAM'S PEAK THROWN ON BIBLE ROCK AT SUNRISE.

It is of *Lanka* (the Resplendent Isle), the 'Golden,' the 'Divine,' as the ancient Eastern poets have variously styled her, *Sinhala dwipa* (the Land of the Lion Race), name later corrupted into Serendib, Ceilao, Ceylon, the *Taprobane* of the Greeks and Romans immortalised in Milton's line, that Sir Emerson Tennent, Colonial Secretary and Lieutenant-Governor between 1845 and 1850, wrote: "There is no island in the world, Great Britain itself not excepted, that has attracted the attention of authors in so many distant ages and so many different countries as Ceylon; there is no nation in ancient or modern times possessed of a language or literature, the writers of which have not at some time made it their theme. Its aspect, its religion, its antiquities and productions, have been described as well by classic Greeks as by those of the lower empire, by the Romans, by the writers of China, Burma, India, and Cashmere, by the geographers of Arabia and Persia, by the mediæval voyagers of Portugal and France, by the annalists of Portugal and Spain, by the merchants and adventurers of Holland, and by the travellers and topographers of Great Britain. . . . The Brahmans designated it by the epithet of *Lanka*, 'The Resplendent,' and in their dreamy rhapsodies extolled it as the region of mystery and sublimity; the Buddhist poets gracefully apostrophised it as a 'pearl upon the brow of India'; the Chinese knew it as the 'Island of Jewels'; the Greeks as 'The Land of the Hyacinth and the Ruby'; the Mahomedans, in the intensity of their delight, assigned it to the exiled parents of mankind, as a new elysium to console them for the loss of Paradise; and the early navigators of Europe, as they returned dazzled with its gems, and laden with its costly spices, propagated the fable that far to seaward the very breeze that blew from it was redolent of perfume."

Topography.

Ceylon is roughly a pear-shaped island, with the "stalk" end to the north, pendent from the southern end of the continent of India. In area it is about 25,000 square miles, rather less than Ireland; its length north to south is about 270 miles; its greatest breadth about 140 miles. The whole of the coast line is low and sandy, and the northern half of the island from sea to sea is a vast unbroken plain. In the remaining portions of the country the low lands extend inland for distances up to 70 or 80 miles, to the foot of the central mountain mass, which covers an area of over 4,000 square miles. On the north the hills rise precipitously from the plains, less abruptly on the southern and western sides. The general trend of the ranges is south-east to north-west, showing that the lifting forces came from the south-west.

[Photo: Plâté, Ltd.

KANDAPOLA ROAD, NUWARA ELIYA.

This mountain region is of great natural strategical strength. The circuit of its wall is unbroken, and access to it is to be had only by a few passes. The best known of these is Kadugannawa, by which the railway and road reach Kandy from the west coast. The south-eastern portion of the hill country, called "Uva," consists of a rolling plateau encircled by higher hills: the remaining and larger part presents a series of steep tumbled mountains intersected by long and narrow valleys, and only in two places are there considerable towns, situated in "cups" among the hills. These are Kandy (1,600 ft.) and Nuwara Eliya (6,200 ft.), the hill-stations of the colony. Kandy is famous in history as the stronghold and last retreat of the Sinhalese kings. The highest mountain peaks range from Adam's Peak (about 7,350 ft.) to Pidurutalagala ((8,300 ft.), the highest point in the island, a noble mountain overlooking Nuwara 'Eliya.

Climate.

The surrounding ocean and the mountains determine the climate of Ceylon. In all parts the temperature is remarkably even: in the low country the variation is only from warm to warmer: in the mountains from cool to cooler. The rainfall is liberal, and there are two well-defined rainy seasons for monsoons—north-east, October to December, and south-west, May to June. The former monsoon is the more general in rainfall effect over the whole island. The mountains rise less abruptly and at a greater distance from the sea in the eastern side, and hence the rain clouds have a more distributed effect. But, in the south-west monsoon, the rains do not reach the eastern side of the central mountain range, and the vapours are condensed against the abrupt western slopes. This process may often be seen strikingly illustrated during the railway journey eastward from Pattipola, the summit of the railway, towards Uva. The railway passes through a short tunnel under the crest of a mountain. Approaching it, the train passes through heavy rain and mists. In a few minutes it emerges on the other slope of the mountain, and the " rolling plains " of Uva are disclosed to the traveller under a smiling sun and blue sky. From the situation of the mountain " massif " and its effect on the rainfall, arises the climatic differentiation of " dry zone " and " wet zone " in Ceylon. The former broadly consists of the eastern and northern plains, the latter of the west and south-west low country and the mountain region. But it is a difference of small degree when compared with the wide divergence prevailing in a continent like India. From the driest to the wettest region the range of average rainfall is from about 25ins. to about 180ins. per annum. The result is that in striking contrast to the vast, arid deserts of India, even the "dry zone" regions of Ceylon are covered with forest and vegetation which presents throughout the year an appearance of fresh verdure.

[Photo: Plâté, Ltd.

SINHALESE GIRL.

Flora.

The opulence of the vegetation is revealed by the fact that while Ceylon is smaller than Ireland it has 3,000 species of flowering plants and ferns, which is three times as many as the British Isles can boast, while that number does not include the mosses and fungi, etc., not yet fully surveyed, but likely to yield an equal number again.

The dry northern zone, as determined by the position of the mountains, approximates more nearly to the character of South India, while the flora of the wetter districts is Malaysian. Briefly, the coconut yields place to the palmyra palm. Indeed, there are not wanting those who find a new beauty in the coastal landscapes of Jaffna with its tide-flats and clumps of palm.

The whole of the wet low country was once under forest, but there has been a great waste of this capital on the part of the villager, who fells, burns off, and then scratches the surface of the ground for a few scanty crops of poor grain. Modern forest conservation has been in time to prevent excessive denudation of the uplands for tea and rubber.

The forests are equatorial and evergreen. The tall trunks of the hard-wood timber trees are smothered in a rank undergrowth, under which again a wealth of herbs is found; in the higher forests European buttercups, brambles, violets, and valerians make their appearance.

The proportion of endemic species (30 per cent.) is very large for a continental island, but it is not these that contribute colour and beauty to the commonest gardens, so attractive to the visitor: flamboyant, temple-tree, shoe-flower, allamanda, croton, lettuce-tree, even the coconut and areca-nut palms, are all aliens. Some of these, like the lantana and the sunflower, have overrun the country, last of the island's many foreign invaders! Acacias, wattles, conifers, and grevilleas, have been successfully introduced in the higher uplands. But one must not fail to notice certain remarkable plants that are native to the country, namely, the na, the ixora, and the murata. Ferns, like the maidenhair and the gold and silver ferns, hothouse specimens of temperate climes, add a

[Photo: Plâté, Ltd.

KANDY, THE BEAUTIFUL LITTLE MOUNTAIN CITY AND ANCIENT CAPITAL OF CEYLON.

[Photo: Plâté, Ltd.

KANDY LAKE FROM LADY HORTON'S WALK

[Photo: Plâté, Ltd.

MONSOON WAVE STRIKING BREAKWATER, COLOMBO HARBOUR.

TRAVELLERS' PALM.

CEDAR TREE.

special element of beauty, crowding every cranny.

The fruits are plentiful and delicious, though again mostly of foreign origin. Almost the only natives are the plantain, as the banana is called locally, and the jambu (Eugenia). Well-known favourites like the mango, durian, jak, mangosteen, nam-nam, guava, pine-apple, cashew, papaw, tamarind, lime, shaddock, pomegranate, sapodilla, lovi-lovi, custard-apple, soursop, and avocado-pear, are such as can be obtained anywhere in the tropics. In fact, the whole of the tropical flora can be found here in brief and convenient compass, and scientific men revel in their opportunity.

Fauna.

Coming to the fauna, the leopard and some cats represent the carnivores, while of mammals the elephant fills the largest room. Gone are the glorious days of Sir Samuel Baker, for elephants are now scarcely shot with the gun, unless they have been proclaimed as dangerous and destructive. They share the forests and the grassy plains with the bears, buffaloes, monkeys, peacocks, and pig; the latter is shot in Ceylon, owing to the nature of the country making "sticking" impossible.

The monkeys are notable, several peculiar species being found. The sambhur and some smaller species of deer are threatened with extinction, but game sanctuaries (an attraction for the animal lover as distinct from the sportsman) have been created to preserve these and other wild species.

Cataloguing the rest, there are jackals, hares, porcupines, squirrels, bats, flying-foxes, crocodiles, cobras, vipers, armadillos, porpoises, sharks, and, more rarely, dugongs.

Myriads of aquatic birds of wide distribution are found in the tank country, and in lagoons and salt-marshes. Eagles, falcons, owls, trogons, hornbills, cuckoos, woodpeckers and parrots provide some peculiar species.

Of songsters there is none of any repute in the low country, though the magpie-robin of the garden has surely missed its public; the Nuwara Eliya robin and thrush emulate their European namesakes. The spurred partridge and the jungle cock have a characteristic call. Game-birds are abundant, and the "sportsman" is well provided for. Of garden birds, the tailor-bird and the sun-bird are notable, while in the country the weaver-birds have an interest all their own with their colonies of retort-shaped nests. The talking myna must not be forgotten; but king of mimics is the king-crow, a species of drongo. Thieving crows and sparrows haunt the bungalows. The cuckoo's scream has earned it the soubriquet of brain-fever bird, while the air is vocal with the calls of barbet and bulbul and the cooing of doves. Butterflies abound, though not of remarkable species; swarms are met with sometimes for mile upon mile. Briefly, Ceylon is the Paradise of the naturalist, and he has not to go far out of Colombo to prove it.

Early History.

Upon Adam's Peak, the apex of the equilateral triangle of the mountains of Ceylon, countless mariners and adventurers from the most ancient times have gazed, and pious pilgrims of four great world religions, Hindus, Buddhists, Mahomedans, and Christians, to this day climb its slopes to worship before the sacred "footprint." Hindus call the mountain "Sivan-adi-padam" (footprints of Siva), Buddhists "Sira-pada" (the sacred footprint); and while Mahomedans travel there to view the spot where, they say, our first

[Photo: Plâté, Ltd.

MAHOMEDAN MOSQUE, COLOMBO.

ancestor, Adam, trod, Christian pilgrims commemorate the visit of St. Thomas, the first Christian missionary to the East. And it is strange to record that even the insect world is said to be affected by the impulse of a pilgrimage to this renowned peak; for in the hot season of the year, between the N.E. and S.W. monsoons, thousands of yellow butterflies can be seen in the central, northern, and western portions of the island, winging their southerly flight in the exact direction of Adam's Peak. The Sinhalese people have, therefore, an alternative name for the mountain, "Samanagala," which means "Butterfly Rock."

This diversity of people making their way towards the great religious mountain is symbolic of the history of Ceylon; for the island, from its position in the midst of ocean currents and winds, and its easy access from the great continent of India by the 20 mile sea passage, with the rocks variously known as "Adam's" or "Rama's"

Bridge, has been the goal of foreign invaders and adventurers from the beginning of its recorded history. It is a history of racial invasions and conquests from the Indian continent, the defeated inhabitants being gradually driven from the northern plains, then splendidly fertile, into the central mountain region, while the conquerors settled down to enjoy the produce of those fertile lands. Meanwhile adventurers from distant Europe had from time to time visited the island and brought back glowing stories of its wealth. Indeed, there is ample evidence of early knowledge of Ceylon in Europe, and of intercourse between the two. Ceylon was known to the Greeks and Romans under the name of Taprobane; and there have been found in the island Roman coins covering five centuries, and bearing the images of twenty-two of the Roman Emperors. Thus early was Ceylon in some sort of relation to the western world.

In the middle of the fourteenth century it was a country of great wealth and greater potentialities; a country with a long written history kept up in poetic form as the famous "Mahavansa," the chronicle of the Sinhalese race, with kings who held despotic power over a population which was undoubtedly greater than is the population in the twentieth century; with a hierarchy of pious and learned priests who had preserved the Buddhist religion in its purest form for centuries; with royal and sacred cities of vast extent, and adorned by splendid temples and palaces, now in ruins and overgrown by jungle; with vast irrigation lakes which, by a system of canals, fertilised all the northern plain. Of all these wonders only the Buddhist religion and its traditions have survived—its symbol the ancient Bo-tree of Anuradhapura, which, with a recorded history of more than two thousand years, may well be called a wonder of the world. The descendants of the last Kandyan kings live in obscure exile in India; their stately cities of Anuradhapura, Polonnaruwa, and others of their homes in the northern plains, lie buried in jungle; the bunds of their vast irrigation lakes have crumbled; and the lands which they fertilised, once the home of teeming populations, who lived on their produce, are now overgrown with forest and peopled by elephant, leopard, and deer. The miserable descendants of the once prosperous subjects of the Sinhalese kings eke out a precarious existence by cultivations of small forest clearings of "dry grains," and are gradually dying out, a prey to the dread malaria which takes such enormous toll of Eastern people.

But there is another side to this picture. If all this decay has occurred in one portion of the country, and on one side of its activities, there is a wonderful record of progress in the hill country and the southern and western plains; and this of progress achieved under manifold difficulties and in the face of great natural obstacles. This double story is the story practically of Ceylon's intimate relationship to the western world.

The earliest known inhabitants of Ceylon are called in the Sinhalese language by the name of "Veddahs," which means "hunters," or alternately, "Yakshas" (devils). Within living memory there were still surviving in the remote southern and eastern jungles sufficient numbers of the races, retaining their primitive habits, to furnish study for the eminent ethnologists, Max Muller and Seligman. The number, however, of these pure-blooded Veddahs who still live by hunting alone and retain their original characteristics is now very small, and is decreasing rapidly. There is strong evidence that through inter-marriage in historic times with the Sinhalese invaders, this aboriginal race has had some influence upon the Kandyan Sinhalese (the inhabitants of the mountains), who in many respects differ from the low country, or maritime Sinhalese.

To a country inhabited by such people the first known invasion on a large scale originated from Northern India in about the 6th century B.C., and these invaders, who arrived under their King Vijaya, were the ancestors and founders of the Sinhalese race.

They came from the region now called Behar, near the banks of the Ganges River. They were of Indo-Aryan stock, speaking Pali, a dialect form of the parent Aryan tongue, which was closely related to the "literary," or written, language Sanskrit, and which developed into the modern Sinhalese. It was this same dialect which was the medium of the preaching of Gautama Buddha.

Warlike and adventurous, these invaders had earned the name "Sinhala" (Lion Slayers), and thence comes the title of the race, "Sinhalese." Their conquest of the northern region of Ceylon, and their partial absorption of the aboriginal Veddahs, are illustrated in the legend of Vijaya's marriage to a Veddah princess, who, in the story, later abandoned and driven forth by her husband in favour of a new Indian queen, sought refuge amongst those of her own kin who had retreated into the mountains.

Then followed, about 300 B.C., the greatest epoch in Ceylon's history, the propagation of Buddhism through the visit of Mahinda, son of the great Buddhist Emperor, Asoka, of Northern India. There is little doubt that Mahinda brought with him the authentic Buddhist canon, and under him, and later Buddhist missionaries, the faith spread through Ceylon. From being merely a form of colloquial speech, Pali became a great literary language, enshrining works, devotional such as the "Tripitaka" or Buddhist scriptures, and historical like the "Dipavansa" and "Mahavansa."

Through a time of peaceful development the Sinhalese kings and their people lived in prosperity. Warriors and conquerors were followed by agriculturists and builders. Successive kings built the royal cities, and more productively dotted the country with those vast artificial irrigation lakes which later fell into ruins, and are now being slowly and painfully restored by the Ceylon Government.

But it could not be supposed that so fair a land, so near, could escape the covetous attention of neighbours in Southern India, themselves warlike, pressed southward by fierce invaders from the Deccan, living in a more inhospitable clime. And so the Tamil invasions began: and thenceforward for many centuries the history of Ceylon centres round the royal city of Anuradhapura, taken by invaders, retaken by heroic Sinhalese kings: a history of battles, of palace intrigues, of usurpations and murders. The ruined palaces, temples, and monuments of Anuradhapura and its sisters, Mihintale and Polonnaruwa, bear authentic testimony to the story of this period, and here the archæological student finds ample scope.

The pressure from India was not to be denied. The Sinhalese were driven southward, and the northern districts of Jaffna and Anuradhapura were more and more peopled by Tamils, or "Malabars." By intermarriage with Tamil princes and princesses the pure royal Sinhalese line disappeared; and by the time of the great European invasions, the kings of Kandy themselves, whose people were considered the Sinhalese *par excellence*, were more Malabar than Sinhalese.

European Invasions and Their Effects.

We may now consider these European invasions and their effects. When the first Portuguese adventurer, Almeida, reached Ceylon in 1505, he found no fewer than seven separate kingdoms in existence: such was the disintegration and decadence that had befallen the country. A few years later the first Portuguese organised an expedition, landed at Colombo, and negotiated a trade agreement with the kings of Kotte, who ruled in the immediate neighbourhood of the place. But the Portuguese aim at that time was not trade, but military glory and Roman Catholic propaganda. And their occupation, lasting nearly 150 years, presents a dark picture of wars, religious persecutions, massacres, broken promises, hostages murdered, and ambassadors betrayed. In these unhappy transactions the Kandyan kings exhibited as much subtlety and vindictiveness as their alien enemies. Leaving aside these "political" events, the Portuguese occupation, which extended only to the maritime low-country districts, to a distance of a few miles from the coasts, has left its traces in forts such as Colombo, Jaffna, Galle, Negombo, in Roman Catholic churches along the coast, and in many family names of Sinhalese, such as Dias, Rodrigo, Fernando, de Soysa, etc. In language, law, and commerce, the Portuguese influence has been very small. It was in the nature of things that the Dutch, the great sea rivals of Spain and Portugal in eastern seas, in the sixteenth and seventeenth centuries, should also endeavour to extend their sphere of influence to Ceylon: and it was in the middle of the seventeenth century that a Dutch expedition arrived at Trincomalee—that harbour of Ceylon's east coast which faces towards the great eastern possessions of Holland. Under the guise of a friendly mission to rescue the Kandyan king from his entanglements with the Portuguese, the Dutch established themselves in the coastal districts with trade agreements, and in 1658, by means of superior armaments and their alliance with the Sinhalese kings, they were able to oust the Portuguese from their footing, but not until a siege of Colombo fort had called out all the horrors of war—a tragedy illumined by the military conduct of the Portuguese garrison. With the capture of Jaffna in 1658, the Portuguese rule in Ceylon came to an end, and the Dutch became practically masters of the whole coastal region, or low country. The Dutch era differs very materially from the Portuguese: the Hollanders who drove out their great rivals were servants of the Dutch East India Company, and their two great objects were trade and sea power. Thus the Dutch occupation was a period of great expansion of the island's trade, and its people as well as commerce was brought more and more into intimate relationship with the men and ideas of the West.

Trade, industry, development of communications, and education of the people were substituted for military glory and religious propaganda. Thus, although the Dutch rule in Ceylon (1658-1796) was actually of less duration than that of the Portuguese, it has had much more substantial and lasting effects. The Dutch in Ceylon, as in all their overseas possessions, were great colonists: they introduced into the country a regular civil instead of a military administration, many important features of which survive still under British rule. Their people, skilful agriculturists as well as traders, were content to settle down in tropical Ceylon and make it their home. The famous spice cinnamon, which was perhaps the chief product of Ceylon for the European trade, was extensively cultivated by them in the districts round Colombo, some of the gardens being of considerable size. They built canals between Colombo and Negombo, Colombo and Kalutara, etc., which are still in commercial use. Many of them founded Ceylon "Burgher" families which have furnished for more than a century the backbone of the Government and mercantile clerical services, and numerous members of these families have risen to great eminence in the legal and medical professions. But the principal surviving Dutch institution is the Roman Dutch law, which, as in South Africa, forms practically the basis of the colony's civil law to this day.

Successful as the Dutch were in these directions, they were unable to make diplomatic progress, and indeed could hardly maintain ordinary friendly relations with the Kandyan kings, who, in their mountain fortresses, kept up a haughty isolation, harassing the foreigners by intrigues and by irksome restrictions on trade in all the districts where they could make their influence felt. Further, the very aptitude and concentration with which the Dutch pursued the progressive and civilising arts of commerce, agriculture, and law, rendered them inattentive to the less profitable, but equally vital, question of military safety. For a hundred years after the expulsion of the Portuguese they had no European rivals in Ceylon. England's maritime power and overseas connections were strong indeed, but the energies of the British East India Company were fully occupied with the expansion of their interests in India, and with the long struggle which they waged against the French for supremacy in that continent. During this period the Dutch remained undisturbed in their island possession. But the English rulers of Madras—though nominally England and Holland were allies at this time—were already, in the middle of the 18th century, exploring avenues towards the acquisition of the prize.

[Photo: Plâté, Ltd.

CORNER OF THE LAKE AT NUWARA ELIYA.

British Advent.

In 1795, when England broke with Holland, a force despatched from India captured the Dutch possessions, meeting with practically no resistance. The capitulation to the East Indies Company took place in 1796. Six years later the maritime districts of Ceylon became the property of the British Crown. It was not long before British Governors turned their attention towards the hill country; but it was the conduct of the Sinhalese kings, rather than the supremacy of British arms, which brought about in 1815 the " Convention " by which the Kandyan provinces acknowledged the sovereignty of England. The cruelties of the last king were so intolerable that his own chiefs begged for British aid to get rid of him. He was captured and exiled to India, and from that time the British rule of the Kandyan country began. A special charter guaranteeing civil and religious liberty, and the protection of the Buddhist religion, was drawn up, and for a time the administration of the hill country under a " Commissioner " differed slightly from that of the maritime district; but the whole was gradually co-ordinated, and at present, with some small exceptions of civil law, the administration has one system for the whole country.

Industrial Development.

Heirs to the good work of the Dutch, the British were able to make great progress towards the development of the country and people in the 19th century. Education has always been an important element of their policy. Among early Governors were some notable road builders, who opened up splendid communications from the plains to the hills. Railways and the telegraph quickly made their appearance; and a great impetus was given to the development of the country by the pioneer planters, who pushed their way to the hill country, cleared forests and jungles, and planted coffee. From 1834, ten years after its first introduction, the prosperity of this industry was so rapid and so extraordinary that Ceylon became a great field for the investment of European capital, and the employment of European planters as supervisors of labour. The natives of the country participated in this prosperity; and, as the uses in the western world of the products of the coconut-palm became more and more extended, the 19th century witnessed, in the low country, a considerable expansion of coconut cultivation, mostly by the indigenous population, often at the expense of the ancient cinnamon industry. After a period of remarkable prosperity there followed, fifty years ago, the disaster of the "Coffee Blight," which brought the coffee-planting industry to practical extinction. The story of the struggles of the coffee planters, many of them rendered penniless, to retrieve their position, of the substitution, first of cinchona (the source of quinine), and then of tea, for the abandoned coffee cultivation, makes a romantic chapter in Ceylon's history. Tea has proved a product not only of great profit to Ceylon, but of vast Imperial importance; and this is true to no less degree of rubber, the cultivation of which has been vastly extended since the first experimental rubber plants were brought from Brazil in 1876. Along with Malaya, Ceylon, with its present exporting capacity of about 60,000 tons of rubber per year, and with more acreages coming into bearing, is an important element in the control which the Imperial Government is able to exercise over the rubber supply of the world. Out of 3,250,000 acres under actual cultivation (omitting 1,000,000 acres of pasturage), rubber and tea plantations, together comprise in nearly equal proportions 900,000 acres, and coconut lands more than 800,000 acres. Coconut, rubber, and tea are, therefore, the three main products of Ceylon which have determined its agricultural and commercial development in the last hundred years. The Agricultural Department, now well equipped in facilities for experiment and research, watches carefully for faint indications of any blight or disease which might threaten these industries with a fate similar to that of coffee, but at present, so far as it is humanly possible to predict, there seems no reason to fear any such disaster; nor is it likely, in present conditions, that there will be any deterioration in the world demand for the products in question.

[Photo: Plâté, Ltd.

PROCESSION OF THE HOLY RELIC, KANDY.

Coconuts, as has been stated, flourish chiefly round the coast. Rubber is cultivated on the slopes of the rainy foothills, mostly in the western, central, and south-western districts, and on lands up to a height of about 2,000 feet.

At the higher elevations tea is the principal product, and there are old plantations at heights up to 7,000 feet or more. But the modern forest policy of the Government, owing to the necessity of regulating rainfall and minimising soil erosion, has dictated a regulation that no land for agricultural purposes, at an elevation of 5,000 feet or more, is alienated by the Crown. This regulation, and indeed the whole land system of Ceylon, depend on the principle that all " forest " lands (including all lands uncultivated over a certain period of years) are the property of the Crown, unless an individual claimant produces some recognised documentary proof of title, such as grants for feudal services by the Kandyan kings, or proof of regular and continuous occupation and cultivation over a certain period. In this manner, Government has had available for sale vast tracts of land. These lands are sold by auction, and the proceeds devoted to public works. At the periodical land sales, blocks of all sizes, from tiny " village " holdings to lands of hundreds of acres, are sold, and the result is that peasants, native gentlemen, and capitalist corporations, are all holders of land.

The progressive success of the three predominant agricultural industries referred to has been reinforced from other industries, less in volume, but still important. Cocoa, cinchona, cinnamon, vanilla, pepper, cardamons, arecanuts, and tobacco, are all flourishing products.

The island is rich in deposits of plumbago, a mineral essential in the construction of crucibles for the manufacture of high temperature steels. The plumbago market is subject to great fluctuations, which render the industry irregular or spasmodic; but in times of great demand, specially during the Great War, it has been an extremely profitable enterprise.

Here, too, may be noted the periodical pearl fisheries carried on under Government control from the oyster bank off the north-west coast. Ceylon pearls bear a high reputation from preclassic times; and though the last pearl fishery statistics available, viz., those of 1925, indicate no great source of revenue to Government, or of " Pearls of Price " to the buyers of shell, the oyster banks in question have been, and will be again, a source of great benefit to the country.

Lastly, mention of the precious stone industry must not be omitted. Rubies, sapphires, " cats' eyes," moonstones, and amethysts are the most important. The operations in connection with these are usually carried on by Sinhalese, in and near the beds of certain rivers, on a lease of " Gemming Rights " from the Government. A marvellous discovery of huge sapphires, one being over 700 carats, in a paddy field near Ratnapura, a year or two ago, caused a sensation among gem merchants, and brought the gemmer a fortune in a day.

Revenue and Public Services.

It will readily be understood that so striking a record of prosperity has resulted in a vast increase of the resources at the disposal of the administration for the improvement of the country. Without entering into cumbersome statistics, the figures of revenue in 1874, just before the coffee blight, and at the present time may be quoted. The rise is from thirteen million rupees to over a hundred million rupees. These increasing resources have been employed in public works (harbours, roads, railways, irrigation), in education, in grants to local Government bodies, and in sanitary and medical services. Free from income tax, Ceylon is a happy haven for the harassed taxpayer of England. The revenue is mainly derived from " indirect " taxes on imports and exports (so devised that necessities are taxed as lightly as possible and luxuries more heavily), and from services such as the railways and harbours. The ancient polltax of a rupee and a half per male adult levied in lieu of labour on roads, and manifestly unfair in incidence, is now practically in abeyance, and will doubtless shortly disappear altogether.

In the domain of public works, reference may here be made to the roads, which are numerous and of a quality far superior to most Indian roads. They are furnished, every dozen miles or so, with excellent " rest-houses " maintained by Government for the accommodation of travellers. The road system is continually being extended and improved.

As to railways, there is a broad gauge line along the west and south coasts, with Colombo as centre, nearly 200 miles in length, and this will be extended. The main line up-country runs from Colombo to Badulla, about 160 miles, and serves the great tea districts. A northern line runs to Anuradhapura, and thence in two branches, one to Jaffna, and one to Talai-manar, for the 20 mile ferry to the South Indian Railway. The length of this northern line is over 200 miles, and a speedy journey of 24 hours can be made to Madras.

A short narrow gauge railway runs up the valley of the Kelani River to the tea and rubber districts below Adam's Peak. Finally, a steam-tramway, to be replaced, when required, by a more substantial line connecting the Northern Railway with Trincomalee on the east coast, has recently been completed, its length being over 100 miles. It is hoped that the opening of this line, and the branch line to Batticoloa, will result in a great agricultural development of the district, now practically jungle, through which it passes.

Education.

Education absorbs yearly more and more of the available revenue. There is an establishment of English and vernacular schools throughout the country, and the various religious bodies maintain good secondary schools, which receive State assistance. In Colombo there are higher schools of training for the legal, medical, and engineering professions; and in the near future Ceylon will possess a State endowed University.

In the matter of medical and sanitary services, Ceylon may fairly claim to take its place among the most fortunate countries. There is a State medical service, with trained apothecaries in every considerable village, and with free hospitals, staffed by qualified doctors and nurses, dotted all over the island. The General Hospital in Colombo is equipped in an up to-date manner, and is constantly being extended, and there is a Pasteur Institute for bacteriological work.

The most prevalent and deadliest disease in Ceylon is malaria; and to cope with it and other tropical diseases a campaign of education in public health has been started. Another scourge of the East, Anchylostomiasis (" Hookworm "), is being combated jointly by Government and by the doctors of the Rockfeller Institute.

Modern Progress.

Such progress has been rendered possible, not only by the availability of ample resources, but by the co-operation and goodwill of the people themselves. From the outset of the British rule, the ancient chiefs and their descendants, and to an increasing degree the educated classes, were taken into the administration, and local organisations were adopted, as far as possible. By the creation of municipalities, such as Colombo, Kandy, and Galle, and of urban District Councils and Local Boards throughout the island, local self-government has been fostered. At the same time, the element of popular representation in the Legislative Council, Ceylon's Parliament, has been so extended that at present the elected representatives of the people have control over the public purse, and unofficials are included in a semi-ministerial capacity in the Governor's Cabinet. It is, indeed, probable that in a few years Ceylon will acquire the status of a self-governing colony. In this process Ceylon has happily escaped the political storms which have convulsed India. It remained untouched by the Mutiny of 1857; its only connection with those events being furnished by the fact that Henry Lawrence, buried far away in Lucknow, was born in the little fort of Matara, in the extreme South of Ceylon.

The peaceful and non-aggressive character of the Ceylonese people, and the comparative ease of climatic and economic conditions, have contributed much to the tranquillity of the country under British rule.

Population.

But it is not to be supposed that all is prosperity and that there are no problems for solution. The centre of gravity of the agricultural population has shifted south, but it is not the Sinhalese who have moved. The overwhelming majority of the labourers on the large tea and rubber estates are Tamils from South India, and this applies in the industrial concerns of Colombo, too—of a total population of about 5,000,000 more than 600,000 are immigrant Indians. Further, the only populous district which supports a totally *native* population, without extraneous capital or alien people, is Jaffna; and again, the natives of Jaffna are Tamils. Petty traders both in towns and villages are nearly all Moormen (Mahomedans from South India); the large importers of foodstuffs are Indians from Bombay and Calcutta; the local financiers are Chetties, a small South-Indian community of money lenders. Thus the Indian invasion still goes on, and the Sinhalese is gradually being pressed out of his position as a peasant proprietor. The Ceylon Law of Inheritance, too, has contributed to this process; instead of primogeniture in the inheritance of land, we find a system of equal division among brothers and sisters. Lands have been subjected to this parcelling process for so many generations that it would be no matter for surprise to find a villager making a claim—and a genuine one—to some such extent as 5-367ths of half an acre.

In the result, a race of agriculturists has become nearly landless—with the exception of a comparatively few wealthy families; and except the learned and clerical professions for those who can afford them, there is no other opening for Sinhalese young men. It is only in recent years that attempts have been made to remedy this state of affairs, by the creation of co-operative credit societies to give assistance in land purchase and cultivation; and, along with this movement must go a bold policy of irrigation and development of the old rich lands now lying waste. This question is intimately connected with the problem of the general food supply of the island. With nearly 900,000 acres under rice, Ceylon normally imports in the neighbourhood of 400,000 tons of rice from India; and in 1919 a sharp reminder of the meaning of this dependence came to the country when, owing to a combination of various circumstances, largely arising out of the war, this stream of imports practically dried up. For months the people were in sight of actual starvation, and for nearly two years were subjected to a food control and a rationing system. At this time an attempt was made by Government, along with utilisation of private capital, to stimulate local food production: and the light railway to Trincomalee was sanctioned, to pass through the chosen district. The undertaking was not prosperous, and with the return of Indian supplies to normal, it has not been strongly pressed. But given the necessary irrigation policy, and bold measures to stamp out malaria, the greatest obstacle, the next few years may yet witness some interesting developments in the direction indicated.

Of the total population of Ceylon (5,000,000) some 9,000 are Europeans, more than 90 per cent. being British, mostly English, the majority of whom are in the plantations. Some 30,000 to 40,000 others are European in outlook, by birth or family tradition, and by training (to an increasing degree in Europe); the latter include all the Burghers, some Eurasians, and the educated Sinhalese and Tamils. The total " literate " population is given as 300,000.

The two main divisions of the population, as determined by the country's history, are Sinhalese and Tamils; the former are more than double the latter and number more than two-thirds of the population. The Burghers are of unique origin, the term "free Burgher " being used by the Dutch to denote the retired servants of their East India Company. Amid the confusions of later times, Dr. Copleston's account of them remains the truest, viz., " Few of these are now of unmixed European descent, but most are of unblemished and some of noble origin." They retained their status under the British occupation, and were of inestimable advantage to the new rulers, alike as a buffer and as a medium of contact between themselves and the people of the country. The result is apparent to-day, both in the striking individual examples of culture and in the general level of educational and social development to be seen in Colombo and other large towns, more especially when it is realised that that result has been achieved (obviously) without any leaven of English youth in the schools.

[Photo: Plâté, Ltd.

SILVER JUGGERNAUT CAR IN INDIAN FESTIVAL, CEYLON.

Scenery.

Having landed in Colombo, which is described elsewhere, it will not be long before the visitor is urged up country to see the 'show places' of the island. No previous description can mar by anticipation the view on the railway journey to Kandy, which has been described as among the most magnificent in the world. After some fifty miles of rapid travelling through flat land, where a wide expanse of rice-fields in their variegated dress of green alternates in a regular rhythm with clumps of coconut, jak, and other shade (and food) trees, under which nestle the hamlets of happy villagers, the steep and sudden ascent of the pass begins. An additional locomotive, a diminished rate of speed, and a new beat in the song of the wheels testify to the stiffer gradient. The earth-cuttings that close in on the track grow more rugged, and one soon realises that they have changed to living rock, gaunt and dripping with moisture. Dark tunnels, through rock-masses that cannot be skirted, increase, and the intervals between them grow less. Then there bursts into vision the mighty panorama that has made the fame of this justly famous railway. Hung precariously in mid-air between a few thousand feet of crag above and a thousand feet drop below, the train skirts the scarped hills along a hewn-out shelf of rock, while cataracts thunder under vibrating viaducts, and every rock-born spring empties its gushing contents into the conduits that guide them to their fall. From our aerial lookout we gaze entranced at the glories spread out as far as the eye can see. The valley is laid in terraced rice-fields, gleaming like mirrors, or in their full gamut of green, the whole forming an amphitheatre with a tesselated floor which borrows a gem-like charm from distance. Homesteads, cattle, and men acquire miniature proportions, and the motor-road is revealed as a thin, white ribbon peeping out at intervals through the opulent vegetation. That is one scale, the scale of the infinitely little. We lift our eyes and the prodigious scale of the infinitely vast alike astounds and exalts the mind. Fold upon fold, the hills are massed together in a stupendous assemblage. The nearer forms wear familiar aspects, castellated, tabular, or biblioid; but as the masses melt into the blue haze, light plays upon them with its magic pencil, and a striking effect of colour enlivens the total beauty of the scene. Such is Kadugannáwa, monument of the imagination and spirit of the engineers of a hundred years ago, who planned and wrought on a scale that must always be a stimulus to future effort, as it is matter for just pride in past achievement.

Keyed up to this high pitch it is not possible long to remain, and the milder charm of the approach to Kandy comes with a natural cadence; but soon further progress through the great central plateau, although it lies through districts 'made' by that industry which is the main pillar of Ceylon's prosperity, and, therefore, presenting less rugged aspects, yet affords a continuous feast for the eye as the train rounds the shoulders of the hills, and valley gives place to valley, gorge to gorge, and here a view of a waterfall or there a vista of the distant landscape, recurring with the successive and tortuous windings of the mounting track, make our 150-mile journey a tireless delight. As the rigour of the tropical sun abates, and evening brings refreshment, the mountain breezes waft a breath of coolness which renews our capacity to receive the impressions of country that is a veritable revelation of earth's fairness.

Reviewing our impressions, we recall that leaving behind the coconut groves of the lowland landscapes, we had in an hour or two climbed from 500 to 1,600 feet, covering no more than 13 miles in the climb. We realise what an impregnable stronghold Kandy was in former times, when fever-haunted jungle barred the trackless approach to the pass. It was a true Sinhalese prophecy which said that the kingdom would be his who cut a road through the rock: the Dawson Pillar at Kadugannáwa sets the seal to the inheritance. We saw Alagalla, the stately peak which towers a few thousand feet above the railway, and, across the valley, standing out from the mass, the castellated rock which was the last refuge of the local Robin Hood; also Bible Rock, with its inspiration to pious emotion. We marked the lone beauty of the talipot palm that rears once in fifty years a multiple plume, twenty feet in height to its hundred feet, and flowering dies. After the break at Kandy we resumed the tortuous climbing among nobler hills, the aspect of which is altered by cultivation or climate. There was found a resemblance to the Sussex Downs in these treeless grass-covered 'patanas,' which now began to fill the picture. Near Patipola (romantic country!) the 'summit level' at 6,226 ft. was reached, and the knowledge was gained that in the south-west monsoon the curious phenomenon of the 'rain-shed' is to be observed there, the train emerging through a tunnel from mist and storm into sunshine and a drier air in the lee of the range.

From Bandarawela, the former terminus of this railway, 150 miles from Colombo, begins the headlong descent to the smiling plains of Uva. On this route Ella affords one of the most wonderful sweeping views of undulating forest country, stretching down to the south-eastern coast.

We pass through historic ground in beautiful Badulla, with its fine amphitheatre of mountains and its grand waterfalls, now the centre of planting country. The country around here is notable chiefly for two things: one is a shrine of the greatest antiquity, sole relic of a time two and a half centuries ago when this spot was the most sacred of a dozen or more sacred localities in the island, and kings lavished upon it their pious gifts; the other is a vast restored irrigation tank to dam which the ancient Sinhalese engineers called into requisition, to eke out their own masonry, two masses of living rock, through which they clove two channels for their sluices.

It has been convenient to localise this account of the scenic beauty of the uplands, confining our going to the railway. But the splendid network of motor roads, though it diffuses the picture, affords now and then a joyous freedom which the railway traveller might envy, for a cascade of sublime loveliness, a frescoed cave-temple or the hidden reaches of a river, or again a plantation bungalow ideally situated on a hill-top, may lure one out of the beaten track, while there are several notable passes and gaps to be visited from which the eye takes in at a single glance the drop to the sea, gleaming like a silver ribbon fifty miles away.

But we are now far afield. Leaving for later description Kandy and Nuwara Eliya, and merely mentioning Ratnapura, the city of gems, and Kurunegala with its stupendous rock-masses, the nomenclature of which links the surrounding country with the fate of the aboriginal queen and her people at the hands of the Gangetic Aryans, it

SINHALESE LADY OF HIGH RANK.

is time to return to the coast to view other features of the varied scenery, including for convenience things of interest which do not belong to that category. Here again the window of the railway train shall be our look-out. It is a hotter journey than the last, but almost throughout the 100-mile ride to Matara, in the south, we keep in sight and hearing of the open sea, and its breezes fan the languorous air. At a first view the endless plantations of coconut, that would otherwise have a fatiguing monotony, present a pleasing attraction in their 'long-drawn aisles with fretted roof,' through which the radiant sunlight is sifted on to an enamelled carpet of sward or to shining sand. League-long rollers curl and dash on the shore in a mass of hissing foam. An unbroken expanse of sea, of the deepest blue, stretches to the sky-line, where the cloud-alps dazzle in the sun. As we proceed the wide strand gradually yields to a sterner coast, where fine natural pools are fed through the funnels of rock, or beautiful rock-bound bays invite the bather. Grand river-estuaries or sea-lagoons suggest romance as one catches a glimpse of thickly-wooded or mangrove-covered banks with Adam's Peak and range in the blue background.

There are other varied elements in the picture: the gleaming bellied sail of an outrigger canoe skimming the crest of the wave shoreward in a favouring breeze; in the offing a coral-fisher's dhow straight from the Middle Ages; the entire male population of a village hauling in with rhythmic chorus the great seine nets, while seagulls dart screaming upon their easy prey, and men wade into the water with agitated splashings; the same on a Sunday, playing village cricket under the coconuts, with a passion worthy of a prize-fight. Nor could we miss, as we pass, evidences of the manifold activities of the district, which embraces one of the principal rubber-planting areas, largely owned by the Sinhalese, the basket-making industry, the cabinet industry, tapping coconut trees for toddy and distilleries for the arrack obtained therefrom, fishing for crab, prawn, and oyster.

With the approach to the port of Galle we may close this section, referring the reader to the description, under their respective headings, of things to see in other parts of the country.

Kandy.

Kandy, the approach to which from the plains can, as already indicated, be scarcely equalled, is reputed to be one of the loveliest cities in the world. Set jewel-like in a verdant hollow, it wears diverse aspects of beauty that can never pall. A charming artificial lake lies at its heart. Bund and drive wind about with the contours of the richly-verdured hills that sweep down to the water's edge. Stately palms and beautiful shade-trees ring the picturesque pool. On the hill-sides commanding the water are pretty bungalows and gardens, and the carriage-drive is a vantage point for a general view of Kandy and its environs over the plush carpet of the tree-tops. Park and greensward heighten the illusion of a sylvan retreat, obscuring the manifold activities of an administrative capital, the clearing-house of the central planting district. Lanes invite to dalliance, while overhead a choir of birds of rainbow plumage sustains its day-long symphony. A forested eminence that flanks the town is roaded as a pleasance in which one might saunter at large and experience in security something of the mystery of a tropical forest, where giant trees hung with giant creepers stand waist-deep in a tangled undergrowth, impervious to sunlight, cool, restful; or recline at ease beside a jungle pool; or stand at an opportune clearing where the eye commands a wide view of remote ranges, opalescent in the sunshine, receding into blue distance.

Wandering farther afield, one finds one's way to a broad river (the longest in Ceylon), where elephants disport in the water or perform variety turns for the visitor's entertainment (and the mahout's profit).

Driving in another direction, past glades of rubber, one traverses a miniature canyon, where the same river dashes over a narrow bed of rock to broaden out in a wide reach dotted with tree-clad islets, while above on either hand virgin forest or tea-garden slopes steeply skyward. Near at hand, on the opposite bank, classified and set in ornamental grouping, interspersed with beautiful sweeps of undulating lawn, and traversed in circles, crescents, arcades, and long avenues, by a shining path, is that wonderful collection of tropical flora, the hundred-year-old Royal Botanic Gardens, famed as the finest of their kind.

Returning to the city, one has leisure to notice the quaint differences in the looks and garb and manner of the conservative hillmen from what had been observed in the plain-dwellers. Stolid villagers troop to market with the fruit of their fields or their artistry. White-robed women wend to temple worship on the days of the moon. Men of the drummer caste may be spied wearing a ritual garb with an effect that obscures their sex. Those are some of the types that catch the eye. Two features of native life in Kandy are there suggested, in their different planes: one is the central market-place, with its chaffering hum, where a wealth of tropical fruits is displayed, and the other that lodestar of the entire Buddhist world, the Temple of the Tooth Relic.

Nor can we do more than enumerate here the appointments of western civilisation in this last retreat of Sinhalese national tradition and sentiment: the old churches and religious seminaries, great schools, palatial hotels, up-to-date clubs, well-equipped hospitals, municipal hall and cinema, fine sporting fields, shops of every class and category, handsome residences, a stately vice-regal palace in beautiful grounds—the *ensemble*, in short, that constitutes the equipment and amenities of an up-to-date city, to which travellers resort not merely for a transitory view, but for a longer or a shorter sojourn.

Nuwara Eliya.

But what of Nuwara Eliya, the unique mountain resort and sanatorium, with a climate and general aspect that recall nothing less than an English (or Scotch) village magically transported to the tropics? Having arrived overnight by the midget train that groaned and creaked up the thousand feet climb in the four short miles from the junction on the main line, as it twisted and doubled back among tea-bushes and the back-yards of the railway settlement, we wake up to a world made new. The languor of the lower climes is gone, and a new zest in living is felt. If we have known beauty before, what language can describe the scene that is now unfolded to our enraptured gaze! Scales have fallen from our eyes. We discern a new mellowness that tones the hard contrasts of sunlit landscapes. The vegetation is less exuberant, and the loveliness of the individual tree finds more expression.

Match me the like of suave Nuwar' Eliya,
Hill-fended, nestling 'mid the grassy vales
Of Lanka's wooded heights, where never fails
A gentle spring. Her balmy airs allure
The alien travellers from far and near.

A thousand ways reminiscence assails
The exile when 'neath garish suns he ails
For greyness, mist, and eager nipping air.
Of northern homeland. Here bracken, gorse, and fir
Reclothe the landscape. Water-meads are starr'd
With daisies; moss-cradled violets lurk obscure;
Forget-me-nots enamel all the sward.
Trout idly glance, slow cattle browse the leas.
—A thought of England in far Indian seas.

(L. A. Arndt, in the *Ceylon Churchman*, 1921).

It is a happy cure for nostalgia, and full well is it availed of. When the heat of the plains grows less endurable at the equinoxes, the Colombo residents go to Nuwara Eliya, which strains its resources of hospitality (first-rate in themselves) to entertain the holiday crowd. Shows, races, gymkhanas, tournaments, and other festivities disturb its wonted peace, but they are a necessary adjunct alike of the routine of the Colombo workers and of the welfare of the settlement, to own house property in which is regarded as the ordinary desideratum of the wealthy of all races.

Those are not the best times, however, for the traveller to enjoy his stay at Nuwara Eliya. Its beauty and charm are savoured in quiet rambles through the woodlands or drives to less accessible spots, which must not be left unvisited. Fatigue is unknown as we tramp past the smooth-curved "patanas," with their pleasing alternation of grassland and forest, where the leopard lurks and the sambhur is hunted in season with hounds and knife. Inexhaustible is the entertainment Nature provides in this favoured retreat. Frosty skies with brilliant nights of stars; a tonic air; secluded paths in cooler shadow; wonderful gorges clothed with tree-fern or other undergrowth; a silvery trickle that takes the imagination a far journey to steaming plains where, grown to a mighty river, it moves in a majestic sweep to the ocean a hundred miles away; waterfalls sparkling in sunlight sifted through a roof of foliage; spray-born rainbows spanning the gullies; lofty eyries commanding the gorse-covered commons or the shining turf of the golf-courses, about which a well-stocked trout stream meanders lazily; many a coign of vantage for panoramic views of undulating country declining gently to the seaboard; a lake in a wilder setting than Kandy's, haunt of the angler for carp, lashed ever and anon to a mimic storm; passes and gaps where the plateau falls dizzily away at one's feet; a short and easy climb through changing belts of vegetation to Ceylon's highest summit, Pedrotalagala, 8,300 feet above sea-level, where the map of the island is unrolled below; cottages with smoking chimneys (last touch of Home), smothered in a wealth of English flowers; orchards bearing English apples, plums, pears, strawberries, gooseberries, and peaches; gardens under cabbages, turnips, radishes, rhubarb and lettuce; clumps of fir and pine; rhododendrons moulded by the wind; and—to round off the interminable list—an English churchyard with an English village church!

A Royal Sport.

There are two outstanding national customs in Ceylon which any visitor may consider himself fortunate indeed to make acquaintance with, if chance takes him to the island at the opportune season or date. One is an annual event timed for the August moon; the other is rarer, occurring at longer or shorter intervals as the policy to preserve a noble wild species dictates.

The latter is a royal sport, the capture of wild elephants. Weeks, or perhaps months, before the date approximately fixed for the final event, the villagers, under a form of feudal service, with axe and gun and simple rigout, enter the forest upon their weary and dangerous task. A solitary pool, retaining a trickle of moisture while the surrounding country is dry, is selected for enclosure within a strong stockade, and towards it in dense forest the beaters work in a great cordon, driving the unseen herd before them with shouting and fires and the beat of many drums. Heroisms are a commonplace of the beaters' days and nights, and not seldom the hereditary chiefs share their peril, one old campaigner recently at the cost of his life. The expectant public is kept posted by the Press; and the Kraal Officer (a senior civil servant), in consultation with the native chief of the district commanding the kraal, fixes the date and hour of the final drive-in. That is the spectacular climax which draws the highest in the land, with many a distinguished visitor, to the town of palm-leaf and bamboo that has sprung up in the jungle. Grandstands are provided for the guests along the stockade of living forest giants, it may be, lashed together to take the shock of the charging beasts that will not tamely yield their native heritage of lordly freedom.

In a crescendo of thrills the day approaches. Closer and closer the cordon is drawn. The sense of hearing is still the only witness to the presence of the invisible monsters, as the ear detects a shriller note in the din, which tells of every nerve strained to avert a last-minute breakaway. Intervals of rest are interposed for the timing of the finale, the beaters' handy camp outfit is requisitioned, great camp-fires rear their heads to flout the sunshine, and a brief peace settles on the scene, until silently the fresh order to advance is communicated to the line, which reforms with military precision, and the herd is driven yet nearer to the masked stockade gate. Suddenly, in ones and twos, followed by the mass of the herd, and with unwilling stragglers in the rear, the actors in the title rôle make their first appearance, and the Second Act of this living drama opens.

The thrill of expectation now gives place to a sense of impending climax, as the herd masses together within the pool in a last stand for dear liberty. The decoy elephants and noosers are let in. A grand beast, hero and favourite of past kraals and pageants, leads the charge, and the jungle comes down in great swathes. The air becomes tense with the danger and the excitement. And then pandemonium breaks loose. The earth quakes under the tramping and trumpetings of the infuriated leviathans. But, with more than human skill and tact, the decoys detach them one by one from the herd. Daring noosers are nimble to seize their opportunity; they slip off their mounts and the sure lasso tightens round a lifted hind-leg to the limit of deterrent pain, and one more royal captive yields up his liberty with a roar of baffled rage.

Desperate are the thunderous charges made by the rest of the herd upon the unyielding fence; madly they retreat from the flaming wall, prickly with thrust spear-points. The decoys pursue their task unperturbed. Calm in their ascendancy over their wilder brethren, they co-operate with their masters in intelligent strategy, to impose their will upon them, and when the last prisoner for the day has been made fast, they march out in orderly file, conscious in bearing and dignity of a great day's sport.

The leaping flames of the fires that have been lighted round the stockade play upon the gaunt, mysterious forms of the captives, still loudly protesting and straining with all the weight of their ponderous carcases at the ropes that secure them.

TYPICAL PEARL DIVERS.

KEELAKARAI DIVERS PREPARING TO DIVE.

BOATS OF THE PEARL DIVERS.

WASHING ROTTED OYSTERS.

[Photos: Plâté, Ltd.

PEARL INDUSTRY OF CEYLON.

The drama moves to its quiet close. The fate of the several prisoners (numbering from a score to a hundred) is determined, and the herd is divided, as the chiefs take their quota, and single units are sold and led away to profitable servitude under various humane and admiring masters, while others, perhaps, happy overplus exceeding the requisite or permitted catch, receive the freewill gift of restored liberty.

A Royal Pageant.

Grown docile with kind usage, some of the captive elephants will soon make another appearance on a different stage, viz., that of the Annual Perahera (or Pageant) in Kandy, an historic custom with an origin shrouded in legend. However that may be, the ceremony, while it is but a pale reflection of the ancient pomp and circumstance of Sinhalese royal power, offers scope to the entire population of the district for a fortnight's carnival. Villages are deserted by the migrating crowds, who bivouac in the open spaces. Booths spring up in the vicinity of the Temple of the Tooth, the focal-point of all the ritual; secular carnival is emphasised by numerous side-shows, which enjoy a paying popularity. Even the European hotels make capital of the occasion to arrange a special Perahera programme centering round the moment when the pageant shall pass by.

The procession is so arranged that from day to day the bounds are wider and the hour altered until from being a midday event it falls at the popular hour of 9 p.m., when it becomes the greatest draw. With duly ordered precedence the elephants and the dignitaries of the different temples (Hindu among them) take their place in the line. Three and three the richly-caparisoned beasts move in stately and unhurried progression. Tinsel and colour recall the magnificence of the past, when the wealth of the city was lavished on this central occasion of national festivity, and the trappings were of pure gold; kings then took part in it, riding in golden chariots drawn by spirited steeds.

The hereditary chiefs, superhuman in their proportions from the multiple swathings of their gorgeous national dress, attended by their satellites, lead each section of the procession. Torchlight and beat of drum and the frenzied dancing to shrill pipes stun the mind into a feeling of unreality, until the stilt-walkers and ludicrous figures germane to carnival bring the necessary comic relief. Dense throngs are merged into the pageant, which assumes the aspect of an advancing victorious host. Every vantage-point on the route, whether boundary-wall or roof or tree, is packed with lookers-on of every degree and station. Nor is a dramatic climax wanting, for the very heart and core of the pageantry, the *pièce de résistance*, is awaited with a general thrill. A gun

THE ROCK OF SIGIRIYA.
An Ancient Sinhalese Fortress.

GAL VIHARE.
Rock Temple with recumbent figure of Buddha, 46 feet in length, cut from the rock. The figure, representing Buddha at his attainment of Nirvana, is the best executed specimen in Ceylon.

MIRISAVETIYA DAGOBA, ANURADHAPURA.

RESTORED STATUES AT RUANWELI DAGOBA, ANURADHAPURA.

SOME OF THE ANCIENT RUINS OF CEYLON.

Although Ceylon is so close to India, and Buddhism originated in India, there are no Buddhist monuments in the peninsula so old as those of Ceylon, which date back to the third century B.C.

is heard, and the leading actor, the elephant of the Temple of the Tooth, descends the temple steps after making ceremonial obeisance. It is worthy of its place at the centre of the spectacle. With the dignity of age and commanding stature, it steps out, the cynosure of every eye, bearing on its back a golden howdah containing what is probably the source and origin of the ceremonial, the venerated Relic. It sweeps the crowd along in its wake, and upon it the curtain may fall, for it would take too long to enumerate the rest of the ritual of a ceremony that never fails to attract visitor and resident alike, and has even been included in special programmes for the entertainment of Royal visitors.

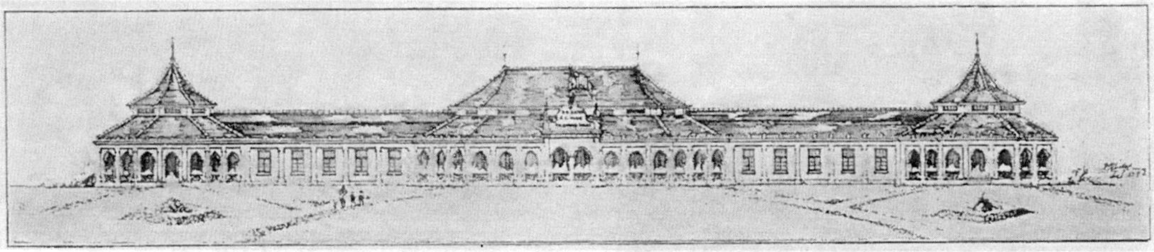

PROPOSED PILGRIMS' REST AT ANURADHAPURA.

Buried Cities.

Nature has resumed her ancient régime in Anuradhapura, where once Ceylon's kings held sway for 1,250 years. Noble forest trees spread their shade over green park country, where every open space not built upon with the growth of the administrative capital of to-day carries some fallen relic of their magnificence or their liberal patronage of religion. The present population of the town is a meagre four thousand, while in the palmy days of the great capital it must have been numbered in hundreds of thousands. A Sinhalese writer, cited by Knighton in his *History of Ceylon*, has thus described the old city as it was about 1000 A.D., on the eve of its decline, and after it had, in fact, ceased to be the capital of the island: " This magnificent city is refulgent from the numerous temples and palaces, whose golden pinnacles glitter in the sky. Its streets are spanned by arches of pliant wood bearing flags of gold and silver, whilst vessels of the same metals containing flowers are observed on every side. In niches placed for the purpose are statues holding lamps. Elephants, horses, carts, and multitudes of people are ever to be seen passing and repassing. There are dancers, jugglers, and musicians of all kinds and of all nations, the latter performing on their chank shells ornamented with gold. The city is 16 miles in length from north to south, and the same in breadth from east to west. The principal streets are . . . all of which are of immense extent, some containing 11,000 houses; to enumerate the smaller would be impossible."

The outburst of the nation's vigorous youth, after the expulsion of a Dravidian usurper from South India in 237 B.C., is thus portrayed by a modern writer: " As if by the waving of a magic wand temples, tanks, parks, gardens, public buildings, resting houses for man and beast, hospitals —also for man and beast—free almonries, schools and colleges for monks and nuns (once numbered in tens of thousands), gymnasiums and public halls were erected throughout the land. There was dazzling magnificence within the sacred city, which contained nine-storeyed houses; and the streets were crowded day and night by throngs of pilgrims and also traders from all parts of the then known world. The atmosphere was saturated with the fragrance of sweet-smelling flowers and delicate perfumes. Elephants, superbly caparisoned, and with gilded howdahs on their backs, and chariots drawn by prancing steeds, paraded the wide ways of the city. The glittering spears, burnished helmets, and coats of iron of the cavalrymen, and foot-soldiers armed with bows and arrows, were seen in the thoroughfares, and the air reverberated with joyous shouts of " Sadhu! Sadhu! " (Hail, hail).

These accounts are corroborated by the celebrated Chinese traveller and monk, Fa Hien, who spent two years in Ceylon, about 413 A.D., and has left an account of the broad, straight streets of Anuradhapura, the beautiful public buildings, the mountain-like monuments, and the ceremonies at the exhibition of the Tooth Relic.

The archæological survey of the last fifty years has laid bare but the sketchy outline of the splendid capital, and that is the magnet which draws curious travellers from all parts of the world, not to speak of sociologists and antiquaries of more serious purpose.

A brief description of some of the things to be seen in this and other " buried cities " may be given here, the reader being referred for a more detailed and scientific account of these historic ruins to an extensive bibliography easily obtainable.

Fittingly placed at the centre is the Bo Tree (a species of ficus), one of the oldest trees in the world, grown from a slip of the sacred tree at Buddhagaya, in India, that was brought to Ceylon 2,200 years ago. It remains an object of veneration to many thousands of pilgrims, who crowd annually to the spot, and treasure the very fallen leaves of a symbolic tree that in itself presents no very striking appearance to the stranger; he would scarcely credit its great age, but that is authenticated by the independent witness of Fa Hien, the traveller already referred to.

Nearly as old is the Brazen Palace, the "Terrestrial Sun," so called from its roof of brazen tiles. It was nine storeys high, and comprised 1,000 rooms. The vast central hall was lined with golden statues of lions and elephants, and at the far end stood an ivory throne, behind which were emblems of the sun, moon, and stars, in gold and silver and brass respectively. What remains to-day is only 1,600 gneiss monoliths, bare of ornament, marking a site 230 feet square.

Built by the same king, his *magnum opus*, which he did not live to complete, being borne out at his desire that he might feast his dying eyes on the gladdening sight, is the Ruanveli dagoba, or relic-house. Its exterior was coated with gold dust. Marred by modern restoration, it still has much interest for the visitor. In its vicinity are many Buddhas, a fine statue of the king, larger than life, altars, carved stones, inscriptions ten to twenty centuries old. Here may be seen the typical "moonstones" — half-moon slabs for doorway and stairfoot, richly carved in high or low relief—the griffin janitors (*makaras*) and the guardian *nagaradjas*—handsome figures of men canopied with hoods of many cobras—and, lastly, the merry elves (*ganas*), carved on step and capital.

Ruins of vast monasteries lie scattered over the park country, all built on a uniform plan (a quincunx), and surrounded by a profusion of ruined cisterns and ponds (notably a fine monolith cistern), until we come to the Thuparama, now restored to its ancient semblance, situated near to the site of the former Temple of the Tooth Relic. Almost virgin territory to the antiquary succeeds this area to northward, marked by one of the most striking features of the city, a towering brick spire surmounting a huge and lofty ruin known as the Jetavanarama.

Passing by more monasteries in various stages of decay and buried in thick jungle, we return to the central Bo Tree, to south of which we are shown the probable site of the tomb of Ehala, a Tamil usurper, which was the object of the chivalry of the Sinhalese king, who slew him in a terrific duel on elephant-back (the monsters sharing in the fight) and, setting up a rock pillar, inscribed upon it this decree: "Let no prince in future pass this way riding in palanquin or litter or with the beating of drums." Some ten centuries later, in British times, a fugitive Kandyan noble, fleeing from the consequences of an unsuccessful rebellion, and passing the same way, but uncertain of the exact site, alighted, worn out as he was, and solemnly walked some distance in scrupulous regard for a noble sentiment.

Mention must also be made of the hill of Mihintale, some eight miles away, and once probably the extreme limit of the city. This is sacred to Mahinda, the royal monk who first preached Buddhism in the island. Pious feet have worn away the surface of the thousand and more rock steps that lead to the summit. The ascent is lined with interesting ruins of sculpture; the Naga Pokuna (Cobra Bath), a large hewn-out cistern with a carving of a great five-headed cobra, is the most notable.

The story of Polonnaruwa, the island's other great capital of former times, is mainly the story of Ceylon's greatest King, Parakrama Bahu the Great. The elder Bishop Copleston discerned in the epic quality of the ancient chronicler's story of his reign the same joyous feeling that prompted the ballad of "King Henry, the Hero of Navarre." In a similar happy comparison he says of this remarkable monarch: "It was given to him to unite the careers of a Julius and an Augustus. We have followed him to the point at which the greater Roman's career was cut short, and leave him prepared to inaugurate the Augustan Age of Lanka." That is comparing small things to great, but it is none the less a just estimate of a king who, from being heir to one of the many small principalities into which the kingdom was divided, not only achieved his ambition to unite the whole country under his sceptre, but even carried his victorious arms to Cambodia and South India, whose kings he compelled to pay tribute. He raised a new Anuradhapura in this city of Polonnaruwa, which now lies desolate.

To describe these ruins would savour of repetition, and mention need only be made of the palace, built like a mediæval castle, with thick walls, and a huge rock-temple with a sleeping Buddha. Prakrama Bahu had a lofty conception of kingship. There is a decree of his extant which runs: "In such a land as this not even the least drop of the water that the rain supplies should go to the ocean without bringing help to man; except places where the mines are, of gems and silver and such-like precious things, in every spot provision must be made for maintaining fields. Not to live for the people's good but merely to enjoy the good things that have come to our hand—such a life is utterly unfit for me!" That brings us to the most eloquent witness to a great past, namely, the vast irrigation systems of Prakrama Bahu and his predecessors. The whole of the northern plain, the ancient granary of Ceylon, is dotted with these tanks and canals, which remain the wonder of modern engineers. To describe one would be to describe all, so that it would suffice to mention the Kalawewa Tank, which is believed to be the Lake Megisba described by Pliny. This magnificent reservoir receives the drainage of 240 square miles of mountain country by three streams, which merge into a wide river. The sluices of the tank are 400 ft. above sea-level, and all the land as far as the sea was irrigated by it. The bund is 5½ miles in length, and in places 65 ft. high; the base width is 250 ft. The area of the tank is 4,425 acres, and its contour 35 miles. Among the canals flowing out of it is the Yodi Ela, 60 miles in length. It was the pride of Sir William Gregory, a former Governor, to have this channel restored, as other irrigation works have been since. The twentieth century engineers made little alteration in the trace of nearly fifteen centuries ago. "This monument of real kings" is the phrase used by Sir William in his gratification at seeing it restored.

We come now to Sigiriya, which must certainly be unique among engineering marvels. Here a patricide prince (479 A.D.), fleeing from a brother's vengeance, found this gigantic boulder of rock, 400 ft. high, and turned it into an impregnable citadel, protected by a moat. A spiral gallery ran round the upper part of the bulging mass, literally hung like a swallow's nest, and emerging at the only point, four feet wide, where there is no overhang. The aerial retreat towers solitary above a sea of forest, but was replete with all the appointments of a royal seat. To get from a lower platform to the upper citadel one walked right into the very jaws of a mighty lion, the claws of which alone are visible to-day, each a man's height. The lower terraces and approaches were protected by a wall of a pink smoothness that remains a marvel to the present day. The surface of the rock was covered with spirited frescoes, traces of which remain where the hollows have protected them from the weather.

Other striking ruins are scattered about the country, notably in the south, showing how the Sinhalese kings were driven from pillar to post by the invading Tamils. Much yet remains to be explored. In one of these retreats was found, more than half-a-century ago, the Sinhalese metrical chronicle on palm-leaves, from which is derived most of our knowledge of the island's history, namely, the Mahawansa (Genealogy of the Great). The first part of it was the work of a Buddhist monk, who wrote back one thousand years to the conversion of the country to Buddhism. Other hands continued it down to 1815 A.D.

Galle.

Under its full name of Point de Galle, this port was well-known to mariners of previous centuries. The present town has grown up on the rocky western arm of a big bay facing south-west, two miles wide at the entrance, and enclosing a wide sweep of water. The shores of the bay are fringed with coconut palms. Opposite to the town is a wooded cliff; and the whole aspect of the place, with hills in the distance stretching up to the great mountain range, is one of great beauty.

Galle has been a port from ancient times, and has even been (conjecturally) identified by Tennent with the Tarshish of Solomon. Its modern history begins with the Portuguese, who built a fort on the western rock, which was later replaced by the Dutch fort. The latter, in wonderfully good preservation, exists to-day, and encloses the official business and residential quarters. A fine V.O.C. (Dutch East India Company) coat of arms, dated 1668, is an interesting survival. The entrance to Galle harbour is extremely difficult for large steamers, being a narrow passage between sunken rocks. There is no artificial protection from the south-west; and, owing to the existence of shallow places, the amount of anchorage is small, considering the great expanse of the bay. It is, however, possible, if future trade conditions require it, that by blasting operations to remove dangerous rocks, and the building of a small breakwater, the available space may be much increased and the harbour used for the relief of congestion in Colombo. As it is, Galle exhibits signs of a trade revival after years of sleepiness. Steamers of the British India, Clan, and Asiatic lines call there regularly, and others at odd intervals. There is a fair and steady import trade in

[Photo: Platé, Ltd.

ESPLANADE AND RAMPARTS, GALLE.

rice and other foodstuffs, and the exports are low-country products, coconuts and their by-products, rubber, citronella-oil, etc. The fort, with its many old and perfectly preserved Dutch buildings, is quaint and picturesque, if unexciting. In its bazaars are to be found the best tortoise-shell and the best workmen in that art in Ceylon; and, as a piece of curious information, it may be mentioned that for two generations Galle has supplied, and still supplies, hereditary barbers to the P. and O. steamers; while the few enterprising emigrants among the lower classes of Sinhalese almost all hail from this town or district. The town is the headquarters of the Southern Province; and the Provincial head official called the Government Agent is the Chairman of its Municipality.

view of coral-gardens and the lace-work of the waves in a tiny bay at its base. Here are to be seen the ruins of a Buddhist-cum-Hindu temple, which, tradition says, once shone out to sea with its thousand statues and columns, bedecked with gold and gems; but the Portuguese despoiled it in the 16th century. Down the coast is lovely Tangalle, and, when we come to Hambantota, with its salt-pans, we are at the portals of the mighty forest which has many secrets yet to reveal, for it played its part in stirring events, hiding in its depths many a fine rocky citadel for fugitive princes and their armies or a retreat for contemplative monks.

There are interesting village activities to be seen in this district, such as the coir, lace, gemming,

[Photo: Plâté, Ltd.

RAILWAY AT THE HORSE SHOE BEND, SCRUBB'S ESTATE, NANA OYA PASS.

While Galle has its own scenic and historic interest, with a fine prospect from Buona Vista, for example, and a beautiful riverscape at Wakwella, and the same social, educational, and sporting activities as we have seen in other towns, it is also the starting-point for interesting trips in the neighbourhood. The pretty town of Matara, the next and terminal station on the railway, is another Dutch relic, with forts in as good preservation as Galle's. According to Sinhalese tradition, Matara had once a great reputation for learning, and the memory of one poet is preserved. Then there is Dondra Head, the most southerly point, fronting the illimitable expanse of ocean, unbroken by any land until the South Polar Continent is reached. A fine lighthouse affords a grand prospect and a

citronella-oil, arrack, and plumbago industries, and most notably the lacquer-work with the dye produced by the lac insect. There is much which it has been necessary to omit in our general survey of Ceylon, more especially that pertaining to unsophisticated village life, so interesting to the western visitor, but there would be leisure on these trips to look around. In prosperous villages, where food is plentiful and the struggle for existence unknown, the huts of coconut-leaf thatch and brick or mud-and-wattle walls have a trim appearance, though where there is distress it appears in the crazy and unkempt aspect of even these easily-rigged dwellings. In the sprucely-kept front-yards, swept bone-clean and hard, under the dense shade of clumps of plantain (as the banana is called in Ceylon), or bread-fruit, jak, or other food-tree, for every one of the commoner fruit-trees is represented in the poorest gardens, the domestic activities of the women may be espied, from the bent and tottering crone to the little three-year-old set to tend her infant successors or, perhaps, to fetch fire from a neighbour's in the form of a blazing torch of coconut leaves or a smouldering fragment of coconut shell cradled in the husk of the same. There would be the grain to dry or the fish or lime-fruit to pickle; or the herbs and tubers to sort for the decoction prescribed by the "vederala," according to the old stanzas memorised in oral tradition; or there would be the rhythmic toil of one or two or three pairs of arms to pound the rice with long pole-like pestles in a tall mortar hollowed out of a log of wood, for the leavened cakes, called "hoppers," which constitute the universal "cereals-and-yeast" of a Ceylon breakfast, and when daintily prepared in the home make a toothsome morsel. Again, there is the *al fresco* bathing in parties (mark of modesty) at a well or running stream, the water being swilled over the body in cool cascades from a gurgling earthenware pot. On festal days the great tomtom, a yard in diameter, will be brought out and heated over a fire of coals for greater tautness, and on it a dozen twinkling hands of laughing women (aged virtuosos among them) will beat out well-remembered melodies with a tireless abandon. Then there is the preparation of cup-sugar from the toddy of the coconut or *kitul* palm; the latter yields the sweeter product, the best Kandy "jaggery," cleanly prepared by known specialists, being a universally popular sweetmeat equal to any in delicacy and flavour, though the stranger is warned off the common market product. Meanwhile, the menfolk, the season of labour in the fields being past, and the crops garnered, and no Government or private works affording employment, dawdle through the day, idle and ripe for mischief, swayed by every wind of rumour as is the way of the peasant all the world over.

Trincomalee

Situated in the middle of the east coast of the island, Trincomalee possesses one of the finest natural harbours in the whole world. It is practically land-locked, is of great natural beauty, and is said to be capable of accommodating the largest naval force ever remotely likely to be concentrated there.

[Photo: Plâté, Ltd.

VIEW FROM FLAGSTAFF, FORT FREDERICK, LOOKING TOWARDS DUTCH BAY, TRINCOMALEE.

At one time "Trinco" was the headquarters of the East Indies squadron, and is still an important station, for gunnery practice is regularly carried out there, and the Admiral commanding has a local official residence. Its naval importance dates from the first landing there of the Dutch: and a military and naval station it has remained since with (fittingly) another claim to fame as the birthplace of the late Lord Fisher.

Commercially Trincomalee has so far an unimpressive history. It is situated in the "dry zone." The coastal fringe is cultivated with coconuts, but the hinterland has been forest and jungle for hundreds of years. With the completion of the railway connecting Colombo with Trincomalee and the hoped-for development of the surrounding districts, as well as the exploitation of the very valuable timber forests, there is some prospect that Trincomalee will assume real commercial importance in the future: and it is possible that, as a port of transhipment for South Indian goods it may to some extent relieve Colombo. Its naval importance it can never lose. There is, in fact, a serious body of opinion which holds that Trincomalee is preferable strategically to the naval base of Singapore.

We are on romantic ground, for Trincomalee has echoed with the thunders of the big wars of Napoleon's day, and many a fighting frigate refitted then in her land-locked waters. Here was the gateway by which Portuguese, Dutch, and British in turn had access to the Sinhalese kings at Kandy, and down this highway their armies marched.

The romantic interest of the country, with its iron coast, is clinched by the demarcation of the railway now running to Trincomalee (China Bay) from Maho on the Anuradhapura line, and the twin-line that branches off to Batticoloa. This area once comprised the granary of ancient Ceylon, and the trace runs past the wonderful irrigation tanks and channels and the interesting temples and dagobas with stupendous Buddha images, melancholy witness, all, to the existence in a bygone day of a vast population of artificers and labourers, and gigantic cultivation schemes. Near Trincomalee, again, is the "White Man's Tree," with a stone (placed in 1893) to inform the passer-by that here Robert Knox was captured by the Sinhalese in 1659. He spent twenty years in exile in Ceylon (his father sharing the first year till death brought him his reprieve), and on his return to England he published his celebrated "Historical Relation," which is an interesting and valuable account of the Sinhalese generally and the Kandyan Court in particular.

Thus the gulf is bridged between the old Ceylon and the new: for it is in this region more than anywhere else that a new chapter lies ready to be opened. Ceylon is an agricultural country, and the call is to her sons to throw open again to cultivation vast tracts that once were smiling rice-fields, but are now for the most part (though the exceptions are notable) given over to jungle and wild animals, and the homes of men are poor and few and far between. Capital is wanted, and enterprise; likewise a determination to employ all known means (and discover new ones) to exterminate the mosquito, which holds up the march of progress in this outlying district of an otherwise prosperous island. A certain measure of sacrifice is inevitable, and a stopping of the ears to the siren-lure of the big towns, where careers are for the few and the unsuccessful are a drag and a deadweight. The writing of this new chapter, the restoration of Ceylon's ancient granary, which would be symbolical of a revival within practical limits, of some of the national arts, e.g., architecture, will be watched with real interest by the friends of Ceylon, both at home and abroad, and they are many.

COLOMBO.

The Port.

If Anuradhapura is the sacred city of Ceylon, and Kandy the home of its "national sentiment of modern history," Colombo is the centre of its commerce, culture, and wealth, and a principal source of its imperial importance. Situated on the great ocean routes between England and Australia, Farther India, and China, and at convenient coaling distance from Aden, Durban, Calcutta, Singapore, and Fremantle, its rise to greatness was inevitable once Galle, at the south-west corner of the island, and with a slight advantage over Colombo in actual position, was abandoned by the P. and O. Company as the port of call for its steamers. The reasons for the change were two-fold: Colombo could more easily and cheaply be converted to a first-class harbour suitable for great steamers, and it was the natural coast terminus for the mountain railway which carries Ceylon's leading products to the sea. Galle is far more distant from Kandy, and the nature of the country vetoed any idea of a railway from Kandy to Galle. As a modern harbour Colombo is only about forty years old, though the Portuguese, Dutch, and English, always made it their capital. It was originally a small roadstead formed by a curve of the coast south of the Kelani River, with slight protection to the west afforded by a short line of rock jutting out northwards. Here were two or three small jetties at which people and goods were landed by small boats, often in heavy and dangerous seas. A comparison of this primitive affair with Colombo harbour to-day shows the amazing progress made in a short time. Three breakwaters—one to the south-west, one "island breakwater" on the north, and one jutting out from the north-eastern shore—now enclose an area of over a square mile, forming one of the largest artificial harbours in the world, and affording accommodation for nearly forty large steamers, besides small sailing craft.

An extra arm was recently thrown out seawards from the south-west breakwater to mitigate the violence of the monsoon seas. Even now, at the height of the two monsoons, the sea within the harbour is choppy, though not dangerous, and on rare occasions of heavy storm, when ships are known to break adrift from their moorings, vessels have to lie outside until the weather abates. The harbour is kept continually dredged to such a depth as to provide water for any ship passing through the Suez Canal; and the stately post-war vessels of the P. and O. and Orient lines, big Cunarders, and Canadian Pacific liners, Dutch and French mail steamers, and battle cruisers, are familiar sights. With the exception of the jetty provided for oiling purposes, there are no alongside berths in Colombo; ships are moored stem and stern to anchored buoys, and the mode of loading and discharging is by lighters brought alongside.

Passengers are carried to and from the shore in steam and motor launches, of which there is a cheap and efficient service: and small rowing boats are available day and night.

In pre-war days every large passenger steamer was surrounded on arrival by a fleet of these small boats, bringing jewellers, trick divers, fruit-sellers, dhobies, and a host of others to amuse—and fleece—the passengers. In the interests of health, order, and the safety of passengers' belongings, this traffic is now stopped; and, while passengers may miss an amusement which tided over the period of waiting for landing or sailing, the new regulation is undoubtedly in the best interests of everybody concerned, except of those deprived of a valuable source of revenue.

The absence of wet docks or of alongside berths would appear at first sight to be a serious disadvantage, both as to time and cost. But, of course, lighters can be worked on both sides of the ship, and vessels are coaled at Colombo as rapidly as anywhere else in the East. From time to time the possibilities of providing alongside facilities have been seriously examined by the Port Authority. There is no doubt that this, and the connected question of increasing the actual ship accommodation of the port, are matters which will engage more and more attention. Accommodation is at present sufficient to cope with normal traffic, given no undue congestion from extraneous causes, such as strikes. But there have been such periods of congestion.

[Photo: Plâté, Ltd.

MAIN STREET, COLOMBO.

A notable occasion was the arrival, late in 1914, of the first great contingent of Australians, on their way to Egypt and the Dardanelles, with their attendant escorts. On that occasion every berth was occupied, and more than twenty vessels rode at anchor outside waiting their turn to enter for coal and provisions. Viewed from the commanding height of the Grand Oriental Hotel roof garden, this Armada of huge liners, with warships of four allied nations, presented a noble and thrilling spectacle. The names Melbourne and Sydney, given to two of the landing jetties, recall the fact that here were landed the wounded British and Germans from the sea fight in which the *Emden* was destroyed. Other instances of congestion occurred when, from reports of enemy raiders in the Indian ocean, or the discovery (through the sinking of two large steamers within sight of the port) of a German minefield in the immediate vicinity, shipping was held up by Admiralty orders.

An emergency amounting to crisis arose quite recently when, by a strike of harbour labour, affecting nearly 15,000 men, the trade of the port was temporarily brought to a standstill. In such a case vessels can be diverted to Galle and elsewhere; but in war-time this course is scarcely practicable, Galle being undefended.

Leaving aside such abnormal occurrences, it seems clear that in the future this problem of accommodation will become pressing. Colombo must be regarded in this connection, not from the point of view of the import and export trade of Ceylon, or of the transhipment of South-Indian cargoes, though these aspects are important, but as a fuelling and provisioning port of world-wide significance. In 1922 in the figures of tonnage of steamers entered and cleared, it stood third in the British Empire, and eighth in the world.

Ocean traffic through these waters is increasing: Colombo has not suffered from the opening of the Panama Canal, and it will become more, and not less, important as time goes on. Its possibilities of expansion are limited. Any attempt on the western or seaward side would simply mean an entirely new artificial harbour, without any natural rocks to start from. The huge mass of sand discharged by the Kelani River, and the existence of the sandy bar at its mouth, render highly uncertain the utility of any effort to make use either of the river itself, or of the shallow water space between its mouth and the north-eastern breakwater.

There is a large swampy area eastward of the harbour which has been suggested as a possible site for a wet dock. But, besides the excavation of the area itself, a long passage would have to be hewn through a low rocky hill, at a very heavy cost.

Finally, south of the harbour and near to it, in the centre of Colombo, is a lake or "lagoon," at present separated from the harbour area by a short canal used by cargo lighters. The utilisation of this area would again be a very costly matter; at present, by constant dredging, a few channels are kept open for lighters to a depth of about six feet. The land between this lake and the harbour, comprising much of old Colombo, is largely reclaimed: it is naturally subject to a tendency towards subsidence, and the construction of a ship canal would greatly accentuate this tendency. In these circumstances attention to-day is mostly concentrated on quick handling and despatch. Greatly increased provision of warehouses and jetties, more and larger cargo lighters, adequate and regular labour, wharfside cranes, ample and quickly moved coal supplies, railway facilities, including, besides sidings, a track all round the harbour with a through connection from each end to the main line, and, finally, a large and modern oil installation at Kolonnawa, in East Colombo, are among the means adopted to the end mentioned.

Situated at some distance from the harbour, and screened from the sea by low hills, the oil installation, under the control of the Port Authority, has large storage for petrol, kerosine, and liquid fuel. Pipe-lines are provided direct to harbour to pump oil to and from steamers, and there is a rail connection.

[Photo: Plâté, Ltd.

YORK STREET, LOOKING TOWARDS THE HARBOUR, COLOMBO.

An interesting feature of the warehousing facilities of the port is found in the two large sets of grain stores, used at present exclusively for rice, known as the Chalmers Granaries and the Manning Market. Built originally on ratproof lines in connection with a successful campaign for the control of plague in Colombo, these stores proved of the utmost value during the food scarcity in 1919. Within them were stored the reserves of rice, and from them were issued the weekly allotments for all districts of the island. They have a total storage capacity of upwards of 60,000 tons, and are held to be the best grain warehouses in the East.

As to further means of dealing with ocean traffic, recent indications seem to point to the development of Galle and Trincomalee, to which reference has already been made. The control of Colombo harbour is vested in a body called the Port Commission, a Government department composed partly of officials connected with the port, and partly of unofficial business men. The Chief Collector of Customs is ex-officio Chairman, and the two executive officers are the Harbour Engineer and the Master Attendant, or Harbour Master. The latter official is responsible for the safe berthing and despatch of vessels, and for the control of harbour traffic, and is head of the Port Commission and pilot service. He has also magisterial jurisdiction over the harbour area.

[Photo: Plâté, Ltd.

HINDU TEMPLE, COLOMBO.

The Harbour Engineer, besides the superintending of all these works, controls the dry dock (situated at the north-east corner, and capable of taking the largest vessels normally using the port) and the oil installation. Pilotage is compulsory: and pilotage fees, entering dues, mooring rents, cargo dues, and fees for various services, constitute the port revenue. The expenditure, after examination by the Port Commission, is incorporated in the annual colonial Budget, and requires the sanction of the legislature. Big capital expenditure has been met by means of loans under Government guarantee, and the excess of revenue over expenditure is applied in interest and debt reduction.

Secretariat Building, containing the Legislative Council Chambers, Colombo.

The visitor's contact with all this officialdom will be limited to his dealings with the policeman who sees his passport, the Port Surgeon, who occasionally glances at him, and the Customs officials who pass his baggage on arrival ashore. And, in general, he will be impressed by the courtesy and speed with which they do their business. His launch journey from the ship will not take more than ten minutes, and within an hour of his vessel coming to its moorings he should be walking from the passenger jetty to the G.O.H. for his cocktail.

The Fort.

Although the page of Colombo's more recent history is crowded with events, no external memorials have survived the successive tides of change that have swept over the city. Named for its good roadstead by the Moors in the 13th century, Colombo has changed, and still changes, with every decade. Once a circumvallated fort, and part still bearing that appellation, it carries no traces of the former fortifications, except perhaps the sketchy remains of an old Dutch wall. Where once the principal ship canal flowed past warehouses on the water's edge, runs now the fine broad thoroughfare into which one steps from the landing-pier; the residence of the Dutch Governors, fronting the harbour, is now St. Peter's Church; the old Dutch cemetery is the Gordon Gardens, commemorating a distinguished Governor, to which has recently been transferred from another site a Jubilee Statue of Queen Victoria enthroned, and at the top end of which, teeming with memories but soon to be replaced by a more modern edifice in the best residential quarter, stands Queen's House, the residence of the Governor.

[Photo: Plâté, Ltd.

SINHALESE WOMEN POUNDING RICE.

Far from carrying traces of its diverse history, the Fort wears quite an English air, with its great blocks of handsome or even imposing buildings, whether hotels or banks, shops or business offices. The wide streets are flanked by pavements or arcades, which carry a foot traffic not specially typical of Ceylon, but approximating to the general type of the cosmopolitan emporiums of the East, and a visitor in search of local colour may experience a feeling of disappointment. His local colour may on occasions be limited to a group of gaping country-folk on holiday, looking lost amid the bewildering strangeness of the big city. Even the apparel of the Moorish pedlar of curiosities and precious stones (or coloured glass) is western as to jacket, pince-nez, watch-chain, and brogues, and he can converse with equal fluency in English and French. Nor do the smaller tobacconists' and curio shops fall short of the standard of their English (and, it may be, Ceylonese) neighbours, while the high-class Moorish jewellers or the Bombay silk merchants make a brave and even alluring show.

Cool tea-rooms and the arcades referred to are a boon to the voyager ashore for only a few hours of the sunniest part of the day, affording a retreat from the bustle of a city busied about a more than empire-wide commerce.

But not commerce alone, for the city is only one part commercial, and political, academic, and social Colombo may meet the stroller's eye as he loafs and culls impressions. A compendious opportunity to realise the comity of races that is Colombo's boast would be a glimpse (if chance so

[Photo: Plâté, Ltd.

SINHALESE LACE MAKERS.

favour) of the ceremonial opening of the Legislative Council, when the representatives of the different provincial and communal electorates in their varying garb of ceremony create an effect of pomp and colour not easily to be matched in a working day.

We have had in mind, so far, the voyager who saunters along the pavements with an eye on his watch, alert not to miss his boat. Not thus is Colombo to be savoured. It is incomplete impressions derived in such fashion that find their way through an undiscriminating publisher to an untravelled public. Nor are licensed native guide and astute gharry-driver, nor even the rickshapuller, nimble-minded as he is nimble-footed, to be trusted to leave the visitor as fully stocked with the most correct and pleasurable impressions of one of the healthiest and happiest towns in the East, as they are likely themselves to be with the rupees of their guests of a day! A hurried run through a residential quarter, a progress through noise and smells to a Hindu temple or two, another to a Buddhist temple, pursued at various points by piratical urchins, clamouring for the price of desistance (and of a posy of wild flowers), it may be even a run to Mount Lavinia (which is no mountain) through the dustiest and most " 'bus-ridden " of the arterial roads—that is what falls to the lot of most callers at Colombo to the detriment of the city's good name.

[Photo: Plâté, Ltd.

GENERAL POST OFFICE, COLOMBO.

We hope to present in these pages a truer picture of Colombo, suggesting an itinerary that will afford the maximum of delight. The north gate of Queen's House shall be our stand for a first comprehensive view of the central part of the Fort. We take up our position, under the eyes of the Sikh sentries, at the foot of a bronze statue of Sir Edward Barnes, Governor, road-maker, and coffee pioneer (1820-1831). At its erection seventeen years after the close of his régime, this memorial received touching marks of reverence from the common people, and it had to be railed off when homage developed into worship, and offerings began to be placed at its base.

[Photo: Plâté, Ltd.

NEW TOWN HALL, COLOMBO.

Looking to the left, we see the block of Government buildings occupied by the Secretariat, including the Council Hall, but this, too, is shortly to be transferred to a grander habitation on a site among the best outside the Fort. Before us, to the right, is the General Post Office, an imposing pile of ambitious architecture. Colombo's " skyscrapers " draw the eye, dwarfing the lighthouse-cum-clock tower " standing where it ought not," in the centre of the vortex of motor traffic, a palpable obstruction. Our coign of vantage affords glimpses of several large English shops and bank buildings, while looking southward is seen in a vanishing perspective the road that will soon take us down the celebrated Galle Face esplanade. We shall pass on the way the Echelon Barracks, where the remarkably efficient Ceylonese volunteer garrison, successor to former regimental garrisons, is worthily housed, together with a company each of Royal Garrison Artillery and Royal Engineers.

Galle Face.

First place in any list of things to see in Colombo will always belong to the local Plymouth Hoe, as beautiful Galle Face has been called. A mile of undulating turf stretches away to vanishing point, bounded on the right by ocean and sky and on the left (partly) by a lake, the beauty of which, after many vicissitudes, has at last been worthily retrieved by canalisation. An upper road carries the motor traffic southward, while below a marine drive and promenade, swept by the salt spray, constitute the principal attraction. At the hottest noontide hour at which it may be the visitor's lot to pass by, when the shimmering heat creates an effect of mirage, and the ricksha-pullers in the distance appear to splash through the heat-haze, little imagination is needed to conjure up the glamour of the scene by moonlight, or its soft charm at sunset or dawn.

It may be of interest to note that when Sir Patrick Geddes was invited some years ago to report on the replanning of Colombo (which is exercising the minds of an ambitious Municipality), he regretted that the hope of any extension of this fine marine drive had been rendered vain by the prior mistake of those who had constructed the south-coast railway on the very edge of the shore; to-day one of the earliest acts of the representative Legislative Council, which has fledged out with enlarged powers, is to prognosticate a vote of 30 million rupees for the diversion of the railway farther inland!

With a glance in salute for the Victory Column and its Roll of Honour, and an ear for the information that near here, on the crest of the undulating ground, is the site of the projected New Cathedral, we move on past the Colombo Club, once the only social club, and, therefore, rich in memories of the "old days" when the race-course was located here, and here were held all the tamashas of a more leisurely time. Here, too, came world-famous singers and other entertainers for the delectation of the earlier exiles.

[Photo: Plâté, Ltd.

CHETTY STREET, COLOMBO.

We catch an early glimpse of a cricket-field, first of many more that constitute a gladdening feature of Colombo landscapes, and contribute not a little to their charm, likewise a church spire, and so we come at last to the Galle Face Hotel, fronting the esplanade with a wing on the seashore.

Mount Lavinia.

We need not follow the route right up to Mount Lavinia. The wide Colpetty Road, with its fine bungalows, fronting or bordering the sea, carries on adequately for some miles, few parts of it being lacking in charm, as we pass by large mansions or lowlier cottages, or even some quaint and typical native boutiques, each standing in its own densely-shaded grounds; but it fails to fulfil its early promise, and, when we reach the limit of the Municipality at Wellawatte, six miles from the Fort, " wild " 'buses and lumbering carts begin to make our going a discomfort. It may be true in a sense that Colombo actually extends as far as Mount Lavinia, but we have no need to anticipate the natural growth of Municipal activities, and, wiser than most guides, we recommend that this Mecca of the passenger be visited by railway instead. The suburban service is a liberal one, and a quick and comfortable run there and back (so it be between the times when the city offices fill up with or empty again their workers) can be included in the briefest itinerary. Fish-tiffins, sea-bathing, tennis, and tea on the seaward lawn amid the antics of thieving crows, constitute the ordinary programme, sometimes drawn out into evening dances and nights in the surf of the lovely bay. Wider sympathies may dictate the inclusion of a visit to the big S.P.G. College of St. Thomas, situated within sight, an old foundation harking back to the first Bishop of Colombo, whose legitimate boast was the transplanting under an Eastern sky of the institutions and traditions of the English public school.

[Photo: Platé, Ltd.

QUEEN'S STREET, COLOMBO.

Cinnamon Gardens.

Returning to the Colpetty Road, there are many points lower down its extension to southward at which we might profitably strike inland into the vast residential area, where is seen an endless succession of sunny bungalows and smiling gardens in contrasting shade, flanking well laid-out roads, all combining to convey an impression of good status and seemly affluence; but there is one point to be preferred above all others for the symbolism of the entry. That is Turret Road, giving access to Flower Road where, a flaming canopy of gold mohurs, or flamboyants, sifts the sunlight into rays of emerald and vermilion, and we make our further progress through a blaze of glory into the famous Cinnamon Gardens. Here we find ourselves in a labyrinth of red lanes with a continuous wall of foliage, pranked with gorgeous flowers, over which peep the red tiles and the gleaming stucco of the mansions where the plutocratic Burghers, Sinhalese, or Tamils lord it in style.

But Nature triumphs over gilded pomp, and the salient impression of the Cinnamon Gardens is what part of the name implies. The cinnamon rows of the Dutch have disappeared, but the gardens-in-a-garden remain. That is best realised by imagining the scale reduced, as in a bird's eye-view or air photograph, though then the vast canopy of shade-trees would obscure the whole, merging into one woolly mass interspersed with shorn patches of greensward.

A garden without birds is a dead garden, and we shall not look in vain for the mango-birds, " boats of gold," in the still green foliage, or a strange hiss may give us just warning enough to look up and catch a vision of flying flames, as the paradise fly-catcher flashes in and out of the bushes; a whirring teetotum of burnished purple would betray the sunbird foraging for honey in the flower-beds; while the needle-craft of the tailor-bird may be the reward of search. The dapper magpie-robin is ubiquitous, and, at the right hour, may entertain us with its sweet note. Fly-catchers and swallows wheel overhead, and a species of lark would run from us in the grass of the parks or duck their heads under the menacing shadow of hovering kestrel or kite. Indeed, the birds of Colombo deserve (and have had) a monograph to themselves!

The Museum.

Before we pass out of the centre of our leafy maze, within which we could be content to roam and dream of eternal summer (so it be that we have avoided the hours of vertical sun), we must spend some time in the excellent Museum, housed in a handsome edifice on beautiful grounds. A fine statue of the founder, Sir William Gregory, Governor from 1872 to 1877, commemorates alike the benefits of his rule and the capacity of the people for a proper appreciation of good government. Here may be noted the attractive specimens of ancient handicrafts, holding out against the mass production of a mechanical age, such as the jewellery, ivory, and tortoise-shell work, damascene, lacquer, pottery, etc., the manifold

[Photo: Plâté, Ltd.

VEDDAHS, OR WILD MEN OF CEYLON.

uses of the coconut and palmyra palms, the natural history collections, the gems, the beautiful hard timbers, the astounding historical remains, key to an understanding of the buried cities already described, the marvellous Sigiriya frescoes, the palm-leaf stylographed books, and the ancient rock inscriptions, etc. A museum is the place of dead bones, as the Sinhalese word has it, but a spirit of research, or even a sentiment of real sympathy, will have power to make these dead bones live, so that here, if anywhere, the visitor will be able to reconstruct in imagination the island's great past, as his study of present-day life and customs will be brought into sharp focus by what he sees displayed here before him in brief and handy compass.

The Museum is set on the edge of the 100-acre Victoria Park, which is one of Colombo's assets. We shall refer again to the beautiful cricket grounds of the Sinhalese Sports Club, and can pass on to where two high-class tennis clubs, English and Ceylonese respectively, offer some spectacular play; or inspect the magnificent new Town Hall, tardy recognition of the good work of the representative Municipal Council, or look in at the Orient Club, which, like the Dutch Burgher Union Club elsewhere, is but another instance to show how readily English institutions thrive in this air, or pass out in the direction of the General Hospital, taking on our way three examples of local philanthropy, one a fountain commemorating George Wall, pioneer, politician, and philanthropist; another a statue of a great Sinhalese, Sir Charles de Soyza, prince of philanthropists, who had the distinction of entertaining royalty on his fine estate now decayed, and the third a composite memorial of the whole country, the Victoria Memorial Eye Hospital, itself enshrining the small original nucleus which was the memorial to another son of Ceylon, Sir Samuel Grenier, the Burgher Attorney-General (1886). As we pass up this street we shall see displayed on the boundary wall of a great store, the hypnotic name of Lipton, which has had the power to send people's minds to sleep, for there must still be many in the British Isles who have not yet waked up to the fact that Ceylon is something more than a tea garden belonging to Sir Thomas Lipton!

Outer Circle.

We might, alternatively, emerge towards the outer circle of the labyrinth, in the direction of Slave Island (which, tradition says, was in Dutch times all that the name implies), passing a fair specimen of a banyan-tree that teaches us to look for its betters elsewhere, catching now a fine vista of cool turf-fringed water. We shall have left behind us the splendid Church of St. Michael and the theatre of the noble activities of the Anglican Sisterhood, which latter maintains good girls' schools and has inspired the foundation of a local Order; and shall be reminded of another high-class girls' school we had seen on entering the Cinnamon Gardens. Leftwise from the old Public Hall we pass into a hybrid area, where commercial factors are beginning to be dominant, and where a crowded and slummy quarter has to be avoided on the return, through one of the finest open stretches, to the Fort, which lies spread out before us across an ornamental piece of water.

Or, again, we might pass out southwards into the academic quarter, where a brand-new University College, starting under the very best auspices with the cream of local scholarship, English and Ceylonese, on its lecturing staff, is initiating traditions against the day, not far distant, when it shall fledge out into the University of Colombo. Meanwhile, the lamp of culture has long been kept burning by various learned societies, branches or copies of their English originals, *e.g.*, the Royal Asiatic, the English Association, Society of Arts, etc. Farther on we shall view the Civil Service bungalows, the pride of the local establishment, and the envy of the Indian. It is a provision thoroughly worthy of a handful of men of lofty purpose, who have brought the country to its present pitch of progress, and will now guide it through the difficult initial stages of a new epoch.

Sport.

Here we find ourselves among spacious green sporting grounds, which remind us that, with these wind-swept lawns, the climate of Colombo could not be as intolerable as we had expected to find it, and that life here must have its alleviations. That would not be far off the mark, for it is only during a short spell of overhead sun, or when a drought has lasted more than a few weeks, or in a sunspot maximum, that one sighs for the hills, for rain quickly works a transformation scene, and in a single night the parched grass is green again.

Here are delightful golf links; a magnificent race-course, with good traditions and a long record among the most fashionable of local amenities; the Colombo Cricket Club, to which the same qualification applies; Havelock Park, successor to the old Burgher traditions of another quarter yet to be seen, with cricket fields and golf-course; and many another open bit of sward where youthful Hobbses wield the willow with a gusto equal to any that England affords.

Cricket is a game so well acclimatised in Ceylon for well nigh three generations that some of its players have caught the public eye on British fields, one at least playing for All Scotland and others for College and County; while, since the days of Lord Hawke (1892) Test teams passing through have delighted to meet the local teams, British and Ceylonese together, or an eleven of each. One name at least must be recorded here, and who knows but these lines may meet the eye of some doughty veteran who will recall his feelings when his wicket was disturbed in disconcerting fashion by Tommy Kelaart, the famous Burgher left-hander, who maintained for more than sixteen years the average of five runs a wicket.

Each of the five communities has its club and grounds, and not cricket only, but all games, and other branches of athletics (with the noteworthy inclusion of scouting) have their keen exponents. The grounds of the Sinhalese in Victoria Park rival in beauty and excellence the old-established Colombo (English) Club. Each of these clubs has at some period put into the field a team of English county class.

Schools.

For that noteworthy result it is the larger public schools that have to be thanked. Two of them, the missionary College of St. Thomas and the Government's Royal College, have a tradition more than half-a-century old for the intensive cultivation of sport, more notably the former as a boarding school. Their classic annual contest, the local Eton v. Harrow, has for nearly all that time been one of the most popular social events of the year. (In Kandy they have a vigorous young rival, Trinity College, whose buildings and playing fields are an ornament even to that lovely town.)

And not sport alone, though that is the cement of good fellowship between East and West. For the task of the Government has been more than three parts done for it by the many different religious bodies, dating back, in fact, to Francis Xavier, that have been engaged in educational work, both in Colombo and in other large towns, for the best part of a century, reaching and maintaining a high standard for a colony and the East. One humble institution, which has recently celebrated its centenary, deserves mention here from its location in a notable district, Cotta, which saw the Indian summer of Sinhalese Royal power under a celebrated Prime Minister in the 15th century.

Loyalty to the old school permeates the whole fabric of life in Ceylon, and the names of former heads and assistant masters are kept green in the loving remembrance of thousands. The annual banquets of Old Boys and the Speech Days are distinguished public functions usually graced by the presence of the Governor or other high official, and marked at times by some momentous statement of policy or like weighty announcement.

At the risk of being fulsome it should be added that the measure of the success of the schools is the crown set upon it by continued academic triumphs at the older English Universities and at the Civil Service Examination, not to speak of other professional honours. Ceylon has a long roll of names of her sons who have made remarkable careers in this and other parts of the Empire, one at least having administered the government of a West Indian Colony.

North Colombo.

Such is the fruit of the labours of the pioneers, including the Dutch, and they embrace missionary and layman alike. The earlier officials and merchants were active in sowing the seed, and the stronghold of the traditions of these men, who, not content with a rootless existence, cultivated a friendly fellowship with the people, is Mutwal, the northern suburb of Colombo, to which we now pass, after crossing a busy area mostly railway territory. Old St. Thomas's College (with the Cathedral Church), Summer Hill, Uplands, Elie House, Hill House, Rock House, Whist Bungalow—these are names to conjure with; and, although the entire district has been commercialised and the Port Commission employees inherit the scene of the former camaraderie, the wit, and the "flow of soul," not to speak of the "beauty and the chivalry" of old Colombo, there are survivors of a former generation who cherish the memory of those larger and more liberal days with wistful regret.

The interest of this suburb is now mainly commercial, and the visitor would mark the spreading tentacles of the port, to which reference has been made; but the aesthetic would not be wholly without witness if, for instance, he could stand on the old College hill in a misty dawn and, looking back upon the harbour, cast his astonished eyes on what is nothing less than a Turner battle-piece, or watch from the water-stairs of Whist Bungalow the eternal battle between the sea and the Kelani River, when the long sandspit is hourly devoured by the hungry waters; or view the fishing fleet come in on the top of the wave with sails bladder-taut in the breeze; or espy, across the strong-flowing river, where the woods come down to the water's edge, the old Dutch canal to pretty Negombo (home of oinnamon) running straight and true under an archway of palms.

And it is here at last that he will find the homes of the common people, scattered among the cottages of the "classes," whom the ebb of migration has left high and dry in a quarter that can only be described as passé. From here, as from other suburbs near and far (notably Kotahena, with its grand Roman Catholic Cathedral, visible from the harbour), an army of workers, filling more or less humble positions in the Fort and Pettah and in the Government railway and other engineering establishments, sallies out daily, coated and sandalled for the most part, and nearly all carrying the indispensable umbrella, which surely is the one peculiar feature of Ceylon streets. The homing throngs in the afternoon and evening hours give the lie to the statement frequently made in books about Ceylon that the Pettah is "where the natives live."

The Pettah.

This is the quarter that has always exercised a fascination for the traveller who is a stranger to the East. Its din and bustle, its colour and its diverse smells; the heterogeneous mob that is never off its streets; the publicity of all its activities with *al fresco* chaffering and trade and eating and drinking; the artless, casual way in which the young fruit-seller from the country, lips carmine with betel-quid, dumps her baskets of polychromatic treasures by the roadside and cuts a side of pine-apple or jak, or opens a young coconut for a passing customer, who will pause to relish it on the spot, innocent of sinks and bins; the scraps of shouted commentary across the narrow street, seeming to merge and mingle into incessant chatter; the block in the traffic when two motor-cars and a tramcar come together and the pedestrian leaps for safety on to a verandah (if he does not come a cropper on a banana peel); the crowds that use the verandahs as pavements, skirting the outdoor stands of the apple-men and the sellers of oily Indian sweetmeats; the importunity of the men at the shop-doors; the constantly shifting yet never-changing scene; the shining, nude backs of coolies at one end of the scale, which runs up through various gradations of undress and over-dress till it terminates in the sleek, half-draped paunch of the Chetty millionaire; and, recapitulating the whole effect, the public market behind the (old) Town Hall, where the entire gamut of sound and the whole spectrum of colour assail eye and ear.

Such is the Pettah; and when the stranger has recovered from the assault to his senses and has begun to think that he has seen the real Colombo, it would be time to inform him that what he has seen is really an Indian settlement entirely alien to the country! The Sinhalese do not take kindly to retail trade (though they are at home in big business), and various Indian communities have taken root here for generations, while the whole fabric of their trade is shot with the financial acumen of the Chetty, whose stronghold in Sea Street should not be missed for its strange combination of literally sunless treasuries, the simple life, and strict Hindu observance.

These shops in the Pettah understudy the European establishments in the Fort, and complete for an overlapping custom, though humbler pockets are also catered for. Drapery, hosiery, books, hardware, groceries, plate and lamp shops, are huddled together in street and cross-street, each with a single narrow frontage, until variety is defeated, and the only marked difference is made by the rare presence of a Sinhalese merchant striking out in more original and ambitious directions.

Nor does the surprise end there. For the further fact remains to be disclosed that this area, which has been allowed in the course of generations, without any heed to town planning, to acquire unto itself the most crazy and squalid excrescences, until it has become to-day a blot and a reproach, with vested interests holding up an enlightened municipality, was once a respectable residential quarter. All that remains to prove it is the Dutch

[Photo: Plâté, Ltd.

GALLE FACE, LOOKING TOWARDS THE ECHELON BARRACKS, COLOMBO.

cemetery, the melancholy appeal of which is being smothered more and more under the ramifications of trade, and the curfew bell and belfry, together with the old Dutch name of Cayman's Gate. But we have, besides, in addition to the traditions of the old Dutch families, the evidence of Walsh's *Military Reminiscences*, where it is stated that "the Pettah had also several good houses, churches, etc., and in the place, altogether, were many respectable inhabitants." Of the churches, the newer (St. Paul's) has just bowed to the inevitable and has a quieter home in Campbell Park, which limits of space prevent describing here, but it is equal to the best in charm; and the other, the Dutch Reformed Church, a real Dutch relic, typical of the architecture of the Low Countries, built in 1749, in Wolvendaal (Wolves' Dale), where former Dutch Governors and mynheers with their pomp-loving vrouws sat to hear long discourses, and where such of their successors to-day as cling to the old Protestantism do the same amid the memorial tablets of the illustrious dead.

[Photo: Plâté, Ltd.

GALLE FACE, LOOKING TOWARDS GALLE FACE HOTEL, COLOMBO.

Later Burgher traditions have centered round the "Racquet Court," which is now given over to the excellent ratproof rice stores already referred to. This was the cradle of Ceylonese cricket, and though it has vanished from the view its memories remain.

Hulftsdorp.

Let us pass from the fine eminence of Wolvendaal, overlooking the sea, to its twin, Hulftsdorp, named after the Dutch General Hulft, which is sacred to the law and the theatre *par excellence* of purely Ceylonese achievement. We shall learn of respected Ceylonese judges and lawyers, remembering that the term includes Burghers, Sinhalese, Tamils, and a few others. We shall note the jealous guarding of great traditions and shall find here the training-ground for larger political and administrative responsibilities.

Conclusion.

It is convenient to close this sketch of Colombo on that note, for the legal profession is typical though not unique; the medical, engineering, and other professions, likewise, offer young Ceylon bare scope for its legitimate aspirations and a field for the display of good qualities of trustworthiness and efficiency. In fact, there is not a single high judicial or administrative post, even up to those of Chief Justice and Colonial Secretary, but a son of the soil has at some period been found worthy to fill it, though policy dictate that it shall be but temporarily. To-day the elective office of Vice-President of the Council, the Supreme Judicature, the highest law offices, the posts of Chief Government Surgeons and Physicians (and practically the whole Medical Service), leading Police, Post, and Telegraph, Volunteer Force, Engineering, and Survey appointments are filled, permanently in some instances, by excellent precedent, though temporarily in others, by Ceylonese, to praise whom would be an impertinence. The cry for more scope for talent and ambition cannot but be heard, and the answer will be in the same generous spirit that moved the early pioneers to give their lives in the spade-work of yesterday, which alone has made possible the foundations of the edifice of the morrow.

Our account of Ceylon's principal city must now end, although it is necessarily incomplete. We have not said much, for instance, of the British colonists specifically, but have preferred to treat the island as a composite unit of the Empire, where all are working together for the good of the whole. There are those who have gone out to Ceylon purely for trade or business or to the big plantations, all undeniably conducive to the welfare of the island and world-commerce. While some of them, however, pull their weight as members of the "Commonwealth," others, it must be granted, prefer in an alien spirit to regard the island as but the temporary scene of their unavoidable exile, failing to understand how their brothers and sisters, cast in a more generous mould, joy to think of it as a second home, which tugs at their heart-strings with a pull strong enough to make them waver in a divided allegiance, while "not once or twice" the election has been in favour of the tinier Isle of Enchantment!

COMMERCIAL COLOMBO.

CARGILLS, LTD., Universal Providers, York Street.

CARGILLS! What a name that is throughout Ceylon, and how vast is the range of supplies which it connotes! All over the island, in the homes of the rich and the poor, the name is a household one that is lisped by little children, who hear it so frequently mentioned in connection with everything pertaining to life's daily routine. Even amongst the people who do not speak English, Cargills is a familiar synonym for merchandise as varied as human necessity itself. Every person who can see or hear, visiting Colombo, must carry away some memory of Cargills, Ltd. The only way for a steamer passenger to escape receiving actual visual impressions of the celebrated firm is to refrain from going ashore; but even then there will be talk about the business when the visitors return with their purchases.

The Cargills establishment looms large and impressive in the immediate perspective of Colombo's chief shopping district, and was the forerunner of many of the fine buildings there. Its colour is the red of life's vitality, and cornucopiæ are appropriately embodied in the stone ornamentation of the great house of plenty that calls to the stranger as well as to the permanent resident with many allurements. Four years were spent in the construction of the edifice, and it was completed in 1905.

In the spacious Cargills arcade the artistic displays in the handsome plate-glass windows can be inspected in comfortable shelter from the tropical sun or rain; but better far to pass through one of the many entrances and make a tour of the pleasant and well-ventilated interior, where everything is arranged on a scale of utility and completeness harmonising in every way with the prominence of the firm in local trade. The person able to differentiate between mediocrity and superiority in general merchandise, but more especially in the infinity of things pertaining to the outfitting of both sexes, will find a visit to Messrs. Cargills' premises prolific of much more extensive purchases than may be intended there. Temptation in that connection is exceptionally powerful in the departments for ladies' clothing, where lovely dresses of the filmiest materials and the latest fashions, in exquisite shades, vie with captivating millinery creations, each of irresistible individuality, and all in so great a variety that uncommon indeed must the requirements be which cannot be met there.

The tailoring departments are characterised by

DEPARTMENT FOR GROCERIES, WINES AND SPIRITS.

LADIES' AND GENTLEMEN'S OUTFITTING DEPARTMENT.

PHARMACEUTICAL DEPARTMENT.

"CARGILLS."

PREMISES OF CARGILLS, LTD., COLOMBO.

all those details of careful selection and operative skill inseparable from every sartorial establishment where output is made subservient to perfection of fit and fashion.

The workrooms for the dressmakers, milliners, and tailors, including European cutters, and the busy activities there, indicate very eloquently how greatly the firm's facilities and resources in that connection are taken advantage of.

But it is impossible within the limits of this restricted sketch to even attempt a description of the many other departments (thirty in all) or to note the claims of each for special recognition in connection with the wealth of its stock or the care with which its organisation has been evolved for the maximum of service and minimum of waste or inconvenience to everyone concerned—groceries and provisions, wines and spirits, jewellery, watches and clocks, electro-plate and silverware, glassware and crockery, gramophones, stationery, fancy goods, pedal and motor cycles, hardware and household utensils, etc. A separate volume could easily be produced for a delineation in detail of the many different departments, each operated like a separate business, but forming one great whole on which is ever concentrated expert knowledge and experience that takes cognizance of all the innumerable idiosyncrasies of local requirement as well as universal demand.

The elegant department for drugs and chemicals, for instance, giving employment to six qualified dispensers, is replete with everything that can be suggested for the relief of pain and illness and the enhancement of physical welfare.

The firm transact wholesale as well as retail trade, and are manufacturers of many of their own preparations, including the well-known and very successful "Cargilineum" mixture for rubber trees, of which mixture they produce about ten tons monthly. Contiguous to the pharmaceutical department is the optical department where sight defects are tested and remedied under the supervision of the only Fellow of the British Optical Association practising in Ceylon.

Extensive as the premises are, the business has outgrown them, and at the time of writing arrangements are being made for additions that will increase the floor space by fifty per cent.

The history of the business dates back to 1844, when it was started at Kandy under the name of Milne, Cargill and Co. When Colombo became a port of call, the firm followed the trend of business there and steadily grew in importance in the city, retaining, however, the Kandy establishment. Later the designation became Cargill and Co., and the firm continued to prosper through the halcyon days of the coffee industry. When that failed, however, the business, like practically every other Ceylon concern, underwent severe vicissitudes, and was one of the few which survived the collapse of the then staple industry of the island. The phenomenal progress of the tea industry of Ceylon led to corresponding development of Messrs. Cargill and Co.'s activities. In 1896 the present limited liability company was formed. The business gives employment to about five hundred persons, including about sixty Europeans, and there are branches of it at Cinnamon Gardens, Galle Face, and Nuwara Eliya, as well as at Kandy, with forage mills in Staples Street, Colombo. The general department store under the designation of **SIME and CO.**, contiguous to Messrs. Cargills' establishment in Colombo, also belongs to the company, but is operated separately under its own name.

The directors of Messrs. Cargills, Ltd., are Sir J. T. Cargill, Bart., Messrs. B. Connell, J. Mathieson, A. J. Martin, and T. R. Mitchell. The general manager is Mr. G. R. Brown. The company's cable address is "Cargills," Colombo, and they use the A B C code.

The London office is at Balfour House, Finsbury Pavement, E.C., and the registered office is at 163, Hope Street, Glasgow.

LIPTON, LTD., Tea Blenders and Exporters, etc., Union Place, Slave Island.

Throughout the world no name is more popularly associated with the tea industry of Ceylon than that of Lipton, Ltd. In cottage and mansion, in village and city, in inaccesible places far remote from civilisation, and in fashionable tea-shops and restaurants in the world's leading centres of wealth and activity, Lipton's tea is in high esteem, and has given to Ceylon an advertisement beyond comparison. When passengers from the steamers land at Colombo for a brief tour of inspection of the city and its environs, there is always at the back of their minds the memories and impressions of the fragrant Lipton tea; and these memories and impressions are recalled vividly and pleasantly by the sight of the premises of Messrs. Lipton, Ltd., in the beautiful district of the Cinnamon Gardens, at the end of Union Place, one of the principal thoroughfares of Colombo. It is so reminiscent of home in Great Britain, Australia, United States, Canada and elsewhere to see the name of Lipton, Ltd.; but to see it in a tropical setting in the lovely island it has made so famous, explains the ejaculations of thousands of visitors to Colombo, when the local premises of the great firm in question suddenly come into the range of their vision.

Much has always been made of the celebrated Lipton tea estates in Ceylon, and their names may be read from afar painted in white letters on the dark curving walls enclosing the Maddema Mills, as the premises in question are designated.

The company's estates, totalling about 8,000 acres, are magnificently situated at a high elevation in dry and invigorating air, peculiarly favourable for the cultivation of tea of the highest quality. The bulk of the company's tea land in Dambatenne is on the slopes of lofty hills, upon which there is no room for buildings as on the other estates; so that the difficulty of preparing the tea there has been overcome by the provision of a system of aerial tramways which transmit the produce as gathered from the gardens to the factory in the valley below. Thousands of Tamil coolies are employed on the Lipton estates, and the utmost attention is paid to the comfort of their homes and their medical and other requirements.

DAMBATENE FACTORY.

DESPATCHING TEA FROM DAMBATENE FACTORY.

DAMBATENE BUNGALOW.

PICKING TEA, BANDIA ELIYA.

MONERKANDE FACTORY.

ROAD IN THE MONERKANDE PLANTATIONS.

SCENES IN THE TEA PLANTATIONS OF LIPTON, LTD., CEYLON.

So fine is the method of plucking on the Lipton tea gardens that many pounds of green leaf are necessary to make one pound of manufactured tea. After the green leaf is gathered it is exposed for some time in the factories in a light, dry atmosphere to wither. It is then rolled by powerful machinery in order that the sap may be crushed out, and is afterwards separated and allowed to ferment, great care being necessary during the latter process. The green leaf is thereafter spread out evenly on perforated trays and fired in a specially contrived drying machine by means of heated air at about 200° F. It is then allowed to cool and is afterwards graded and packed for shipment to all parts of the world.

A bulky and interesting volume could be written about the huge business built up by Sir Thomas Lipton, and the great influence exerted in its development and success by his lucky acquisition long ago of the magnificent estates whence the celebrated Lipton tea of Ceylon is derived. Suffice it to say, however, that the record price of £36 15s. 0d. per lb. has been obtained in the Mincing Lane sales room for a parcel of Golden Tipped Flowery Orange Pekoe from Lipton's Dambatenne estate.

The company's manager in Ceylon is Mr. H. H. Sutherland, who has been connected with the firm since 1911.

DARLEY, BUTLER and CO., LTD., General Merchants and Commission Agents, 69, Queen Street, Fort.

The large and handsome office buildings erected in Colombo during recent years have greatly changed the appearance of the city from what it was when the writer first knew it in 1900. Consequently the busy, sunny, island capital provides great contrasts between the old and the new, more especially in and around the Fort district, where the former Dutch colonists centred their affairs before Ceylon became British in 1796. Here and there are some old structures which are delightfully reminiscent of the long forgotten past; but none used for commercial purposes is more worthy of notice than the premises in which the business of Messrs. Darley, Butler and Co., Ltd., has been carried on for many decades. These premises are much more extensive than might be inferred from their outward appearance. A fire in 1924 destroyed the top floor of the office building and all the interesting records of this famous old concern, but it did not injure the thick and strong walls; so that the aspect of the establishment as it stands to-day, with its square turreted top, is probably exactly the same as it was in the eighteenth century. The date of its erection cannot be ascertained, but in one of its ancient sections there is a remarkable strong-room where, it is asserted, the last King of Kandy, the notorious Sri Vikrama Rajasinha, was imprisoned before he was sent in 1816 to the fortress of Vellore, in the Madras Presidency, where he died in 1832. The cell, or dungeon, in question has a convex roof, and is so strong that it would undoubtedly remain intact if the whole of the structure into which it is built collapsed about it. The great thickness of its walls is discerned by the two narrow air vents on each side of the old steel entrance door. When the writer inspected it for the purpose of this sketch, its contents included some fine old wines—and what could be more highly prized in these days of fantastic legislation and spurious imitations of the liquors of long ago!

Behind the main building is a curious old courtyard—surely the oldest and quaintest in Colombo. Sloping down towards it are the red-tiled roofs of extremely old warehouses, where the impressions of the past are very vivid. What a place it could be, and probably is, for ghosts of long dead persons who had to do with merchandise of every description!

On one side of the courtyard is a building called the King's Warehouse devoted entirely to the firm's bonded stock, access to which can only be obtained in the presence of a Customs official. Messrs. Darley, Butler and Co., Ltd., are one of the few firms in Colombo with such a facility on their premises.

Other buildings opening into the courtyard are so old and unsuited to modern storage requirements that they are utilised only for the accommodation of boxes and things of general utility. The floors of these old warehouses are a succession of ups and downs, and some of them have been so frequently repaired that in some places not much of the original timber remains.

The sections in which the trade activities of Messrs. Darley, Butler and Co., Ltd., are conducted are very different, and provide ample indications of the care there exercised for the perfection of everything relating thereto. The firm are amongst the largest exporters of Ceylon tea, and were amongst the first to engage in that industry after the failure of Ceylon coffee in 1876. Rubber and all the productions of the island are handled by them. They may be regarded as pioneers in the piece-goods trade of Ceylon, and in that connection still transact an extensive trade. As general commission agents they have connections throughout the world.

PREMISES OF DARLEY, BUTLER and CO., LTD.

The business is probably the oldest in Colombo, and was founded in 1847 by Mr. E. J. Darley and Mr. (later Sir) Samuel Butler, who had previously been partner in the firm of Ackland, Boyd and Co. Mr. Darley, who died in 1870, is commemorated by Darley Road, one of the important business thoroughfares of Colombo. In 1860 Sir Samuel Butler retired to London and supervised the firm's interests at the office which was then opened for that purpose there. In 1863 the late Sir William Mitchell became partner and proceeded to Colombo, where he lived for fifty-two years. Sir William Mitchell was the representative of the mercantile community in the Legislative Council for about twenty years, and was the first elected Chairman of the Chamber of Commerce in 1869, serving as a Committee member for thirty-five years.

During the administration of Sir Arthur Havelock, Governor of Ceylon, Sir William (then Mr.)

Mitchell was created a C.M.G. in recognition of his public service to the colony. He was Chairman of the Wharf and Warehouse Co. for many years. He was also connected with the Colombo Hotels Co., Ltd., The Colombo Apothecaries Co., Ltd., The New Colombo Ice Co., Ltd., Spinning and Weaving Mills, and many other concerns. He was a member of the Colombo Harbour Board from its inception, and manifested a lively interest in all matters pertaining to the development of the port. In the agitation for the establishment of a Port Trust, which occupied the attention of the mercantile community for a number of years, he took a prominent and leading part.

Sir William represented the mercantile community at the Diamond Jubilee of Queen Victoria in 1897, and had the honour of presenting the address of the Chamber to Her Majesty in person. He represented the Chamber at the Paris Exposition in 1900. While he was there, news reached Ceylon that amongst the birthday honours was a Knighthood for him in recognition of the services he had rendered to the colony during his long and distinguished career.

Meanwhile Sir Samuel Butler had retired from the business in 1884, and it was thereafter carried on by Sir William, who was joined in partnership in 1896 by Mr. J. F. Headrick and Sir William's son, Mr. W. E. Mitchell—the latter having been connected with it since 1886. In 1911 Mr. Headrick retired, and after Sir William's death in 1915, the business was conducted by Messrs. W. E. and F. S. Mitchell as sole partners until July, 1920, when the present limited liability company was formed with an authorised capital of Rs.5,000,000.

The Board of Directors now comprises Messrs. F. S. Mitchell (Chairman); W. E. Mitchell; W. A. Cole; O. P. Rust; J. M. Souter, and S. G. A. Julius.

The company's telegraphic address is "Darley," Colombo, and the codes used are Bentley's and the A B C 5th edition.

Messrs. Darley, Butler and Co., Ltd., are agents for the following:

- Darley, Butier & Drew, Ltd., London.
- A. Provant & Co., Manchester.
- George Woolley & Co., Ltd., Manchester.
- Sternberg Bros., Manchester.
- Mellon & Co., Manchester.
- East Asiatic Co., Ltd., Bangkok and Singapore.
- S. H. Ewing & Co., Montreal.
- Scottish Union & National Insurance Co.
- American Trading Co., Ltd., New York.
- S. L. Jones & Co., San Francisco.
- Gollan & Co., Adelaide, Melbourne, Sydney, and Wellington.
- Chargeurs Reunis Line of Steamers.
- Maritime Insurance Co., Ltd.
- Northern Assurance Co., Ltd.
- Union Insurance Society of Canton, Ltd.
- Queens Insurance Co., Ltd.
- The Home Insurance Co.
- Western Assurance Co.
- Underwriters at Lloyd's.
- The Gangwarily Estates Co. of Ceylon, Ltd.
- The Ceylon Land & Produce Co., Ltd. (S.A.).
- The Gartmore (Ceylon) Tea Co., Ltd. (S.A.).
- The Piccadilly Rubber & Tea Estates, Ltd.
- The Lugaloya Tea & Rubber Co., Ltd.

BROOKE BOND CEYLON, LTD., Assambrook Mills, Slave Island.

THE name of Brooke Bond is famous to the uttermost parts of the earth. Anyone not versed in what it stands for is uneducated in modern commercial enterprise, which must always have examples of comparison and achievement. Even the lowliest of people, whose range of knowledge is of the most circumscribed character, have an appreciative familiarity with the name of Brooke Bond, and would uphold it against all competitors. Brooke Bond is almost in the dictionary as a synonym for tea; and it may be regarded as amongst the dozen best-known commodities of modern trade. The eminent firm which it designates have huge warehouses in London, Manchester, Leeds, and elsewhere; and in grocery shops throughout Great Britain the Brooke Bond packages are demanded with an emphasis that will not be put off with other brands.

The great Brooke Bond business, like other celebrated undertakings, has certainly been built up largely by advertising, but not altogether. Millions of pounds may be spent in booming anything, but if the commodity is not worthy of its publicity, the money will surely be wasted. No people in the world are better judges of tea than the British. We cannot do without it, and its absolute indispensability has raised the standard of necessary quality very high indeed, which explains Brooke Bond.

In the south of India the Brooke Bond Company have about 50,000 acres of tea estates, and very large premises at Calcutta and Bombay. In Ceylon, where they have been operating since 1919 under the name of Brooke Bond Ceylon, Ltd., their tea lands, Allakolla, Ratnatenne, and Udaveria, aggregate 3,185 acres, and are amongst the best in the island.

The company's Assambrook Mills, in Slave Island, Colombo, are amongst the largest industrial establishments devoted to tea and produce in Ceylon. These mills have recently been completely remodelled, and considerable additions made to them. They occupy about 3 acres, and give employment to about 800 persons. The busy scenes there afford exceedingly interesting and instructive object lessons in the methods of preparing tea and other products for shipment abroad. Certain hand operations—and they are many—cannot be enhanced by any mechanical process, and will continue as long as tea is consumed, which will doubtless be for ever; nevertheless, there are many remarkable contrivances in the Assambrook Mills which reduce labour to a minimum, and ensure beyond peradventure the accuracy of qualities and measurements in leadfoil packages, in standard chests, in marks and labels, etc. All the work is executed in a chain of specialised activities, each dependent upon and influencing the other; and throughout it all is manifested undeviating regard for the exemplification of the superlative in every detail; hence the continual expansion of the Brooke Bond business.

In addition to tea, great quantities of other Ceylon products, such as desiccated coconut, cocoa, rubber, etc., pass through the Assambrook Mills, and are shipped to all parts of the world. The mills have their own printing department for labels, etc., and the company also import estate supplies on a large scale.

The managing director of Brooke Bond Ceylon, Ltd., Mr. R. E. Southwood, is a tea expert of long and extensive experience; so also is the other director, Mr. W. Trevellick Hicks. The company's cable address is "Assambrook," Colombo, and the code used is the A B C 6th edition.

Messrs. Brooke Bond Ceylon, Ltd., are agents and secretaries for Brampton Tea Co., Ltd.; Koralle Tea Estates, Ltd., consisting of Glenloch Estates, Wewesse Estates, Riverside Estates; The Downside Estate Co., Ltd.

COLOMBO APOTHECARIES CO., LTD. (SMITH CAMPBELL and CO.), Chemists and Druggists, General Merchants, Outfitters, Furniture Manufacturers, Printers, Booksellers, Stationery Manufacturers, etc., Fort.

Colombo Apothecaries Co. That well-known name is suggestive of the days of long ago when the alchemists sought the elixir of life, and the establishments of the apothecaries had not evolved from the crude limitations of the remedial agents then in vogue into the pharmacies of the modern highly-trained chemists and druggists; but even the latter are now, in most centres of population, being merged to a considerable extent into departments of the huge general stores that are playing so prominent a part in the consolidation of modern retail trade. So it is at Colombo, where the large business of the Colombo Apothecaries Co., Ltd., is quite at variance with the restrictions which might be suggested to the uninitiated by its title. Throughout all the ramifications of the undertaking in question, the novelties of last year or last month are replaced by substitutes of improved utility and attraction. The great assortments of merchandise quickly come and go; department after department is added; indeed, other concerns are merged into the ever-expanding business, but the name remains unaltered as it was when it was the designation of the little chemists' shop opened in 1883 in the de Soysa Buildings, Slave Island. Why should that humble little venture have been followed by such remarkable results? Thousands of little chemists' shops, or, should we say, chemists' little shops, have been established in thousands of promising places, but in those that continue to exist the passing years show no change in the dimensions of their trade or character. The district of Slave Island was not particularly good for a chemists' shop—at least not in the latter part of last century, and the proprietors, Mr. W. M. Smith and Mr. James Smith Findlay, being men of ambition, removed their little business into another establishment at the corner of York and Prince Street, Fort. Their new pharmacy was also small, but it had the advantage of being close to the jetty, where the people from the steamers landed, and was thus prominent in the line of attraction of the great tide of passenger traffic that ever flows through Colombo. Such was the commencement of the extensive business that today gives employment to about 500 persons and caters to that traffic, as well as to the requirements of the inhabitants of Ceylon, with a thoroughness that includes everything pertaining to life's daily routine on land and sea.

PREMISES OF COLOMBO APOTHECARIES CO., LTD.

The story of its rise and progress in detail would occupy many pages and must be curtailed. In 1904 the gentlemen's tailoring and outfitting business of Smith, Campbell and Co., and also the one that had been carried on by Mann and Co., manufacturers of saddlery and harness, importers of footwear, etc., were acquired by the Colombo Apothecaries Co., Ltd. These were followed in 1917 by the absorption of The Anglo-Oriental Furnishing Co.

The building housing the many departments of the Colombo Apothecaries Co., Ltd., was completed in 1915, and covers an area of 15,000 square feet. It has four floors, each connected by an electric elevator, as well as by broad staircases, and each of these numerous departments is operated as a separate business. Those for ladies' outfitting are ever a source of great attraction to the fair sex, for in them are to be found the latest styles from Paris and London, with particular regard to specialities of fabric and fancy for use in the tropics as well as in more temperate zones.

The gentlemen's tailoring and outfitting sections are still carried on under the name of Smith Campbell and Co., and as all the workshops are

C.A.C. PRESS, SLAVE ISLAND.
Printing Works of Colombo Apothecaries Co., Ltd.

DISPENSARY OF
COLOMBO APOTHECARIES CO., LTD.

on the premises, customers have the satisfaction of knowing that their orders are fulfilled under the most commendable and sanitary conditions—a point of great importance in the Orient regarding the execution of tailoring work. The following is from the firm's handsomely got-up catalogue entitled *Gifts—Suggestions for Men.*

"Fine kerchiefs for gay gallants. So runs the legend. And as the gallants of the 'periods' trip past the shop which displays the gay silk squares, each in his turn pauses. For the many-coloured handkerchief is a thing of beauty and its purchase a delight. The Early Stuart, elegant with voluminous cloak; the Restoration beau, very straight; the much bewigged gallant of 1700, our fine fellows from the 'Beggar's Opera'; the snuffy fop of George the First—Oh, and many others right up to the large-trousered young man we know so well. He! What part has he with these highly-coloured gentlemen of the past? Just this, that his finishing touch of personal distinction is still the brilliant handkerchief—more elegant to-day than ever before in its long and glorious history.

"On the following pages are just a few selections from the colossal handkerchief assortment of Smith, Campbell and Co., enlivened with coloured illustrations of the actual silk handkerchiefs we have in stock."

That extract is eloquently suggestive of the skill and good taste pervading the company's alluring sartorial service and supplies.

The whole of the second floor is devoted to household requisites and suites of every description, office equipment well calculated to please the most fastidious demands, and all the odds and ends of things comprised under the term furniture in an exceedingly interesting diversity of design. They are made of Ceylon and other Eastern woods at the company's factory in Slave Island, previously carried on by The Anglo-Oriental Furniture Co. already mentioned.

On the ground floor is the pharmaceutical department, which amply justifies the retention of the company's title, and would be a very notable business by itself. Four qualified Europeans are employed in its dispensing department, contiguous to which is the section for Kodak goods and photographic materials of all kinds, where a special organisation has been evolved for the rapid as well as perfect development and printing of customers' films and plates in view of the comparatively short period during which passengers remain in Colombo.

But it is impossible in this brief review to do more than merely indicate the other departments, such as books and stationery, silver and plated goods, watches, clocks and jewellery, general fancy goods, travelling requisites, glass, crockery, hardware, wines and spirits, groceries, provisions and confectionery, etc.

Probably the most impressive of all the many sections of the business is the company's large printing works, occupying about half an acre in Slave Island, where everything pertaining to printing and its allied activities, such as the manufacture of stationery and account books, machine-ruling, bookbinding, block-making, etc., is carried on with skill and enterprise. The printing plant was originally established in 1901 for the company's own requirements, and the development it has attained is in keeping with the expansion and progress characteristic of the entire business since its commencement.

The general manager is Mr. F. Trollope, who has been connected with the concern since 1896. The cable address is "Apothecary," and the codes used are the A B C 4th and 5th editions.

H. L. DE MEL and CO., Exporters and Importers, Insurance Agents, Owners of Estates, Graphite Mines, Mills, Brush and Broom Factory, etc., etc., De Mel Building, Chatham Street, Fort.

No family in Ceylon has been longer nor more influentially connected with the development of the commerce and industry of the island than the "De Mels," who can trace their lineage back to 1534. One of the modern office buildings in the Fort of Colombo is called the De Mel Building, and on its third floor are the offices of the proprietors of that structure, Messrs. H. L. De Mel and Co., whose extensive combination of commercial, industrial and agricultural undertakings, employing upwards of 3,000 people, contributes to the importance of Ceylon as one of the richest exporting colonies of the British Empire. The great interests of Messrs. H. L. de Mel and Co. represent the accumulated knowledge and experience of generations of De Mel business men, each handing down to his succeeding son continually increasing assets in land and buildings, industrial achievements, and commercial connections encircling the globe.

The present head of the "De Mel" firm is Mr. H. L. De Mel, C.B.E., J.P., whose father, the late Mr. Jacob De Mel, did probably more than any of his ancestors in making the "De Mel" name prominent and influential in Ceylon's economic development. Owning and managing coconut, cinnamon, and tea estates, of an aggregate area of about 5,000 acres, large fibre mills at Madampe, in the Chilaw district, and flourishing commercial undertakings in Colombo, the activities of the late Mr. Jacob De Mel were many and varied. Nevertheless, in 1870 he turned his attention to the great potentialities that lay in the development of Ceylon plumbago, and became the pioneer of that industry. It was he who discovered the rich Ragedera mine at Kurunegala, which was photographed by a representative of Nobel's Explosives, and was the first mine in the East where explosives in mining for plumbago were used. That was the surest foundation of the De Mel plumbago industry, and for the purpose of learning something about the business, the present writer was courteously received and shown over the firm's remarkable factories and other premises, occupying more than thirteen acres of land on the "Model Farm Estate," at Colombo, where, amongst many other operations, the plumbago, as received from the mines, is prepared for shipment to all parts of the world.

The plumbago, or true vein graphite, of Ceylon will be familiar to the ordinary reader as black lead, which, in its chemical relation, is totally different from all other forms of carbon. The Ceylon plumbago is the purest and best in the world, and is exceedingly refractory. A piece of Ceylon plumbago with sharp needlelike projecting angles can be subjected to a heat which melts steel and yet not have any of its finest points affected in any way. Plumbago with 99 per cent. of graphitic carbon, or only 1 per cent. ash, can be supplied by Ceylon only. It is used chiefly in the manufacture of crucibles, stove lead, pencils, greases, paints, and electrodes. Its invaluable character in the manufacture of explosives and the great modern steel guns, armour plates, and

The world renowned plumbago mine in Ragedera Kurunegala, Ceylon, opened by the late Mr. Jacob De Mel in 1870, now the property of Mr. H. L. De Mel, C.B.E., J.P. Chairman of the Ceylon Merchants' Chamber.

The photograph, taken in 1881, shows the pit head gear and hauling tackle, also workmen descending by ladders. The mine, which stopped working a few years ago, was 1,000 feet deep.

armaments led to Ceylon being called upon by Great Britain and her Allies during the War to double the amount of plumbago which she had been exporting prior to the outbreak of hostilities. Thus, in contrast to the 15,000 tons exported from Ceylon in 1913, the amount during the years 1916 and 1917 rose to not less than 59,607 tons, of a value of 24¼ millions of rupees. Mr. De Mel's mines are in different parts of Ceylon, and his plumbago has been awarded gold medals and diplomas at the Paris, Chicago, St. Louis, London, Colonial, Wembley, and other Exhibitions.

After the Armistice Mr. H. L. De Mel studied in America, Germany, and other countries, the modern requirements in connection with Ceylon plumbago, with the result that now at his factory in Colombo there are in operation methods and machinery embodying everything that can be suggested for the perfection of the work done there to meet up to date economic conditions. In the well-equipped chemical laboratory the plumbago is tested and guaranteed according to its various specified grades and characteristic constituents.

The great De Mel establishment in Colombo has been evolved into a self-contained little world of its own, where the welfare of the many hundreds of people employed is studied with affectionate care, and the old patriarchal system is made to fit in with modern conditions. The houses of the workers are very comfortable, and the spacious garden and grounds are tastefully laid out, full provision being made for all kinds of games and athletics. One of the buildings is used as a creche for the babies of working mothers, who follow their various occupations in the happy knowledge that their little ones are well taken care of during their absence. As the children grow up, they are educated in another building utilised as a school, which has in front a pleasant garden containing a tree planted by Sir Hugh Clifford when His Excellency paid a visit of inspection to the place in January, 1926. The children as they grow up are also trained to become experts in the particular branches of work for which they are selected according to their capacity and inclination. Properly equipped play-grounds for the juveniles, parallel bars and a volley ball court for the men, demonstrate the interest taken in the physical development of the labourers.

The head of this noteworthy business, Mr. H. L. De Mel, had been connected with it since 1900, when he joined his father and took over a share in its management, prior to which he had been practising as a lawyer. In 1908 he was elected member of the Municipal Council for the Slave Island Ward, and in 1909 he was elected member of the Board of Agriculture and the Ceylon Chamber of Commerce. In 1916 he was elected Chairman of the Low Country Products Association, having been its founder and Secretary for eight years previously. In recognition of the services he rendered during the War, he was made a Commander of the Most Excellent Order of the British Empire by his Majesty the King, being the first in Ceylon to receive that honour, and was also created a Chevallier de l'Ordre de la Couronne de Belgique by His Majesty the King of the Belgians. In 1920 Mr. De Mel was elected Member of the Reformed Legislative Council, representing the Low Country Products Association of Ceylon, and in 1921 he was Chairman of the Reception Committee of the Ceylon National Congress.

In conferring on him the highest local birthday honour—a Commission of the Peace for the Island of Ceylon—on June 3rd, 1917, His Excellency Sir John Anderson, then Governor of the island, said:

> "On many occasions Government had to apply to you for advice and assistance, which were freely and promptly given, and never more so than at the present critical time."

His public philanthropy and private generosity are well known, and he has done very much for local education. In 1925 he organised the work of a newly-constituted Committee on "Free Education" of the City's children, and has been elected its Chairman. In addition to the schools which he has on his estates and factories, there are six others managed by him, in which more than 3,000 children are educated free; and two other schools have recently been built in order to provide for some 10,000 children in the whole city.

When H.R.H. the Prince of Wales visited Ceylon in March, 1922, Mr. H. L. De Mel was the only Ceylonese Chairman of Committee, and successfully organised a pageant of 18,000 school children, who were drawn up on a length of a mile and a half right through the Cinnamon Gardens with only 500 Boy Scouts instead of the Police to maintain order.

Although Mr. De Mel has been a Member of the Chamber of Commerce for more than twenty years, he was the founder of the Ceylon Merchants' Chamber inaugurated in August, 1926. Thus a large number of local merchants were enabled to form themselves into a Chamber to safeguard and advance their own interests, which are not always identical with the interests served by the Ceylon Chamber of Commerce. Mr. De Mel was elected President for three years, and the offices of the new Chamber are also on the third floor of the De Mel Building.

There is no space here, however, to recount all the worthy things performed by this highly esteemed gentleman, but sufficient has doubtless been said to indicate the prominent and honoured position which he occupies. He is assisted in the management of his business by his son, Mr. R. F. S. De Mel, and the firm's reputation has been well maintained by their numerous managers and assistants who have grown grey in service.

Messrs. H. L. De Mel and Co.'s telegraphic address is "Elsmere," Colombo, and the codes used by them are the A B C 5th and 6th editions, Bentley's, Western Union, and private. They are agents for the New India Assurance Co., Ltd., of Bombay, and Mr. George F. Pettinos, of Philadelphia (U.S.A.). They have also agencies at Antwerp, Hamburg, Bremen, Berlin, London, New York, Melbourne, Sydney, Calcutta, Bombay, Madras, Rangoon, Durban, and in Italy, Japan, and Java.

MILLER and CO., LTD., Wholesale and Retail Merchants and General Outfitters, York Street.

THE number of department stores bearing the name of Miller throughout the British Empire is truly remarkable. The present writer has described dozens of them, including one giving employment to 5,000 persons. There must be something that makes for expansiveness in the Miller psychology, something that finds its best expression in large business undertakings, in supplies of the most necessitous materials, and in that highest of all ideals, service, which is the import of all the creeds. What could be more indispensable, for instance, than food, clothes, and medicines, to say nothing of the infinity of other things necessitated by the ever-growing comextensive department store in Colombo's chief shopping thoroughfare. General department stores are, as a rule, very much alike in organisation and goods. The one under notice differs by reason of the fact that, although displaying the most comprehensive stock, there is a specialisation in certain departments that raises them above plexity of modern life! The business of Messrs. Miller and Co., Ltd., has been highly appreciated for its service and supplies in that connection for upwards of seventy years; so that there are very good reasons for the continual ingress and egress of customers through the many doors of their the level of ordinary achievement, and has earned for the firm a reputation peculiarly their own throughout Ceylon. In no direction, for instance, is this more in evidence than in the one for things eatable and drinkable, that so well upholds the name of Messrs. Miller and Co., Ltd., in homes all over the island. An inspection of its interesting assortments provides an object lesson in the enormous range of modern preserved foods. By means of these numerous choice comestibles it is easy to impart to the daily fare of the ordinary home that piquancy and variety which whet jaded appetites and create delightful surprises and uncertainty as to what is to be served. The groceries and provisions obtainable from Messrs. Miller and Co., Ltd., enable their many customers to solve most pleasingly and economically the domestic problems regarding meals which confront every home where good and varied food is a matter of primary importance. Fresh fruits and vegetables, and confectionery put up in new and alluring ways, are included in the comprehensive supplies. The facilities thus provided by Messrs. Miller and Co., Ltd., are greatly appreciated when occasions arise for special additions to the daily bill of fare; and many a dinner that would otherwise be in the category of mediocrity, is raised to the superlative by the choice dainties in question.

Similar encomiums are applicable to the firm's exhaustive selections of wines and spirits, which embrace a large proportion of the best-known brands on the market. The firm import much of their liquor in bulk, and consequently their bottling department in Dawson Street is a busy and important place.

Another department in which Messrs. Miller and Co., Ltd., excel is the one for drugs, medicines, and toilet articles, where the best pharmaceutical traditions are exemplified in all those details that are inseparably associated with high-class pharmacies in Great Britain.

As exponents of the latest styles in ladies' and gentlemen's outfitting, Messrs. Miller and Co.,

PREMISES OF MILLER and CO., LTD., COLOMBO.

KANDY BRANCH OF MILLER and CO., LTD.

NUWARA ELIYA BRANCH OF MILLER and CO., LTD.

Ltd., are similarly popular and influental, and in the tailoring, dressmaking, and millinery departments are employed experts whose clever interpretation of fashion and fit takes cognizance of the ever-varying idiosyncrasies of individual requirements in all that relates to accuracy of measurement, suitability of material, chromatic harmony, and good taste.

Much could be written regarding the departments for tobacconists' supplies, glassware, crockery, and household requisites of every description, watches, clocks and jewellery, gramophones, photographic materials, sports goods, etc. But to describe these even briefly would entail more inches than there are pages at our disposal.

The history of the concern goes back to the early fifties of last century, when Mr. Cramond Miller started at Kandy a small business in general merchandise, which later became known as Bell, Miller, and Co. In 1858 that name was changed to Findlay, Miller and Co., and in 1862 it became Miller and Co., which continued until 1921, when the firm was incorporated as a private limited liability company. The business now gives employment to about 600 persons; and to its very successful development no one has contributed more than Mr. W. Philps, the former managing director, who retired in 1926 after 36 years' service. Messrs. Miller and Co., Ltd., have other large stores at Kandy, Nuwara Eliya, and Bandarawella, also forage mills and warehouses in Dawson Street, Colombo. The company's cable address is "Millers," Colombo, and the codes used by them are Western Union (five letter), A B C 5th edition, and Bentley's.

HEATH and CO., Exporters of Tea, 9, Park Street.

The famous tea of Ceylon is tested, blended, graded, and packed for shipment abroad in the premises of Messrs. Heath and Co. at 9, Park Street by methods representing all the knowledge and experience that have evolved for the perfection of process and result in that connection. Ceylon tea varies considerably in flavour, according to the elevation and district in which the estate is situated. Teas from the estates in the low country have practically no distinctive flavour; while a choice flavour is produced by estates of medium elevation; and a very choice lemon flavour is characteristic of tea grown in certain areas and in districts over 6,000 feet above sea level.

After the tea has been graded each grade is packed separately in wooden boxes lined with sheet lead and carefully soldered, for it is of the utmost importance that the package should be as air-tight as possible, since tea is exceedingly quick in absorbing moisture from the air, and then becomes rapidly mouldy and useless. Before packing, each grade of tea is always fired at a temperature round about 180 deg. Fahr. The tea is then graded and packed.

Messrs. Heath and Co. are one of the best-known firms in the tea trade, and are shippers of tea to Australia, Canada, United States, Great Britain, and other parts of the world. Their business was started in January, 1862, by Mr. Rodewald, who was subsequently joined by Mr. A. H. Heath, and the firm then became known as Rodewald and Heath. With the expansion of the tea trade in India and Ceylon, the firm opened branches there, the Colombo branch being established in 1896 and the one at Calcutta in 1904; while an office was also established at Batavia, Java, in 1920. In 1900 Mr. Bodewald retired. The business was then transferred to Messrs. A. H. Heath and A. R. A. Heath, and has since been carried on under the name of Heath and Co. The partners now are Messrs. A. R. A. Heath, G. L. Lyon, and C. H. Griggs. Messrs. Heath and Co. are agents for the China Fire Insurance Co., Ltd., incorporated in Hongkong. Their telegraphic addresses are "Heather," Colombo; "Heathbird," Calcutta; and "Heather," Batavia. The codes used are the A B C 4th, 5th, and 6th editions, Lieber's, and private.

LEE, HEDGES and CO., LTD., Import and Export Merchants, Estate, Shipping, Insurance and General Commission Agents, Colpetty.

Unlike many other seaports in the East where firms come and go with astonishing rapidity, Colombo's commercial community comprises quite a number of fine old houses that have been established for many decades. Amongst these are Messrs. Lee, Hedges and Co., Ltd., whose name is honourable and prominent in local commercial records since 1858, when the firm was founded, and when merchandise to and from Ceylon was carried in sailing ships round the Cape of Good Hope. Messrs. Lee, Hedges and Co., Ltd., used to be amongst the largest exporters of Ceylon coffee, and after the failure of that industry in 1876 turned their attention to its successor, tea, in which they were one of the pioneer firms and helped considerably in making that fragrant product of the island famous throughout the world. Their trade in tea is very extensive, as is well evidenced by the interesting sights in that connection to be witnessed at their new premises in Colpetty, where every existent condition is the result of careful study and long experience of the best ways and means for the reception, preparation and shipment of the commodity.

Messrs. Lee, Hedges and Co., Ltd., have always had their stores at Colpetty, but it was only recently that they removed their offices to that admirable district from 55-57, Queen Street, where they had been for many years. The premises in Colpetty are about five acres in area, and on the top floor of one of the new buildings, covering 36,000 square feet, are the clerical departments, where much valuable time is now saved that was formerly wasted through the separation of offices and works so far distant from each other. Besides tea, Messrs. Lee, Hedges and Co., Ltd., are also amongst the largest exporters of cinnamon, rubber and coconut products, etc.

They transact likewise an extensive trade as general importers, more especially of teak and other foreign timber, momi chests, building materials, estates' requisites, explosives, cartridges, etc. The directors are Messrs. A. S. Berwick, A. P. Waldock, C. S. Burns, J. M. Pittendrigh and J. W. Oldfield. The firm's telegraphic address is "Hedges," Colombo, and they use all the standard codes. They are agents for the following:—

Grace Bros. & Co., Ltd., London, Liverpool, Manchester, Genoa, etc.
W. R. Grace & Co., New York, San Francisco, Chicago, Seattle, Panama, Valparaiso, Lima, etc.
Grace and Co., Ltd., Montreal, Kingston, Jamaica, etc.

For Shipping:

Dollar Steamship Lines, Ltd.
New York and Pacific S.S. Co., Ltd.
Atlantic and Pacific S.S. Co., Ltd.
Grace Steamship Co., Ltd.
Societa Nazionale di Navigazione.
The Standard S.S. Owners' Protection and Indemnity Association, Ltd.

For Insurance:

The Commercial Union Assurance Co., Ltd., Fire, Life, Marine and Accident Guarantee and Motor Car Insurances.
Union Insurance Society of Canton, Ltd.
Underwriters at Lloyds.
Imperial Live Stock and General Insurance Co., Ltd.
The Gripoly Belting Co.
The Morgan Crucible Co., Ltd.
Curtis's and Harvey, Ltd., London.
The State Saw Mills, Government of Western Australia.
The Atlas Preservatives Co., Ltd.
Bells United Asbestos (India), Ltd.
Sumner's Ty-phoo Tea, Ltd.

Agents & Secretaries for:

The Kanapediwattie Tea Co., Ltd
The Vogan Tea Co. of Ceylon, Ltd.
The Lanka Rubber Co., Ltd.
The Pelmadulla Valley Tea & Rubber Co., Ltd.
The Honiton Rubber Co., Ltd.
The Mirishena (Kalutara) Rubber Co., Ltd.
The Kandy Rubber and Tea Co., Ltd.
The Hatton Tea Co., Ltd.
The Alpitakarde Tea & Rubber Co., Ltd.

WALKER and GREIG, LTD., General Engineers, Slave Island

Although the premises of Messrs. Walker and Greig, Ltd., occupy an area of about five acres in the centre of Colombo, they are hidden in a secluded district beside the lake, and, therefore, are not likely to be noticed by the stranger making a brief and unaided tour of inspection of the city and its environs. In that important establishment hundreds of skilled workmen, supervised by European experts, are engaged in the wide range of general engineering for which Messrs. Walker and Greig, Ltd., are famous, especially in those phases of it pertaining to the manufacture, installation, and repair of machinery for the various agricultural industries of the island. Owing to the continual development of the business, the firm's Slave Island premises, to which allusion has just been made, have become inadequate for the demands made upon them, and accordingly Messrs. Walker and Greig, Ltd., are building larger and better premises on the other side of the lake. Their wood-working plant has already, at the time of writing, been transferred into the new works; and when the entire transference will be completed, it will inaugurate a new era of progress and expansion for the firm, and enable them, by their greatly increased facilities and resources, to demonstrate even more impressively than before their capacity for the fulfilment of big contracts for the remodelling of all kinds of plants and the erection of all kinds of buildings.

Messrs. Walker and Greig, Ltd., specialise in the manufacture and installation of machinery for tea and rubber factories.

The business is one of the oldest industrial undertakings in Ceylon, and was founded by Mr. John Walker, who arrived in the island in 1836 for the purpose of erecting sugar machinery for Messrs. James Finlay and Co. Thereafter he started operations as a general engineer on his own account at Kandy, and was very successful. At that time the cultivation of coffee was the principal agricultural industry, and Mr. John Walker's coffee pulping machine was one of the most popular and best known contrivances of the kind then in use. Mr. John Walker was essentially an engineer. In order that he might have an absolutely reliable person to look after the commercial side of his business, he sent for his brother William, and together they carried on the concern from 1854 as John Walker and Co. Advancing with the times, and to meet the requirements of the coffee planters of Uva, Mr. John Walker opened at Badulla and Haldummulla branches under the style of Walker and Wilson, which was changed in 1874 to Walker and Greig. With the growing importance of Haputale, the old workshop at Haldummulla was closed, and a new one opened at the top of the pass, where the business was carried on, the firm eventually removing into their present premises at Haputale. Badulla workshop likewise underwent reconstruction, and is now an imposing establishment.

About the year 1873 the head office (John Walker and Co.) at Kandy started a branch in the Dikoya district in a small store close to the firm's present well-stocked premises at Glencairn, also a branch at Craiglea, Dimbula, which they took over from Messrs. Lee, Hedges and Co. About the same time they started building a store at Tillicoultry, Lindula, and in 1876 took over the business of Gordon, Massie and Co., at Devon, Dimbula, and Agrakande, Lindula, transferring the Craiglea store to and incorporating it with that at Devon. In the early eighties Mr. John Walker retired from the firm of John Walker and Co., taking over the various up-country businesses, and —leaving Kandy to his brother William—carried them on under the style of Walker and Greig. With the death of Mr. John Walker in 1890, the concern passed into the care of trustees, and was eventually managed and bought from the trustees by Mr. John Walker, son of the founder of the firm.

In 1910 the firm was incorporated with a capital of Rs. 1,500,000, and the new company, still retaining the up-country establishments, opened the works in Slave Island, Colombo, already referred to.

The telegraphic address of Messrs. Walker and Greig, Ltd., is "Reklaw," Colombo, and the codes used are Bentley's, A B C 5th and 6th editions, Marconi's, etc. Messrs. Walker and Greig, Ltd., are agents for the following:—

Gandy's Belting Co., Ltd.
J. M. Henderson & Co., Aerial Ropeways.
Allan, Whyte & Co., Wire Ropes and Shoots.
John Yates, Estates Tools.
Carron Iron Works.
Strathcylde Paint Co., Ltd.
Adolphe Crosbie, Ltd.
W. Gunther & Sons.
Martin Earle & Co., Ltd., Cement.
Dennis Lorries.
Planters Engineering Co., Ltd.; Rubber Mills and Gass's Back Washers.
Darlaston Galvanizing Co., Ltd.
Norris Henty & Gardners, Ltd., Gardner Engines.
Ruston & Hornsby, Lincoln, Gas Engines.
Hans Renold, Chain Transmission.
Hele-Shaw Oil-Hydraulic Transmission.
Flux Pump Co.

THE CEYLON WHARFAGE COMPANY, LTD.

THE Ceylon Wharfage Co., Ltd., was formed in 1899 for the purpose of taking over and extending the old-established business of the Wharf and Warehouse Co., Ltd., founded in 1875. The company at its inception leased from Government a large part of the Customs premises, to which it has since made many improvements, both as regards facilities for landing and delivering cargo and in increased warehouse accommodation. In 1899 all rice and bag cargo was landed at an extensive sandy beach by coolies wading into the water and bringing the bags to shore on their heads. All that has now been changed, and quay walls having been built, the former sandy beach has been transformed into a miniature wet-dock, well supplied with travelling steam-cranes and all appliances for the rapid handling of cargo. Large additions have also been made to the company's fleet of cargo, coal, and water lighters. The total tonnage of the fleet of lighters is already close on 20,000 tons. For the rapid movement of this fleet the company owns nine tugs of the latest design. The tonnage of the water fleet amounts to an aggregate of 2,100 tons, with ten steam pumps and boilers. For the upkeep of this fleet there are two yards, one—the building yard—on the Kelani River, and the other—the repairing yard—on the north-east side of the harbour. At the latter point the company has several patent slips for convenience in the repair of its tugs and barges.

The company lands and ships all coal for the P. and O. Co., British India Steam Navigation Co., and the Messageries Maritimes Cie., and handles annually on an average three quarters of the trade of the port.

The company is also the cargo-landing and boating contractor for the P. and O., British India, Orient Royal Mail, Bibby Line, Harrison Line, Messageries Maritimes, Asiatic S. N. Co., Nippon Yusen Kaisha, Clan Line, City Line, Holt Line, Anchor Line, and others; and it ships cargo to every steamer line entering Colombo. This large undertaking necessitates, of course, a big labour force, and it is estimated that the company controls a staff of about 5,000 men.

The manager at Colombo is Mr. W. Y. Fleming. The head office of the company is at 9, Throgmorton Avenue, London, E.C. The chairman is the Right Hon. the Viscount Inchcape; the managing director is Mr. James A. Ridge. The other directors are Mr. Edwin Darlington, C.I.E., Commander August B. T. Cayzer, R.N., Mr. Alfred Geoffrey Turner, and Sir Kenneth Anderson, Bart., G.C.M.G.

BOIS BROS. and CO., LTD., Estate Agents, Merchants, and Financial Agents, Queen Street.

THE business of Messrs. Bois Bros. and Co., Ltd., was established in 1891 by Mr. (later Sir) Stanley Bois and his brother Percy, both of whom had been engaged with the now defunct firm of Alston, Scott, and Co. for many years. Amongst the first agencies held by Messrs. Bois Bros. and Co. was that of the British India Steam Navigation Co., which developed very greatly with the growth of the port of Colombo; so much so that at last that company opened its own office there.

Sir Stanley Bois was very influential in the public life of Ceylon, and was knighted for his services in that connection. He was a member of the Legislative Council, Colombo Municipal Council, Chairman of the Chamber of Commerce, and Commissioner of the Ceylon Exhibition at the St. Louis Exhibition. He and his brother Percy are now resident near London; but Sir Stanley is still intimately connected with the Colombo firm bearing their name, which was formed in 1920 into a limited liability company, of which the present directors are Messrs. G. C. Slater, Neill G. Campbell, and L. G. Byatt.

Messrs. Bois Bros. and Co., Ltd., have at Colombo very large warehouses, where tea, rubber, cocoa, and the other products of the island are prepared for shipment to all parts of the world. The firm's telegraphic address is "Boisdale," Colombo, and the codes used are

Marconi, Bentley's, A B C 6th edition, and private. They are agents for the following:—

The Anglo-Ceylon & General Estates Co., Ltd., 20, Eastcheap, London, E.C.
Robertson, Bois & Co., 12, Fenchurch Street, London, E.C.
M. P. Evans & Co., 30, Mincing Lane, London, E.C.

INSURANCE:

The Standard Life Assurance Co. (Life).
The Alliance Assurance Co. (Fire, Marine, Motor Car, and Burglary).
The Royal Exchange Assurance Corporation (Marine).

SHIPPING:

Struthers & Barry.
Managing Agents, U.S. Shipping Board E.F. Corp.

STERLING COMPANIES:

The Anglo-Ceylon & General Estates Co., Ltd.
The Ceylon Upcountry Tea Estates, Ltd.
The Ceylon Timber & Rubber Syndicate, Ltd.
The Craighead Tea Co., Ltd.
The East India & Ceylon Tea Co., Ltd., London, E.C.
The Hanwella Rubber Estates, Ltd.
The Lindoola Tea Co., Ltd.
The Tyspane Tea Co., Ltd.
The Vellikellie Tea Co., Ltd.

AGENTS AND SECRETARIES (RUPEE COMPANIES):

The Apthorpe Estates, Ltd.
The Ceylon & Eastern Investments, Ltd.
The Eastern River Tanneries Co., Ltd.
The Jambulande Tea & Rubber Estates, Ltd.
The Kaluganga Valley Tea & Rubber Co., Ltd.
The Katiapola Rubber Co., Ltd.
The "L. L. P." Estates, Ltd.
The Macaldeniya Tea & Rubber Co., Ltd.
The Morakelle Rubber Co., Ltd.
The Mulhalkelle Tea Co., Ltd.
The New Colombo Ice Co., Ltd.
The Oaklands Tea & Rubber Co., Ltd.
The Palmerston Tea Co., Ltd.
The Roeberry Tea Co. of Ceylon, Ltd.
The Rubber Plantations of Kalutara, Ltd.
The S. Helier's Tea Co., Ltd.

CORRESPONDENTS FOR:

Charles Lane & Sons, 7-8, Idol Lane, London, E.C.
Drexel & Co.
Hasler & Jaeger, 21, Mincing Lane, London, E.C.
Morgan, Glenfell & Co.
Morgan, Harjes & Co.
Rownson, Drew & Clydesdale, Ltd., 225, Upper Thames Street, London, E.C.4.
Scott & Co., Mauritius.

NEW COLOMBO ICE COMPANY, LTD., Glennie Street, Slave Island.

THE word new in the name of a business undertaking, like the one indicated above, suggests improvement upon what that concern had formerly been or had attained. The records of the preceding Colombo Ice Co., Ltd., include nothing out of the ordinary. It had been established for many years and went into liquidation. Such is its brief, bald history. But from it arose, Phœnix-like, a totally different company; and in order that its greatly improved character should be proclaimed, the word New was added to the former title. Thus in 1920 the New Colombo Ice Co., Ltd., began to serve the people of Colombo and elsewhere in new ways of efficiency that made them "sit up and take notice."

In Colombo the famous foreign aerated waters are expensive; and so residents in Ceylon's capital and visitors to it were agreeably surprised when they found that the Elephant brand of non-alcoholic beverages of the New Colombo Ice Co., Ltd., compared favourably with the foreign waters and were procurable at much less cost. The New Colombo Ice Co., Ltd., has proved the fallacy of ginger beer in stone bottles, which has always been regarded as the slogan of correct preferment in that connection. Fearful things creep into stone bottles, and remain there undetected in death, however great care may be exercised in prevention. Clear glass bottles are not suitable for ginger beer, as the sunlight deteriorates the contents considerably. The ginger beer of the New Colombo Ice Co., Ltd., is always in amber glass bottles; and the insides of all the bottles are subjected to minute scrutiny before and after being filled.

The new methods of washing the bottles are amongst the most outstanding characteristics of the work done in the busy Elephant Brand factory. After the bottles receive their preliminary washing they pass through the new Dawson Patent Washer, where the insides are scoured with great force by jets of alternating caustic soda and hot and cold water, this being an improvement upon the method of revolving spiral brushes which has hitherto been regarded as the most effective system.

The department for the mixing of the sugar and flavouring essences affords, with its fly-proof and dust-proof arrangements, impressive demonstrations of the care exercised by the company in regard to safeguarding the absolute purity of the materials from any possible contamination, as well as in ensuring absolute accuracy and uniformity in the quality of the finished products. The boiling of sugar, as is frequently adopted in other aerated water factories, is, through crystallization tendencies, apt to lead to injurious effects in the manufactures. Accordingly in the factory in question the pure cane sugar used is made soluble by what is known as "the cold process," and is filtered through paper pulp, when its purity is attested by the fact that it is almost without colour, like water. The flavouring fruit syrups and essences are then added by ingenious contrivances that operate with automatic precision in determining the amount necesary for each particular beverage; and the mixtures are conveyed through pure tin pipes to a remarkable aluminium filler which inserts the mixtures and their specified quantities into the bottles. The latter are thereafter conveyed by machinery to the bottling apparatus, which adds to their contents the twice-filtered water and carbonic acid gas. The bottles are then crown corked and labelled, and pass on to the storage departments, whence they go in thousands of dozens daily to gladden thirsty people throughout Ceylon. The factory is permeated by an ingenious transit system of gravity tramways, on which are conveyed in continuous succession the bottles as they pass through the evolution that commences with their cleansing and ends with their completed contents ready for the market.

As its name indicates, the New Colombo Ice Co., Ltd., is primarily engaged in the manufacture of ice, of which it turns out about thirty tons daily, and supplies almost all the shipping visiting Colombo. The ground occupied by the company is about 2 acres, and it gives employment to about 200 persons. For its deliveries it has 14 motor lorries and 40 bullock carts. Arrangements are now being made for rebuilding the factory on a much larger scale and for the addition to it of large cold-storage chambers. The managing director is Mr. G. C. Slater, who is also general manager of Bois Bros. and Co., described in the preceding article. The other directors are Messrs. A. R. Quarme, D. Julius, and E. W. Keith. The general manager is Mr. C. McMillan Mathieson. The company's telegraphic address is "Zero," and Bentley's code is used.

HENDERSON and CO., Export Merchants and General Commission Agents, 19, Queen Street.

In no country in the world is more tea consumed in proportion to its inhabitants than Australia, and Messrs. Henderson and Co. were amongst the earliest and most influential pioneers in introducing and popularising Ceylon tea throughout that country. Their name is well known in tea circles all over the world; and while exporting Ceylon tea very extensively they are even still larger shippers of India and Java tea. Nowhere is tea more carefully and scientifically prepared for export than in Messrs. Henderson and Co.'s factories in Foster Lane and Colpetty, Colombo, where several hundreds of people are employed. The equipment of these establishments represents everything that experience can suggest for the enhancement of the work done there. The manner in which the packets of tea of different sizes are put up with labels of variegated designs is an object lesson in the efficiency which has been attained in connection with that class of operation. Messrs. Henderson and Co. have also done very much in the development of the rubber and coconut industries of Ceylon, and are large exporters of all the agricultural products of the island.

TEA TASTING DEPARTMENT.

PACKING DEPARTMENT.

DESPATCHING THE TEA.

SCENES AT HENDERSON and CO.'S, NILWATTE FACTORY, COLOMBO.

The history of the concern dates back to the early eighties of last century, when Mr. J. A. Henderson and Mr. H. Tarrant, both previously engaged in the wholesale tea trade in London, commenced business in partnership under the name of Tarrant, Henderson and Co.; but in 1896 the partnership was dissolved, and Mr. Henderson continued business on his own account under the name of Henderson and Co., every year showing a development in his trade. Mr. Henderson attends to the firm's interests at the London buying office in "Ocean House," 24/5, Great Tower Street, E.C.3. The other partners are Messrs. H. J. Hanscomb and G. K. Logan, who reside at Colombo.

Messrs. Henderson and Co.'s telegraphic address is "Quality," and they use all the standard codes. They are agents for the following:

The Dalkeith (Ceylon) Rubber Estates, Ltd.
Pindenioya Rubber & Tea Estates, Ltd.
Allerton Estates (Ceylon), Ltd.
Kudaganga Rubber Co. of Ceylon, Ltd.
Walagama Rubber Co., Ltd.
Balahela Rubber Co.
Trafford Hill Rubber Estates, Ltd.
Hangranoya Tea Estates, Ltd.
Richlands Ceylon Tea Estates, Ltd.
The Kirivaula Coconut Plantation Co., Ltd.
Tilton (Ceylon) Tea Estates, Ltd.
Danzil Estates Co., Ltd.
The Union Marine Insurance Co., Ltd.
The State Assurance Co., Ltd.
The Western Assurance Co.
The Queensland Insurance Co., Ltd.
The Phœnix Assurance Co., Ltd.
Lloyd's Underwriters.
The Nilwatte Tea Packeting and Packing Factory,

WHITTALL and CO.,

General Merchants, Shipping, Insurance, and Estates Agents, 14, Queen Street.

THE prominence of Messrs. Whittall and Co. in local trade is well demonstrated by their mills and warehouses, occupying about four acres at Mortlake, Slave Island, and giving employment to some hundreds of persons. From these premises are shipped large quantities of the products of Ceylon, especially tea and rubber.

The tea departments are particularly interesting. The firm's tea tasters, like those in the other similar establishments in Colombo, have to taste from 1,000 to 2,000 teas every week. In the tasting of the tea a weight of tea equal to a sixpenny piece is dropped into a small pot, and about an eighth of a pint of boiling water is poured thereon. The lid is then placed on the top of the pot, and after standing from five to six minutes all the liquid is poured into a small china bowl of suitable size. The infused leaves are tapped from the pot on to the lid, which is inverted for that purpose. The taster then starts his examination, testing the tea first by the liquor, next by the scent or brightness of the infused leaf, and finally by the appearance of the dry leaf of the sample, forming his opinion by the combination of the points noticed. Ceylon tea varies considerably in flavour according to the elevation and district in which the estate is situated. Teas from the estates in the low country have practically no distinctive flavour; while a choice flavour is produced by estates of medium elevation, and a very choice lemon flavour is characteristic of tea grown in certain areas and in districts more than 6,000 feet above sea level.

The tea, after being graded is packed in the familiar lead-foil packages and loose in wooden boxes lined with sheet lead hermetically soldered; for it is of the utmost importance that each package should be as air tight as possible, as tea is exceedingly quick in absorbing moisture from the air (up to 16 to 17 per cent.) and then becomes rapidly mouldy and useless.

Messrs. Whittall and Co.'s premises include their own printing plant for labels, stationery. etc.

The firm not only sell the products of the various tea and rubber companies for whom they are agents, as detailed at the end of this sketch. but they also buy for them the comprehensive range of articles comprised by the term of "estates supplies," including large quantities of rice and other foodstuffs.

The business of Messrs. Whittall and Co. was established in 1859 at Kandy under the name of Keir, Dundas and Co., which was continued until 1873 when the firm moved to Colombo and became known as Duncan Anderson and Co. In 1880 the present title was assumed.

It is worthy of note that Mr. G. W. Carlyon, one of the former partners in the firm, introduced about 1890 the first ricksha into Ceylon. Mr. Carlyon retired in 1906, but the puller of the historic little vehicle remained a pensioner of the firm until his death in 1924.

The present partners are Mr. C. H. Figg, Sir James T. Broom, Mr. A. S. Collett, and Mr. P. H. Fraser. Messrs. Whittall and Co.'s telegraphic address is "Whittall," Colombo, and they use all the standard codes. They are Agents and Secretaries for (Rupee Companies)

The Agra Ouvah Estates Co., Ltd.
The Clunes Estates Co. of Ceylon, Ltd.
The Coconut Estates of Perak, Ltd.
The Colombo Fort Land and Building Co., Ltd.
The Dorset Rubber Estate Co., Ltd.
The Drayton (Ceylon) Estates Co., Ltd.
The Estates Co. of Uva, Ltd.
The Fernlands Tea Co., Ltd.
The Glasgow Estate Co., Ltd.
The Colinda Tea & Rubber Co., Ltd.
The Hatbawe Rubber Co., Ltd.
The High Forests Estate Co., Ltd.
The Kalutara Co., Ltd.
The Kanana Rubber Estate Co., Ltd.
The Lady Havelock Gardens Co., Ltd.
The Maha Uva Estate Co., Ltd.
The Niriwatte Co., Ltd.
The Oonoogaloya Tea Co., Ltd.
The Pimbura Rubber Co., Ltd.
The Ruanwella Tea Co., Ltd.
The Sunderland (Ceylon) Rubber Co., Ltd.
The Telok Bharu Coconut Co., Ltd.
The Torrington Tea Estates, Ltd.
The Uplands Tea Estates of Ceylon, Ltd.
The Upper Maskeliya Estates Co., Ltd.
The Vincit Tea and Rubber Co., Ltd.

AGENTS FOR (STERLING COMPANIES):

The Alliance Tea Co. of Ceylon, Ltd.
The Balmoral (Ceylon) Estates Co., Ltd.
The Bandarapola Ceylon Tea Co., Ltd.
The Bibile Rubber Co., Ltd.
The Demodera Tea Co., Ltd.
The Ganapalia Estate Co., Ltd.
The Haydella Tea & Rubber Estates, Ltd.
The Imperial Ceylon Tea Estates, Ltd.
The Kobonella Estates Co. of Ceylon, Ltd.
The Mazawatte Tea Co., Ltd. Densham & Sons, Ltd.).
The Seremban Rubber Estates, Ltd.

MANAGING AGENTS FOR (STERLING COMPANIES):

The Panawatte Tea & Rubber Estates, Ltd.
The Yatiyantota Ceylon Tea Co., Ltd.

AGENTS FOR:

The Yorkshire Insurance Co., Ltd. (Fire and Marine).
The Northern Assurance Co., Ltd. (Fire & Burglary).
Hongkong Fire Insurance Co., Ltd.
London Guarantee & Accident Co., Ltd. (Fidelity Guarantee, Motor Car, Motor Cycle, and Vehicle Insurance).
Canton Insurance Office, Ltd. (Marine).
Northern China Insurance Co., Ltd. (Fire and Marine).
Triton Insurance Co., Ltd. (Fire).
Eagle, Star & British Dominions Insurance Co. (Fire, Loss of Profit, Marine and Baggage).
The Orient Line.
The Glen Line.
The Dollar Line.
The Admiral Oriental Line.

JAMES FINLAY and CO., LTD.,
General Merchants and Commission Agents, 63, Queen Street.

The fine old block of office buildings on the left side of Queen Street, looking from the lighthouse towards Galle Face, is practically as it was many decades ago, and has housed some of the principal firms in Colombo for generations. But no concern there is comparable in history and achievements with that of Messrs. James Finlay and Co., Ltd., whose business, founded about 1750 in Glasgow, has contributed very considerably to the development of British trade, especially in the East. An account of it will be found on pages 60 and 61, in the section on Calcutta, in which city the firm have their headquarters for the Indian Empire.

At Colombo Messrs. James Finlay and Co., Ltd., are large exporters of all the products of Ceylon. Their Ambawatte Mills, in Vauxhall Street, occupy $5\frac{1}{2}$ acres, and are excellently equipped for their purpose. In that interesting establishment may be seen the famous tea of Ceylon undergoing the various operations preparatory to its being packed in the well-known "Acme" lead-lined tea chests for shipment to all parts of the world; also rubber, cinnamon, cocoa, desiccated coconut, etc. The firm are likewise extensive importers of piece-goods, sugar, rice, etc. Their telegraphic address at Colombo is "Mercator," and they are agents there for the following:

South British Insurance Co., Ltd.
Royal Insurance Co., Ltd.
National Insurance Co. of Great Britain, Ltd., Glasgow.
United Insurance Co., Ltd., Sydney
Ulster Marine Insurance Co., Ltd.
Morrison Pollexfen & Blair, Ltd.
The Osaka Marine & Fire Insurance Co., Ltd.
The Automobile Insurance Co. of Hartford, Conn.
The Insurance Co. of North America.
The Samarang Sea & Fire Insurance Co., Ltd.
The Consolidated Tea & Lands Co., Ltd.
The Amalgamated Tea Estates Co., Ltd.
The Anglo-American Direct Tea Trading Co., Ltd.
The Kanan Devan Hills Produce Co., Ltd.
The Mahawale Rubber & Tea Co., Ltd.
The Pelmadulla Rubber Co., Ltd.
The Wellandura Tea & Rubber Co., Ltd.
The Ceylon Land Dovelopment Co., Ltd.
Clan Line Steamers, Ltd.
Osaka Shoen Kaisha Line.
Houston Line of Steamers.
Wilson Line of Steamers.
Scottish Shire Line of Steamers.
C. & S. Popoff Freres, Moscow and London.

GRAND ORIENTAL HOTEL (COLOMBO HOTELS COMPANY, LTD.).

At no port in the East do more passengers land than at Colombo, and the many thousands who pass through there must carry away memories and impressions of the Grand Oriental Hotel, situated opposite to the landing jetty. It is a meeting place of the East and the West, a famous resort of passengers between Europe, Australia,

GRAND ORIENTAL HOTEL.

and the diverse countries of the Orient. The many signatures in its guest book present as varied caligraphy and nomenclature as may be found anywhere, and include the names of celebrities in all walks of life. The extensive lounge hall is equipped, as are all the other public sections, with overhead electric fans and comfortable chairs, settees, tables, etc., for *dolce far niente.* In that spacious place the people en route from home to the ports farther on get their first impressions of Oriental hotel service and the various much appreciated ice-cold beverages of tropical custom and necessity; while those on vacation from the lands of the East or South meet there in the happy abandon of rest from business and in full enjoyment of the holidays upon which they have entered.

The adjoining dining-room, with seating accommodation for 300 persons, is very ornate in its white and gold decorations, and is overlooked on three sides by balconies. One of these is pleasantly and attractively furnished as a reading and writing-room, and always contains the latest illustrated papers, etc., from Great Britain and elsewhere. The dining-room opens on the left-hand side into a charming old world garden with a well-kept lawn, tropical trees, plants, fountain, benches, etc. At one end of the garden is St. Peter's Church, which used to be the residence of the Governor of Ceylon before the island passed from the possession of the Dutch in 1796; and the old garden was then part of the Residency grounds.

Many of the hotel bedrooms look into this delightful garden, and those on the upper floors command a beautiful view of the sea and the shipping entering and leaving Colombo harbour. The hotel has 220 bedrooms, and they are all nicely and suitably furnished. Each has its own large overhead electric fan and washbasin with hot and cold running water. Many of the apartments have their own bathrooms attached, and include also suites fulfilling all requirements.

The G. O. H., as it is popularly called, has recently undergone very extensive additions and improvements with special regard to the maximum of comfort, convenience, and adaptability to tropical conditions. The new entrance hall is exceptionally handsome, and over it on the first floor is the beautiful new ballroom equipped with projecting coloured lighting arrangements. Overlooking the entrance hall is a round gallery on each floor, and the great unobstructed space thus created, extending from the ground floor to the distant roof with its artistic coloured glass, contributes very much to the coolness and airiness as well as impressive appearance of the internal ensemble.

No feature of the G.O.H. is more noteworthy than its splendid roof garden, whence a memorable view is obtained of the city and the sea. In that cool and lofty rendezvous cinema displays are given on Wednesday and Sunday nights.

The G. O. H. has its own ice factory and all modern conveniences, such as billiard room, electric elevators, hair-dressing saloon, and telephones on each floor with unrestricted connection throughout Ceylon.

The hotel was started in 1870 on a small scale, and has evolved to its present extent with the great development of Colombo as one of the chief ports of call in the world. The establishment is owned and operated by the Colombo Hotels Co., Ltd. The managing director is Mr. Thomas Walker, and the other directors are Messrs. S. P. Hayley, F. H. Layard, F. T. Wright, and Col. T. Y. Wright. The secretary is Mr. T. S. Rowe, and the manager Mr Frank Winfield. The telegraphic address is "Grand," Colombo, and the A B C code is used.

PLÂTÉ, LTD., Photographers, Publishers, Booksellers, Art House Decorators, etc., Colpetty.

BY no firm in the East is the art of photography in all its branches more efficiently demonstrated than by Messrs. Plâté, Ltd., whose Colpetty premises, originally a private residence, have been gradually enlarged and adapted to the requirements of the business, which now presents a very noteworthy combination of art and utility that has evolved as the natural outcome of the firm's continuous endeavour to exemplify the superlative in all their operations. The evolution through which photography has gone during recent years is amongst the wonders of modern science. The work of Messrs. Plâté, Ltd., in that connection can only be adequately realised by actual inspection of their processes and results. Their portraits, including those of Royalty and many celebrities throughout the world, are characterised by all the details inseparable from the highest phases of the art. The numerous examples of their ability in depicting the best expression of their sitters in positions and poses best adapted to each individual seems to have behind them much psychological intuition, as well as very great experience of studio routine.

PREMISES OF PLÂTÉ, LTD., COLPETTY.

Specially noteworthy are the firm's beautiful enlargements and hand-coloured photographs, showing Nature's wealth of chromatic loveliness on land and sea. They have the largest selection in existence of photographs of all parts of Ceylon, and transact an important trade in commercial photographs of every kind. The supplies of Messrs. Plâté, Ltd., include everything for photograph·· and they are sole agents in Ceylon for Kodak, Ltd. They are also agents for the Autotype Fine Art Co., Ltd., London; The Platinotype Co.; Ross, Ltd., London; Ilford, Ltd., London; The Adhesive Dry Mounting Co.; The Autotype Co., London; W. W. Curtis, Ltd.; and Fine Art Printers, Coventry, England.

Messrs. Plâté, Ltd., recently turned their attention to the manufacture of motion pictures, and are now busily engaged in developing that branch of trade, which will include the production of films dealing with local history, folk-lore, customs and current events, etc.

The firm are likewise booksellers and publishers, and amongst their productions are the well-known *Plâté's Colombo Directory* and the popular book *Ceylon*, which deals in a very interesting and comprehensive manner with the island. At their Colpetty premises they have a circulating library containing more than 4,000 volumes.

Another very highly appreciated department of their business is the one devoted to all kinds of artistic house decorations. They are also manufacturers of furniture, and hold themselves in readiness at all times to submit designs for special requirements, or to carry out customers' own specifications in any class of wood work or upholstery. In that connection they are agents in Ceylon for Hall's Sanitary Washable Distemper and the "Keystone" oil paints. Their versatility in the manufacture of picture frames of every description is the natural outcome of their photographic activities, and their stock of mouldings is well calculated to meet the most diverse needs. They have a department for printing, and are manufacturers of all kinds of illustration blocks.

The business was started in 1890 in a small studio at the Bristol Hotel by Mr. A. W. A. Plâté, who was joined in partnership soon afterwards by Mr. H. H. Heinemann. After the advent of the latter gentleman, it developed very rapidly, and when picture post-cards came into vogue, the firm began turning these out in enormous numbers as they still do. After the retirement of Mr. Plâté the firm was incorporated in 1900 with Mr. Heinemann as managing director, the other directors now being Mrs. Clara Plâté, E. J. Hayward, and C. W. Thompson. Branches of the business are established at Galle Face Hotel, Colombo, and at Kandy and Nuwara Eliya.

The company's telegraphic address is "Platewalk," and the codes used are the A B C 5th edition and Bentley's.

LEWIS BROWN and CO., LTD.,
General Merchants and Estate Agents, Prince Building, Prince Street.

A very great deal of the business activity in Colombo is carried on by firms operating as agents for the numerous tea, rubber, coconut, and other companies, whose properties are scattered throughout the island. One of the most prominent of these firms is that of Messrs. Lewis Brown and Co., Ltd., which was founded in the late seventies of last century by Mr. Robert Lewis Maitland Brown, who died in 1898. The firm was incorporated in 1916, and the directors are Messrs. Robert Davidson, David Scott, A. F. Patterson, and G. K. Stewart. Their telegraphic address is "Lewis," Colombo, and the codes used by them are The International Mercantile, Lieber's, A 1, A B C 5th and 6th editions, Western Union, Bentley's, and Broomhall's (Rubber edition).

Messrs. Lewis Brown and Co., Ltd., are agents and secretaries for the following:

The Ceylon Ice & Cold Storage Co., Ltd.
The Wanarajah Tea Co. of Ceylon, Ltd.
The Ribu Rubber Co., Ltd.
The Langat River (Selangor) Rubber Co., Ltd.
The Ankande Estate Co. of Ceylon, Ltd.
The Uva Rubber Co. of Ceylon, Ltd.
The Monte Cristo (Ceylon) Tea & Rubber Co.. Ltd.
The Cocoawatte (Ceylon) Rubber & Tea Estates, Ltd.
The Arcadia Coconut Estates, Ltd.
Sir Harry Dias Coconut Estate, Ltd.
The Hillwood Tea Co., Ltd.
The Ragama Tea & Rubber Co., Ltd.
Martin Coconut Estates of Chilaw, Ltd.
The Nyanza Tea Co. of Ceylon, Ltd.
The Burnside (Ceylon) Tea Estates, Ltd.
Parkside (Neilgherry Hills) Estate Co., Ltd.
The Ambalawa Estate Co. of Ceylon, Ltd.
The Walakande Rubber Co., Ltd.
Horrekelly Estate Co., Ltd.
The Woodside Estates, Ltd.

Agents for:

The Woodend (K.V. Ceylon) Rubber & Tea Co., Ltd.
The Lochnagar (Ceylon) Produce Co., Ltd.
The Neboda (Ceylon) Rubber & Tea Estates, Ltd.
The Parambe Rubber & Tea Co. of Ceylon, Ltd.
The Tismoda Estates Co., Ltd.
The Galphele Tea & Rubber Estates, Ltd.
The Ukuwela Estates Co., Ltd.
The Aboyne Clyde Rubber Estates of Ceylon, Ltd.
The Motor Union Insurance Co., Ltd.
The Royal Insurance Co., Ltd.
The Queensland Insurance Co., Ltd.
Parry & Co., Madras.

FREUDENBERG and CO.,
Importers, Exporters and General Commission Agents, De Mel Building, Chatham Street.

The business of Messrs. Freudenberg and Co. was established in 1873 by Mr. Phillip Freudenberg, who went to Ceylon to buy coffee and to develop direct trade between the island and the continent of Europe as the result of the new era of opportunity ushered in by the opening of the Suez Canal in 1869. When the coffee industry of Ceylon failed in 1876 Messrs. Freudenberg and Co. turned their attention to its successor tea and the various other native products. As time passed their operations increased very considerably, and they became owners of the Hultsdorp Oil Mills and Manuring Works, which form the oldest industrial establishment in the island, having been founded in 1835 in connection with Price's Patent Candle Co., London. In 1898 the old oil mills were burnt down, and were replaced by a much larger and more up-to-date plant, occupying an area of 13 acres, and giving employment to nearly 1,000 persons. Early in the nineties of last century experiments with Messrs. Freudenberg and Co.'s artificial manures for tea growing were first made on a scientific basis, with such satisfactory results that the demand for them underwent great development.

Messrs. Freudenberg and Co. also became bankers and had world-wide connections as general, shipping, and insurance agents, their agencies including the North German Lloyd and East Asiatic lines and the leading German insurance companies and banks.

The outbreak of the Great War led to the liquidation of the business; but it was resumed in 1924, and is now being operated with the enterprise and ability that characterised it in former decades. Messrs. Freudenberg and Co. are exporters of tea, rubber, desiccated coconut, cocoa, fibre, and all products of Ceylon; while as general importers they handle all kinds of building materials, estate supplies, motor cars and accessories. They are agents for the Mercedes, Benz, Adler, Opel, Bean, Jowett Paige cars and the Moreland and White trucks. They are also agents for the Bosch sparking plugs, Carl Zeiss optical goods, the North German Lloyd and the Deutsch-Australische-Damfschiff-Gesellschaft (Cosmos line), etc. The partners are Messrs. W. Freudenberg, S. Freudenberg, E. Wild and H. Gauger. The head office is at Bremen under the name of Freudenberg, Boehringer and Co. The firm's telegraphic addresses at Colombo are "Frudenberg," "Boehringer," "Nordlloyd" and "Austral," and the codes used by them are A B C 5th and 6th editions, A 1, Lieber's, Bentley's, Mosse, and private.

GEORGE PAYNE and CO., LTD., Tea, Coffee, and Cocoa Merchants, Ambewatte Mills, Slave Island.

As might be expected, some of the best known tea firms in the world have branches at Colombo. Amongst them are Messrs. George Payne and Co., Ltd., in whose premises at Ambewatte Mills, Slave Island, the choice teas of Ceylon are dealt with in a system of operation that well substantiates the firm's fame for the excellence of their teas throughout the world. Messrs. George Payne and Co., Ltd., specialise in blended tea, and in that connection are second to none. At the Ambewatte Mills, as well as in their great premises in London, the firm's experts accurately blend the different growths together and produce just that fragrant, invigorating and delicious flavour for which their blends are so celebrated. When it is realised that the tea from practically every estate in Ceylon and India has its separate characteristics and varies considerably, it will be seen how necessary and important is the tea blender's art. Certain growing districts produce tea of light flavoury character, others of full, rich, and strong liquor, while others are known for their pungency. All these different virtues have to be so arranged as to form a blend suitable for the particular locality for which it is required. The long experience and study of Messrs. George Payne and Co., Ltd., enable them to produce blends to suit also the water of each district. For that purpose they store on their London premises samples of water from all parts of Great Britain and abroad, and these supplies are constantly replenished.

The head office of Messrs. George Payne and Co., Ltd., is at Tower Bridge, London, E.C., and besides their great warehouses in Queen Elizabeth Street, Boss Street, Goat Street, Three Oak Lane, and their export blending establishment in Lafone Street, in the metropolis, they have also extensive premises at Waddon, Surrey, Manchester, Liverpool, Glasgow, Cape Town, Durban, Winnebah and Saltpond, Gold Coast, and Calcutta.

They have been established at Colombo since 1904, and their manager there is Mr. W. F. Wood, who is assisted by Mr. W. R. A. McLellan. The firm's telegraphic address is "Pouring," and the codes used by them are the A B C 5th and 6th editions, Bentley's, and private.

EASTERN GARAGE, LTD., Galle Face; Proprietors of THE COLOMBO TAXICAB CO. and LOVER BROS.

THE works of this well-known company, not far from the Galle Face Hotel, occupy about 5½ acres, and employ about 300 persons. Upwards of 1,000 gallons of petrol is sold daily at the two pumps at the entrance. In these works there is in operation an organisation of men and machinery representative of all that knowledge and skill have produced for the perfection of process and result in everything pertaining to motor engineering. Body building, painting, upholstering, electro-plating, etc., are performed there by the latest methods, and in a system of specialisation whereby each worker acquires a proficiency that would otherwise be impossible.

If a car meets with mishap anywhere in Ceylon and cannot run on its own wheels, Eastern Garage, Ltd., will, on notification, have it conveyed to its works on a special contrivance fitted with a powerful crane, which is always kept in readiness for such contingencies.

The stock of spare parts and general motor accessories kept by the company averages in value about £6,000. Whatever may be the requirements in such things the company is sure to be able to meet it—if not in exact design or pattern asked for, something better doubtless will be forthcoming.

Eastern Garage, Ltd., is sole agent for the Standard, Armstrong-Siddeley, Hupmobile, Chrysler, and Salmson cars and the Commerce, Victor, and Federal trucks, and disposes of hundreds of these famous vehicles annually. The company is also sole agent for the Valspar Veedol oils and the Stephenson jacks, which latter have relegated the ordinary jack to the limbo of the obsolete.

The business was originated in 1903 in a very small way, and gradually expanded in keeping with the development of the local motor trade. It went into liquidation in 1919 and was purchased by Mr. G. F. Clayden, of extensive business experience in Great Britain, India, Indo-China, etc. Under his direction the concern was completely metamorphosed and has become one of the most noteworthy undertakings of the kind in the East. In 1925 Mr. Clayden formed the present company, of which he is managing director, and since then the development which has taken place in all its affairs has been very considerable, including ownership of The Colombo Taxicab Co., which is the largest of its kind in Ceylon, where it was the pioneer in the introduction of taxicabs. It has a fine fleet of vehicles, in charge of careful and skilful drivers, for tours all over Ceylon at moderate rates. In that connection it may be mentioned that Eastern Garage, Ltd., issues an extremely interesting booklet entitled *Motor Tours through Ceylon*, which should be seen by everyone desirous of viewing the beauty spots of the island. The Eastern Garage, Ltd., also owns the business of Lover Bros., and in July, 1926, it purchased the Grand Motor Depot in Nuwara Eliya. It has also a branch at Haputale, where it has a fleet of powerful motor lorries, engaged in the transportation of tea and other produce from 28 estates, including those of Lipton, Ltd. The company has also a lock-up garage opposite to the Galle Face Hotel. The telegraphic address of Eastern Garage, Ltd., is "Hustle," Colombo, and the codes used are the A B C 5th edition, Motor Trade, and Bentley's.

DISPLAY OF EASTERN GARAGE, LTD., AT THE ALL CEYLON MOTOR AND GENERAL ENGINEERING EXHIBITION, COLOMBO, IN 1927.

THE CEYLON ICE AND COLD STORAGE COMPANY, LTD., Galle Face.

Life in Colombo to-day is certainly very different from what it must have been when there were no service and supplies like those of The Ceylon Ice and Cold Storage Co., Ltd., which contribute very considerably to the preservation of the health and happiness of the community. Its importance may be gauged by the fact that it is the only cold storage undertaking at present in Colombo, and from its well-stocked refrigerating rooms, having a storage capacity of about 50,000 cubic feet, are issued daily beef, mutton, fowl, fish, fruits, vegetables, dairy produce, and other perishable commodities of every description, which are delivered in the company's motor vans to the homes and hotels throughout the city and its environs.

The company manufactures ice at the rate of 25 tons daily, and has also one of the best establishments in Ceylon for the production of all kinds of aerated waters, of which it turns out about 500 dozen bottles daily. Ceylon water is said to be the best in the Orient, but at the factory in question it is filtered twice before being converted into the company's delicious beverages.

The business originated as a small ice and aerated water concern during the last decade of the 19th century. In 1899 it came under the management of Mr. H. S. Mackenzie, and the present company was formed in 1901. Since then the business has developed pro rata with the growing requirements of the city. The premises cover an area of about two acres, and give employment to about 120 persons.

THE LIGHTFOOT REFRIGERATION COMPANY, LTD.

This company have a branch at Colombo, and are reviewed on pages 197 and 198.

E. B. CREASY and CO., General Merchants and Commission Agents, Shipping, Clearing, Customs, and Express Agents. Head Office: 12, Baillie Street.

MODERN science is revealing many wonders, but probably none more so than the sensitiveness of material things to receive and retain the impressions continually impinging upon them, and the life forces and influences to which they are exposed. Consequently the psychometrist would doubtless find very much to read from the establishment of Messrs. E. B. Creasy and Co., for it is one of the oldest of the local buildings, and, situated as it is in the midst of the bustle of local trade, has been for many decades associated with the reception and despatch of goods of every description. Its appearance is exactly as it was when the writer first saw it more than a quarter of a century ago. Then, as now, it had a sign indicating that it was the London and Colombo Forwarding Agency—forwarding goods to all parts of the world. Then, as now, the Royal Coat of Arms of Norway indicated that it was the Norwegian Consulate; and on its flag pole the crowning and passing of monarchs, occasions of national rejoicing, and other events, have been recognised by " banners fluttering in the breeze."

All over the world the name of E. B. Creasy and Co. is known in connection with local and mercantile transactions, for the firm have correspondents at every port, and there is no limit to the size or weight of shipments which they are prepared to undertake as clearing, forwarding, and general commission agents.

Messrs. E. B. Creasy and Co. have long been prominently associated with the supply of momi tea boxes, veneer tea chests, hoop iron, nails, solder, hessians, acetic acid, galvanized corrugated roofing, cement, sanitary fittings, Jeyes' disinfectants, coal tar, paint, oils, varnish, and Solex carburettors.

They are the agents for Wakefield's "Castrol " and lubricating oils.

Besides their establishment in Baillie Street, they have very much larger premises in Skinner's Road South.

The business was founded in 1881 by Mr. E. B. Creasy, who died in England in 1921. On his retirement in 1899 he was succeeded in the control of the concern by his son and namesake, the present proprietor, who is Consul for Norway. He, too, has a son bearing the same name as himself.

Messrs. E. B. Creasy and Co.'s telegraphic address is " Cresco, Colombo," and the codes used by them are Bentley's, Western Union, A B C 5th and 6th editions, and Broomhall's Rubber edition.

TARRANT and CO., Import and Export Merchants and General Commission Agents, Union Place.

FROM the premises of Mesrs. Tarrant and Co. a considerable quantity of the famous tea of Ceylon, as well as rubber, coconut, papain, spices, and other products of the island, is shipped to all parts of the world. That firm are also large importers of general merchandise, and operate as insurance and general commission agents. Their business was started in 1886 by Mr. Herbert Tarrant, who had been for some years previously in the tea trade in Mincing Lane. It was carried on at first under his own name, but after a short time was changed to Tarrant, Henderson and Co., and in 1896 it assumed its present designation. Its highly esteemed principal, Mr. H. Tarrant, is one of the oldest residents in Colombo. In partnership with him are Messrs. T. W. Jones and N. Walsgrove. The firm have an office in Baillie Street, Fort, and their London correspondents are Tarrant, Winn and Leighton, of 20 and 21, St. Dunstan's Hill, E.C.3. Messrs. Tarrant and Co.'s cable address is " Figites," Colombo, and the codes used by them are A B C 4th and 5th editions, Lieber's, Premier, Western Union (5 letter), Bentley's, and Imperial. They are agents for :—

Western Assurance Co. of Toronto.
The North British & Mercantile Insurance Co., Ltd.
The Eagle, Star & British Dominions Insurance Co., Ltd.
National Provincial Plate Glass Insurance Co., Ltd.
The National Guarantee & Suretyship Association, Ltd.
The Railway Passengers Assurance Co., Ltd.
Tarrant Winn and Leighton, London.
The Central Agency, Ltd., Glasgow.
Reckit & Sons, Ltd., Hull.
Chiswick Polish Co., Ltd.
National Roofing Co., New York.
The British Portland and Cement Manufacturers, Ltd., London.
Chr. Thomas & Bros., Ltd.
"Glaxo."
Bovril, Ltd.
W. Angliss & Co. (Aust.) Pty., Ltd., Melbourne.
T. Brunton & Co., Melbourne.
Macphail and Co., Ltd., Singapore.
Macgregor and Co., Ltd., Rangoon.
Henry Gardner & Co., Ltd., London.
Caledonian Insurance Co., London.
Bismag, Ltd.
J. & E. Waters, Ltd.
Burgoyne, Burbridges & Co., Ltd.
Siamese Steamship Co.
Zee Kol Manufacturing Co., Ltd.
International Chemical Co., Ltd.
R. M. Roberts & Co., Ltd. (Yemcolid Disinfectant).
W. R. Davies.
Hazelhurst & Sons, Ltd.
Price's Soap Co., Ltd.
Crown Cork Co., Ltd.
International Icilma Trading Co., Ltd.
Wm. Crawford & Sons, Ltd.
Studley Preserving Co., Pty., Ltd.
Finsbury Distillery Co., Ltd.
H. Hanna & Co., Pty., Ltd.
Maclaine, Watson & Co., Ltd.
Steel Products, Ltd.
F. Chivers & Co., Ltd.
E. Cook & Co., Ltd.
Juan Sanjanume Sen. C.
Michaelis, Hallenstein & Co., Pty., Ltd.

CLARK, YOUNG and CO.,

Importers, Exporters and General Commission Agents, Lauriston Stores. Offices: Prince Street.

Lauriston Stores, as the premises of Messrs. Clark, Young and Co. are called, employ many persons in connection with the principal commodities sustaining the export and import trade of Ceylon. Plumbago, tea, rubber, desiccated coconut, oils, and the other products of the island are there handled with the discrimination that instantly detects superiority and inferiority; and is equally swift in effecting anything that may contribute to the maximum of satisfaction in service and supplies.

LAURISTON STORES OF CLARK, YOUNG and CO.

Messrs. Clark, Young and Co. are also very large importers of all classes of goods, but chiefly teak, rice, flour, Java and China sugar, piece-goods, etc.

The business was started in 1894 by Messrs. T. S. and E. S. Clark and the late S. D. Young, and has grown into one of the most noteworthy mercantile undertakings in the island. The firm's telegraphic address is "Centrum," and they use all the standard codes. They are agents and correspondents for the following:

MacKinlay & Co., 121, Chiswell Street, London, E.C.
Bengal Coal Co., Ltd.
Carr & Co., Ltd., Carlisle.
General Accident, Fire and Life Assurance Corporation, Ltd.
Eagle, Star & British Dominions Insurance Co., Ltd.
Yorkshire Insurance Co., Ltd.
Scottish Metropolitan Assurance Co., Ltd.
G. W. Goodwin & Son, Manchester.
Slater, Rodger & Co., Ltd., Glasgow.
John Jefferies & Co., Edinburgh.
J. T. Benkers, Schiedam.
Societe Anonyme des Usine Destree, Belgium.
Abdulla & Co., Ltd., New Bond Street, London, W.
China Underwriters, Ltd.
Steel Bros. & Co., Ltd., Rangoon.
North British Rubber Co., Ltd., Edinburgh and London.
East Asiatique Français, Paris and Saigon.
Gillespie & Co., New York.
Thos. G. Hill & Co., Ltd., Manchester.
Barton & Catlow, Manchester.
Jardine, Matheson & Co., Ltd., Hongkong.
Wellestein, Krause & Co., Batavia.
Anglo-Burma Rice Co., Ltd., Rangoon.
Ellerman Arracan Rice & Trading Co.
The Commonwealth Trust, Calicut.
James Taylor & Co., Manchester.
Geldard, Griffiths & Co., Bradford.

H. W. CAVE and CO., Printers, Booksellers, Stationers, General Importers, Builders of Pianos and Organs, etc. Head Office: Gaffoor's Building.

Most of the large shopping emporiums in Colombo are general department stores. The establishment of Messrs. H. W. Cave and Co. differs from them in that it is not concerned with fashions in ladies' and gentlemen's apparel, nor with groceries and liquors, medicines, hardware, furniture, nor general domestic utensils; but its lack of these is more than made up by the exceptional completeness of the departments of trade in which the firm operate. An inspection of these reveals ample evidence that the discriminating policy of specialisation by which the business is conducted is thoroughly well justified.

Civilisation has developed nothing of greater importance and influence than the multiplicity of its literature, and the stock of books and other reading matter kept by Messrs. H. W. Cave and Co. is an interesting and accurate index to public tastes and requirements in that connection. The books obtainable from them range through every class of the publishing trade—grave and gay, educational and amusing, fact and fiction, philosophy and romance, in a great variety of bindings, from the cheapest editions to handsomely bound volumes with gilt-edged leaves.

Their large assortment of stationery is likewise comprehensive, and, indeed, in that respect, has a greater diversity than is necessary in similar undertakings in Great Britain, for, in addition to the requirements of the vast number of people passing continually through Colombo, must be considered the minute necessities of the commercial and industrial interests of the island in relation to all manner of documentary specifications and account books, etc.

Messrs. H. W. Cave and Co.'s department for office equipments, such as filing cabinets, cash registers, adding machines, typewriters, etc., provides object lessons in what has been achieved for the minimum of labour and the maximum of accuracy and efficiency in all clerical work. Many clever inventions and uncommon specialities may be noticed amongst their supplies of athletic goods and gymnastic apparatus, fishing tackle, billiard tables, surveyors' requisites, silver ware, watches, pictures, artists' materials, tobacconists' sundries, etc. As importers of musical merchandise and builders of pianos and organs, no firm has attained greater prominence throughout Ceylon than Messrs. H. W. Cave and Co. They are agents for all the leading makes of pianos, and in their piano and organ workshops very skilful work is done in the repair of worn-out instruments, and in the building of new ones to withstand the ravages of climate and insects.

Visitors to Messrs. H. W. Cave and Co.'s establishment will appreciate its large and attractive tea-room, where all kinds of light refreshments are procurable. The delicious cakes and confectionery for which that place is noted, are made of the finest ingredients in its own conterminous bakery and under conditions of scrupulous cleanliness.

There is, however, no branch of trade in which Messrs. H. W. Cave and Co. are more noteworthy than in printing and its allied activities. The firm's printing works, in Slave Island, occupies an area of 25,000 square feet, and gives employment to about 300 people. It was built specially for them in 1918, and from time to time its equipment has been added to and improved. In 1926 about £4,000 was spent on new machinery, which now includes no fewer than 41 printing machines of various sizes. In the compositors' rooms are linotypes and one of the Ludlow typographs that has revolutionised typesetting. The speed and economy of the latter invention can only be appreciated by actual inspection of it in operation.

The infinity of interests necessitating the use of printed matter is impressively shown by the work performed by Messrs. H. W. Cave and Co. They turn out, for instance, many millions of tea labels, and their beautiful photographic reproductions in natural colours are masterpieces of artistic achievement. The firm are contractors to Government, and undertake printing in all the leading languages in Ceylon.

In the manufacture of all kinds of printing blocks, and as machine rulers and manufacturing stationers, Messrs. H. W. Cave and Co.'s versatility is in keeping with their typographical efficiency.

PRINTING WORKS OF H. W. CAVE and CO.

The founder of the concern was Mr. H. W. Cave, M.A., F.R.G.S., who went to Ceylon from England as Secretary to the Anglican Bishop, and started work there by editing the *Ceylon Diocesan Gazette*, the first Church paper in the island. In 1876 he began importing religious books, and from that modest beginning has developed the business of H. W. Cave and Co., which now gives employment to upwards of 400 persons. In literary circles Mr. H. W. Cave, who died in 1913, is known in connection with his very interesting writings on Ceylon. His famous volumes " Golden Tips " and " Book of Ceylon " passed through many editions, and received high encomiums from the leading journals of England.

The partners in the firm now are Messrs. E. A. Bartlett, C. S. Brown, F. A. Dawkins, and C. H. Wratten. The telegraphic address is " Cave," and the codes used are Bentley's and the A B C 5th edition.

BROWN and CO., LTD., Wholesale and Retail Hardware Merchants, Chatham Street. Engineering Works: Darley Road, and Lanka Garage, Union Place.

A Scottish firm! That description of a commercial house in the Orient seems to carry more weight than accrues from even domicile in the Home country. In the lands beyond the seas, especially in the East, the Scottish character, silhouetted against foreign conditions and elemental necessities, stands out with sharper delineation than it does when viewed in the aggregate of national idiosyncrasy and procedure in the Northern Kingdom. For that there must be cogent reasons, not associated with the accredited orthodox standards of monetary considerations—reasons that go down into the heart of things and make for confidence and esteem, for development and progress in all branches of commerce and industry. The name of Brown and Co., Ltd., does not sound exclusively Scottish, but intercourse with the principals of the business which it designates leaves no doubt regarding their race.

An inspection of the showrooms of Messrs. Brown and Co., Ltd., reveals to the discerning eye very much regarding the improvements that are ever being made in the vast range of materials embraced by the terms ironmongery and hardware, including the comprehensive assortment of such things pertaining to household requirements. Utility is there exemplified by many contrivances for the reduction of labour and the maximum of comfort and convenience—electrical and engineering accessories, tools, paints, distempers and varnishes, push and motor bicycles, agricultural implements, typewriters and office appliances, firearms, electro-plated and silver goods, etc., etc.

But the various departments in the firm's stores in Chatham Street are only of minor impression in comparison with their Lanka Engineering Works in Darley Road. That important undertaking occupies an area of about four acres, and gives employment to hundreds of workmen who are engaged under highly skilled Scottish engineers and supervisors in all branches of general engineering, but more especially in work relating to the manufacture, installation, and repair of tea, rubber, and coconut machinery, in which Messrs. Brown and Co., Ltd., specialise with marked success. One of the warehouses at the works, completed in 1918, and occupying an area of 12,870 square feet, is an excellent example of the company's skill as general structural engineers.

In Union Place, not far from the Lanka Engineering Works, is the company's Lanka Garage, which is devoted entirely to the productions of the Ford Motor Co. It covers about an acre of ground, and gives employment to about 80 workmen, who are engaged entirely in the work pertaining to the famous Ford vehicles. Consequently, by specialising in his respective job, each workman attains a proficiency therein that would otherwise be impossible. A noteworthy example of this proficiency is seen in the rapid dexterity and accuracy with which the Ford cars are assembled from the compact masses of separate parts as they arrive from the factories of the Ford Co. The owner of a Ford car has the great advantage of being able to obtain spare parts without any delay—indeed, no company in the world offers better service in that connection than the Ford Co., and in the Lanka Garage the comprehensive stock of spare parts and accessories of every description is in keeping with the noted thoroughness of the Ford organisation at all its service and supply depots throughout the world.

The business of Messrs. Brown and Co., Ltd., was started in 1875 by Mr. James Brown at Hatton, Ceylon, under the designation of Brown, Rey and Co., and branches were opened at Dickoya and Maskeliya. In 1892 the firm was formed into a limited liability company under its present name. The capital, originally Rs.500,000, is now Rs. 3,333,000. In 1897 the company began business at Colombo, and have branches at Hatton, Nawalapitiya, and Kandy. The managing director is Mr. W. Boak. The London office is at 270, Mansion House Chambers, Queen Victoria Street, E.C. The telegraphic address is "Metal," and the codes used are the A B C 4th and 5th editions, Western Union, Bentley's, Marconi International, and private.

Messrs. Brown and Co., Ltd., are agents in Ceylon for the following:—

Ruston & Hornsby, Ltd.
Joseph Robinson & Co.
T. A. W. Clarke, Ltd.
George Scott & Co., Ltd.
Smith & Grace, Ltd.
Quirk, Barton & Co.
Electrical & Ordnance Accessories Co., Ltd.
John Tullis & Sons, Ltd.
W. N. Brunton & Son.
The British Mathews, Ltd.
Wm. Marples & Sons, Ltd.
The Black Diamond File Co.
Dobbie, Forbes & Co.
Alexander Shanks & Sons, Ltd.
The Paraffin Paint Co.
The West Kent Portland Cement Co.
The Yale and Towne Manufacturing Co.
Colthurst and Harding.
The Standard Varnish Co.
The Hoyt Metal Co.
S. L. Allen & Co.
Massey-Harris Co.
Newton, Chambers & Co.
The "Empire" Typewriter Co.
Royal Typewriter Co., Ltd.
The Midland Gun Co.
The Triumph Cycle Co.
Kynoch, Ltd.
Hendee Manufacturing Co.
Phelon and Moore, Ltd.
Ford Motor Co., Toronto, Canada.
Albion Motor Co., Ltd.
The Machine Gas, Ltd.
Kee Lox Manufacturing Co.
Anderson's Oil Expellers, etc.
Thos. A. Edison.
Coleman Lamp Co.
Royal Insurance Co., Ltd. (Fire, Motor, Marine, etc.

PREMISES OF BROWN and CO., LTD., CHATHAM STREET.

MACKWOODS, LIMITED, Importers, Exporters, Estate, Insurance and General Commission Agents, Gaffoor's Building.

THE aspect of Colombo is very deceptive, so far as its commercial and industrial development is concerned, for the reason that the city has several distinct business districts, and the large mercantile firms have their mills and warehouses scattered about in places not readily noticeable by visitors making only a brief tour of inspection of the busy island capital.

One of the largest and oldest of the mercantile concerns is that of Messrs. Mackwoods, Limited, whose stores and mills in Maradana occupy an area of 12 acres, and give employment to many people. Through these extensive premises passes a considerable amount of Colombo's inward and outward merchandise.

The firm's importations are very comprehensive, and include piece-goods, hardware, corrugated roofings, barbed wire, nails, iron and steel bars, metal sheets, agricultural implements, cement, crockery, cutlery, enamelled ware, perfumery, biscuits, toys, etc., also rice, sugar, flour, etc. Many of the traders in Pettah, the busiest of Colombo's business centres, get their supplies from all parts of the world through Messrs. Mackwoods, Limited.

The firm are also amongst the large exporters of Ceylon produce, as is well demonstrated by the scenes in their tea, rubber, and desiccated coconut stores. Copra, coconut oil, cinnamon oil, fibres, cocoa, etc., are likewise shipped by Messrs. Mackwoods, Limited, throughout the world.

The records of this notable business date back to 1839, when it was founded by Mr. William Mackwood, and carried on in his name until 1844, when it became known as Mackwood and Co. The present company was formed in 1919, and the directors are Messrs. F. M., F. E., F. O., and E. O. Mackwood, H. F. Parfitt, J. C. Kelly, and J. F. Sibbald. The concern was one of the few old houses that survived the collapse of the coffee industry of Ceylon, and has played an important part in the rise and development of the island's great tea trade.

The cable address of Messrs. Mackwoods, Limited, is "Mackwoods," and the codes used are the A B C 5th and 6th editions, Bentley's, and private. The firm operate as follows:

AGENTS FOR STERLING COMPANIES:

The Central Province Ceylon Tea Co., Ltd.
Hewagam Rubber Co., Ltd.
The Beau Sejour (Ceylon) Tea & Rubber Co., Ltd.

AGENTS AND SECRETARIES FOR:

The Rayigam Co., Ltd.
The Pine Hill Estates Co., Ltd.
The St. James Uva Tea Co., Ltd.
The Uva Highlands Tea Co., Ltd.
The Uva Ketawella Tea Co., Ltd.
The Gallebodde Estates Co. of Ceylon, Ltd.
The Girindi Ella Tea Co., Ltd.
Damblagolla Rubber Co., Ltd.

SECRETARIES FOR:

Eastern Garage, Ltd.

AGENTS FOR (INSURANCE):

Royal Exchange Assurance (Fire, Marine, Life and Motor Car).
Law Union & Rock Insurance Co., Ltd. (Fire and Life).
Northern Assurance Co., Ltd. (Motor Car, Burglary and Theft).

MOUNT LAVINIA HOTEL.

THE most popular trip for visitors to Colombo is a motor run to the celebrated Mount Lavinia Hotel, only seven miles away from the city. The run to Kandy, seventy miles distant, is not always possible, as many steamers do not stay long enough for that purpose; but there is always ample time for the cheap and exceedingly pleasant little tour along the interesting highway to Mount Lavinia Hotel, where a very delightful time may be spent under conditions such as do not obtain at any of the other notable hotels in the island.

In former times the handsome and palatial building now forming the Mount Lavinia Hotel was a residence of the Governor of Ceylon; and since it was taken over in 1924, from the former proprietary company, by its present owner, Mr. Arthur Ephraums, considerable improvements have been effected in its equipment and administration; so that visitors will be pleased with the facilities and resources in vogue there for their comfort, convenience, and pleasure.

The position of the hotel is very attractive. It stands on a lofty knoll at the extremity of a projecting point of the sea beach on the beautiful palm-fringed west coast. The area occupied by the hotel is $2\frac{1}{2}$ acres. The grounds are charmingly laid out, and on the well-kept lawns are chairs and tables where refreshments of all kinds are nicely and promptly served. The spacious

SEA-FRONT OF MOUNT LAVINIA HOTEL.

public reception rooms have been planned and furnished in a system that makes for the maximum of coolness and utility, and the long verandahs facing the ocean receive the full benefit of the prevailing inshore breezes.

In the principal dining-room 150 guests can be accommodated with ease at one time, and the meals served there are noted for their excellence and variety. The hotel has 50 bedrooms, all furnished on a scale of amplitude conformable to the standards of first-class requirements. It is lighted throughout by electricity generated on the premises, and has also a billiard room, with two tables, and tennis courts. Probably the most attractive feature of the establishment is its unsurpassed facilities for sea bathing in perfectly safe conditions. Close to the sandy beach is its large and well-built pavilion with dressing rooms, where the fullest provision is made for all requirements in bathing costumes, towels, etc. Not far from the hotel is Mount Lavinia Railway Station, providing a frequent service of trains to and from the city, the journey occupying about twenty minutes.

Mr. Ephraums is also owner of the Bristol Hotel, Globe Hotel, and the White Horse Hotel, Colombo, the Anuradhapura Hotel, Anuradhapura, and St. Andrew's Hotel, Nuwara Eliya, all of which provide comfortable accomodation, good food, and service at very moderate rates. The most famous of them is the Bristol Hotel, situated in the midst of Colombo's great shopping emporia. He is also lessee of the railway refreshment cars and rooms.

Mr. Ephraums is the principal of A. E. Ephraums and Co., who are agents and secretaries for The Colombo Pharmacy, Ltd., which has its registered offices at 27, Upper Chatham Street, Colombo; and owns also the two establishments known as "The City Dispensary," in Norris Road and Union Place, Colombo, and the I. C. Drug Store, Bambalapitya, Colombo.

DELMEGE, FORSYTH and CO., LTD.

General Merchants and Commission Agents, Victoria Arcade Building.

Throughout Ceylon the Asiatic Petroleum Co. (Ceylon), Ltd., is providing facilities and resources that are contributing very considerably to the country's economic progress, especially in relation to road transport by motor vehicles. That influential concern has in Ceylon no fewer than 75 installations for bulk petroleum and 21

DISTRIBUTING VEHICLES OF ASIATIC PETROLEUM CO. (CEYLON), LTD., COLOMBO.

installations for liquid fuel, which practically means that the motorist will find at every town and village a depot for the famous "Shell" motor spirit and motor oils.

The agents for the Asiatic Petroleum Co. (Ceylon), Ltd., are Messrs. Delmege, Forsyth and Co., Ltd., who are one of the principal firms in Ceylon, where they have been established for about eighty years. Their business, started at Galle, and transferred in due course to Colombo, when the latter became the chief port of the island, has developed pro rata with the growth of Colombo, especially in connecton with its coaling and shipping interests. In that association Messrs. Delmege, Forsyth and Co., Ltd., operate on an extensive scale, as is indicated by the busy bunkering scenes at their large coaling yards at the harbour.

The directors of the company are Messrs. T. W. Hockley (Consul for Portugal and Vice-Consul for Spain), O. L. Beresford-Hope, T. H. Tatham, and A. R. Quarme.

Messrs. Delmege, Forsyth and Co., Ltd., are Admiralty contractors and agents for:—

- The Asiatic Petroleum Co. (Ceylon), Ltd.
- The Anglo-Saxon Petroleum Co., Ltd.
- The Burrakur Coal Co., Ltd., Calcutta.
- St. George's & Natal Navigation Coal Companies, Natal.
- F. W. Heilgers & Co., Calcutta.
- Marine Insurance Co., Ltd., London.
- Guardian Assurance Co., Ltd., London.
- Board of Underwriters of New York.
- The National Board of Marine Underwriters, New York.
- The London & Lancashire Insurance Co., Ltd., London.
- The Magadi Soda Co., Ltd.
- Ledward & Taylor, Manchester.
- The Ocean Steamship Co., Ltd.
- Anchor, Brocklebank and Well Line of Steamers.
- Natal Direct Line of Steamers (Bullard, King & Co.).
- Prince Line (James Knott).
- The Cunard Steamship Co., Ltd., Liverpool.
- Red Star Line, Antwerp.
- Shell Line of Steamers.
- Suzuki & Co., Kobe and London.
- Carreras, Ltd., London.
- Macfarlane, Lang & Co., Ltd.
- Bryant & May, Ltd.
- John Robertson & Co., Ltd., Dundee.
- The British Fire Insurance Co., Ltd.
- The Prudential Assurance Co., Ltd.
- Bureau Veritas, Paris.
- Shell Transport & Trading Co., Ltd.

The firm's brokers are:

- Delmege, Allen & Co., London.
- James Burness & Sons, London.
- Wm. Cory & Son, London.
- Mann, George & Co., Ltd., London.
- M. Samuel & Co., London.
- Sinclair, Hamilton & Co., London.
- Carleton & Moffat, New York.

RUBBER AND PRODUCE TRADERS (CEYLON), LTD., Gaffoor's Building.

The story of the development of rubber is one of the romances of modern commerce and industry, and the uses to which that indispensable material is now put have a range altogether beyond that which was thought possible a few decades ago before the introduction of modern inventions and their corresponding multiplicity of requirements. The cultivation of rubber in Ceylon has developed very greatly, and amongst the noteworthy firms engaged in its exportation is the Rubber and Produce Traders (Ceylon), Ltd., formed in 1926 as successors to Wilson Holgate and Co. (Ceylon), Ltd., established in 1918. As its title indicates, the company is also engaged in general produce, such as copra, desiccated coconut, cinnamon oil and leaf, citronella oil, etc. It has an office in London at 21, Mincing Lane, E.C. The manager is Mr. L. P. Hayward. The telegraphic address is "Colrub," Colombo, and the codes used are the A B C 5th and 6th editions, Lieber's, Bentley's, and private.

ROWLANDS GARAGE, Turret Road.

No phase of the business activity of Colombo is more noteworthy than the extent to which the automobile trade has been developed there. The city in that connection can hold its own with any in the Orient; indeed, in some respects, the facilities and resources which Colombo provides in everything associated with motor vehicles are probably unsurpassed anywhere east of Suez. Rowlands Garage, for instance, must be referred to when the motor trade of Colombo is under consideration, and cannot fail to impress the stranger who may visit it with erroneous ideas of what has been accomplished locally in motor engineering. It occupies an area of about seven acres, and gives employment to more than 400 persons. That alone might be sufficient to indicate its prominence and importance; but only by actual inspection of its numerous departments can the perfection of its service and supplies be properly appreciated. The work done there covers a range of operation that includes everything relating to motor vehicles in all conditions in which they can be considered. A motor vehicle can be built there in harmony with the most acceptable ideals of orthodox design, or embodying any uncommon feature in capacity or appearance that may be desired.

It has become a comparatively simple matter now in all up-to-date garages to effect with skill and rapidity the ordinary kind of repairs consequent on accident, neglect, or ignorance; but the best makes of cars sometimes develop extraordinary idiosyncrasies of imperfection that baffle even extremely experienced motor experts; and it is in difficulties of that kind, as well as in repairs of every description, that Rowlands Garage substantiates its fame. Its machinery equipment is of the most comprehensive kind, including acetylene welding, electro-plating, and vulcanising; and any part of the mechanism of any car, including gear wheels, can be produced at Rowlands Garage with a celerity truly astonishing.

DISPLAY OF ROWLANDS GARAGE AT THE ALL CEYLON MOTOR AND GENERAL ENGINEERING EXHIBITION, COLOMBO, IN 1927.

Rowlands Garage is agent for the Rolls Royce, Sunbeam, Crossley, Hillman, Chevrolet, Oakland, Pontiac, and Chandler cars, which are displayed in its large and handsome showroom. An interesting department of the business is one for second-hand cars, which are taken in part-payment of new ones; and many an excellent bargain is there procurable by the discerning.

Rowlands Garage is an evolution of the former motor department of the business of H. W. Cave and Co., and has developed enormously since it was taken over in 1923 under its present name by Mr. F. C. Gibbs (previously partner in that firm) and Mr. A. P. Rowlands. It is interesting to note that Mr. Gibbs early in his career was employed in the "City Press" works of Messrs. W. H. and L. Collingridge, printers and publishers of this volume.

The telegraphic address of Rowlands Garage is "Prowlands," Colombo, and the codes used are Bentley's and private. The London agents are Robertson and Malcolm, 5, Bishopsgate, E.C., and the New York agents Robertson and Malcolm, Singer Building.

NESTLÉ and ANGLO-SWISS CONDENSED MILK COMPANY, "Nestlé House," Union Place.

When the business of the Nestlé and Anglo-Swiss Condensed Milk Co. was founded in 1866 it marked the commencement of a great era in food preservation, and inaugurated a vast improvement in the commissariat of all peoples, but especially those in the tropics, where life during the preceding centuries had been, for natives of the temperate zone, much more trying than in these days of remarkable inventions for the enhancement of health and comfort. Nothing is more necessitous for the young and sick than milk, and many lives were lost that would otherwise have been saved had there been at hand the celebrated product of the Nestlé Co., whose huge interests now encircle the globe, and whose goods are to be found wherever civilisation has penetrated, and in many places where it has not. The Nestlé business is the largest of its kind in the world, and has condensaries not only in Switzerland, but also in France, Holland, Norway, England, United States, Canada, and Australia. For many years the company transacted their trade in Ceylon through local agents, but in 1912 opened at Colombo a branch which has since developed very considerably. As in all other parts of the world, the company's sweetened and unsweetened condensed milk, sterilised natural milk, (whipped) cream, malted milk, milk food, "Lactogen," as well as their Peter's, Cailler's, Kohler's, and Nestlé's cocoa, chocolate, and bonbons, are very popular in Ceylon, and in great demand.

The company's manager at Colombo is Mr. T. A. Ryde. The telegraphic address is "Nestanglo," and the codes used are the A B C 5th edition, Western Union, Bentley's, and private.

LEECHMAN and CO., Exporters of Ceylon Produce, Estates and General Commission Agents, National Mutual Building, Chatham Street.

The business of Messrs. Leechman and Co. was established in 1864, when coffee was the principal product of Ceylon. On the failure of that industry, through leaf disease, about ten years later, Messrs. Leechman and Co. were among the pioneers who introduced into the island the cultivation of cinchona and tea. Later, too, they were similarly distinguished in connection with rubber, both in Ceylon and the Federated Malay States.

The founder of the business was Mr. G. B. Leechman. He also established in 1866 the firm of G. and W. Leechman, who leased and operated for about twenty years the Hultsdorf Coconut Oil Mills, and thereafter the Colombo Oil Mills, until the end of 1911.

The present partners in Leechman and Co. are Messrs. J. J. Wall, D. T. Richards, and J. S. McIntyre. The firm are exporters of tea, rubber, and all the products of Ceylon, and have connections throughout the world. Their telegraphic address is "Leechman," Colombo, and their codes are the A B C 4th and 5th editions, Bentley's, and Broomhall's (Rubber). They are agents for the following:

- Carolina Tea Co. of Ceylon, Ltd.
- Nuwara Eliya Tea Estates Co., Ltd.
- The Choisy Tea Co. of Ceylon, Ltd.
- The Beverlac (Selangor) Rubber Co., Ltd.
- Panagula Rubber Co., Ltd.
- Ederapolla Tea Co. of Ceylon, Ltd.
- The Highland Tea Co. of Ceylon, Ltd
- Westward Ho Tea Co. of Ceylon, Ltd.
- Kongsi Rubber Co., Ltd.
- The Yokohama Fire, Marine, Transit & Fidelity Insurance Co., Ltd.
- Norwich Union Fire Insurance Society.
- New Zealand Insurance Co.
- London & Scottish Assurance Corporation, Ltd.
- Norwich & London Accident Insurance Association.
- Norwich Union Life Office.
- Underwriters at Lloyds.
- Lyall, Anderson & Co., London.
- Shand, Haldane & Co., London
- Grindlay & Co., Ltd., London, Calcutta, and Bombay.

THOMSON, TETLEY and CO., Importers of Piece-goods, etc., Prince Building.

The one great outstanding class of British merchandise in the Orient is that of piece-goods; and while these materials are regarded by the uninitiated as primarily of little, if any, individual or collective interest, it is, nevertheless, true that no productions are more regulated by custom and idiosyncrasy, by tradition and climate than the enormous variety of modern textiles. The patterns and designs in vogue in one district are not always popular in other parts of the same country; so that throughout the great territory of the Orient are to be found many contradictions in preference for chromatic effects and quality of texture. Ceylon provides many striking examples of the vast difference existing there in regard to demand and supply in the connection indicated; but, as the Sinhalese, who form the bulk of the population, prefer more expensive materials than the other Eastern peoples, Colombo is, in the piece-goods trade, regarded as a "fancy" market, to which Messrs. Thomson, Tetley and Co. contribute considerably, being, as they are, the leading piece-goods firm devoted exclusively to that trade in the island. They do a great deal of indenting for native traders, and have been established at Colombo since 1910; but transacted trade with Ceylon for many years previously through local agents. The director at Colombo is Mr. E. D. Molyneux. The firm's telegraphic address is "Shipment," Colombo, and their codes are Parker's, Premier, A B C 5th and 6th editions, Bentley's, and private. At Manchester and Madras the firm are established as Tetley and Whitley, Ltd., and well known in piece-goods circles throughout India.

GORDON FRAZER and CO., LTD., Estate and Insurance Agents, Gaffoor's Building.

THE business of Messrs. Gordon Frazer and Co., Ltd., chiefly estate agency, was established in 1890, and is one of the principal concerns of its kind in Colombo. The firm have recently opened new warehouses and mills at Wekande, where tea, rubber, and other products of Ceylon are carefully prepared by the most accredited methods for export to all parts of the world. The directors are Messrs. G. E. Woodman, F. J. Hawkes, F. H. Lavard, and F. F. Roe. The telegraphic address is "Frazerco," Colombo, and the codes used are the A B C 5th edition, Broomhall's (Rubber), and Bentley's.

Messrs. Gordon Frazer and Co., Ltd., are agents for:

Scottish Union & National Insurance Co.
South British Insurance Co.
Royal Exchange Assurance Co.
The Relugas Tea Estates, Ltd.
Augusta Tea Estates Co., Ltd.
Rajawella Produce Co., Ltd.
Tea Corporation (1921), Ltd.
The Alluta Rubber & Produce Co., Ltd.
The Lavant Rubber & Tea Co., Ltd.
Kadienlena Tea Estates, Ltd.
Kenilworth Tea Co., Ltd.
Lethenty Tea Estates Association, Ltd.
Taldna Rubber Co., Ltd.
The Bowlana Tea Estates, Ltd.
Kurunegalla Rubber Co., Ltd.
Glentaffe Tea Estates, Ltd.

AGENTS AND SECRETARIES FOR:

Arratenne (Ceylon) Tea & Rubber Co., Ltd.
Aviswella Tea & Rubber Co., Ltd.
The Clifton Rubber Co., Ltd.
Dartonfield Estate, Ltd.
Gallawatte (Ceylon) Rubber Co., Ltd.
The Kalutara Rubber Co. of Ceylon, Ltd.
The Kallande Rubber Co., Ltd.
The Kelani Valley Rubber Co. of Ceylon, Ltd.
The Lower Perak Coconut Co., Ltd.
The Mentenne Rubber Co., Ltd.
The Moneragalla Rubber Co., Ltd.
The Muppane Valley (Ceylon) Rubber Co., Ltd.
Pembroke Estate, Ltd.
The Perak Kongsi Coconut Co., Ltd.
The Pettiagalla Tea Co., Ltd.
The Sittagama Rubber Co., Ltd.
The Tuan Mee (Selangor) Rubber Co., Ltd.
The Udapolla Rubber Co., Ltd.
Yatapola Estate, Ltd.
Panakura Estates, Ltd.
The Craiglands Tea & Rubber Co., Ltd.
H. Bastian Fernando Estates, Ltd.
The Labugama Rubber Estate, Ltd.
Midford (Ceylon) Tea Estates, Ltd.
The Ceylon Financial Investments, Ltd.
The Murraythwaite Rubber Co., Ltd.
The Kegalla Rubber & Tea Co. of Ceylon. Ltd
The Biddescar Rubber Co., Ltd.
Darton Development Co., Ltd.
The Gammikande Rubber Estates, Ltd.
The Perak River Coconut Co., Ltd.
The Nakkala Rubber Co., Ltd.
The Heenpannawa Coconut Co., Ltd.
The Theberton (Ceylon) Tea Estates, Ltd.

HOLLAND-CEYLON COMMERCIAL COMPANY, Gaffoor's Building.

THE commercial community of Colombo is not so cosmopolitan as that of the great ports of the Far East, and most of the local firms are English, Indian, or Sinhalese. A noteworthy exception is afforded by the Holland-Ceylon Commercial Co., which has a title reminiscent of the time when the island was a Dutch possession. That company, which well upholds the best traditions of Dutch commercial enterprise, was established in 1916 with a capital of one million guilders, and is engaged in the exportation of all kinds of Ceylon produce, especially copra, desiccated coconut, cinnamon, and oils, which it ships chiefly to Holland, Great Britain, and the United States. The import trade of the company is principally in piece-goods. The company has at Colombo large warehouses well adapted for the storage of their merchandise, the section for copra having a capacity of about 12,000 tons. The directors at Amsterdam comprise Mr. W. Ruys, Managing Director of the Rotterdam-Lloyds Steamship Co., Mr. W. H. J. Oderwald, Managing Director of the "Nederland" Steamship Co., and Messrs. M. Bury, W. Stork, and Dr. Th. M. Verster. The manager at Colombo is Mr. L. van der Spoel. The telegraphic address is "Hollandco," Colombo. The following are the agencies held by the company:—

H. P. Gelderman & Zonen, Oldenzaal van Gelder Zonen, Amsterdam.
P. F. van Vlissingen & Co., Helmond.
Koninklijke Weefgoederenfabriek v/h C. T. Stork & Co., Hengelo.
Nederlandsche Plantenboter Fabriek, Amsterdam.
Batavia Sea & Fire Iusurance Co., Batavia.

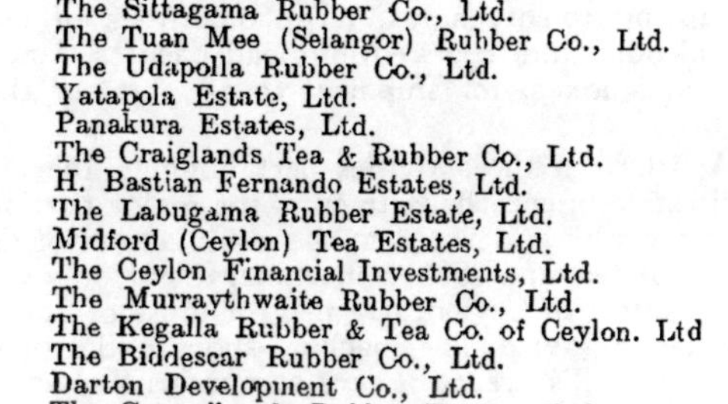

Packing Copra for Shipment in the Stores of the Holland-Ceylon Commercial Co.

The Netherlands Insurance Co. (Est. 1845), The Hague
The Phœnix Assurance Co., Ltd., Liverpool, Marine Department.
Jurgens Margarine Works, Nymegen, London.
The Anglo-Dutch Milk & Food Co., "Hollandia," Vlaardingen.
Claim and Settling Agents for Nord-Deutsche Versicherungs Gessellschaf (and affiliated companies), Hamburg.
Claim Agents for Mannheim and Continental Insurance Co., Mannheim.

COLOMBO COMMERCIAL COMPANY, LTD., Fort and Union Place.

The Colombo Commercial Co., Ltd., was founded in 1876 for the purpose of acquiring estates in Ceylon for the production and export of coffee. A few years later, however, the coffee industry declined owing to the spread of the coffee-leaf disease, and, like the other planting firms in the island, the company mentioned turned its attention to the cultivation of tea.

In addition to the production of tea on its own estates, the company acts as agent for a number of sterling and rupee companies, and purchases largely for its export trade from the teas offered on the local market. In its premises at Colombo, occupying twenty acres, large quantities of tea are blended and repacked into lead packets, fancy tins and boxes, for shipment to all parts of the world.

Apart from the activities pertaining to the tea and estate agency departments, the major portion of the works is devoted to the manufacture of all kinds of tea and rubber machinery, not only for the planters of Ceylon, but also for those of South India and Java. The machine shops and wood-working mills are on a very comprehensive scale and fitted with up-to-date plants.

In general constructional engineering the Colombo Commercial Co., Ltd., operates with similar completeness, and many buildings at Colombo and elsewhere in Ceylon bear witness to its capacity in that connection.

The Colombo Commercial Co., Ltd., has greatly benefited Ceylon by the attention it has paid to suitable fertilisers for the island's agricultural products and the very extensive business it has developed in their manufacture. It has large fertilising mills beside the main railway line at Hunupitiya, and has recently erected other big mills along the Kelani Valley railway line, about nine miles from Colombo.

The company has also engineering workshops at Badulla and Kandapola specially devoted to the requirements of estates. Contiguous to the Colombo premises is the factory of the Colombo Lead Mills, Ltd., for which it is agent. In that establishment is produced the linings of the chests in which the tea of the Colombo Commercial Co., Ltd., and that of many of the other exporting houses is shipped from the island.

The two-storeyed building containing the company's administration offices in Colombo is known as Acland House, and was originally the mess quarters of the Ceylon Rifle Regiment. It stands in extensive grounds, and the upper portion forms the residence of the manager.

The company's London office is in Thames House, Queen Street Place, E.C. The codes used are Bentley's, Kendall's, and Lieber's.

Among the agencies held by the company are the following:—

SOLE AGENTS FOR:

Birkmyre Bros., Calcutta; hessians and gunnies.
C.C.C. tea rollers, roll-breakers, desiccators and scrap washers.
David Bridge and Co.'s rubber machinery.
"Day Elder" lorries.
Gillingham "Red Hand" cement.
I XL pruning knives.
Leyland Motors, Ltd.
Penman's auto-expressors.
Savage's tea cutters.
Solignum wood preservative.
Southwark cotton belting.
Tangyes, Ltd., oil and suction gas engines and tea rollers.
Venesta, Ltd.
"Vulcan" disinfectant.
W. Gunther and Sons' turbines and Pelton wheels.

AGENTS FOR STERLING COMPANIES:

Colombo Lead Mills, Ltd.
Ellawatte Ceylon Tea Estates, Ltd.
Hunasgeria Tea Co., Ltd.
Mayfield (Dimbula) Tea Co. of Ceylon, Ltd.
Mooloya Estates, Ltd.
Ouvah Ceylon Estates, Ltd.
Rani Travancore Rubber Co., Ltd.
Spring Valley Ceylon Estates, Ltd.
Telbedde Ceylon Estates, Ltd.

AGENTS AND SECRETARIES FOR RUPEE COMPANIES:

Agra Tea Co. of Ceylon, Ltd.
Baddegama Estate Co. of Ceylon, Ltd.
Bank of Uva, Ltd.
Cullen Estates, Ltd.
Kalkudah Coconut Estate Co., Ltd.
Pitakande Tea Co. of Ceylon, Ltd.
Rye Estate Co. of Ceylon, Ltd.
London and Lancashire Insurance Co., Ltd., London and Liverpool.
Thames and Mersey Marine Insurance Co., Ltd., London.

A. F. JONES and CO., General Exporters, Stratford Stores, Slave Island.

Stratford Stores, the name of Messrs. A. F. Jones and Co.'s premises, is arresting, especially to people interested in the commerce and industry of Colombo. It might be regarded as indicating a general department store, such as obtains in Stratford, catering to universal demand. Stratford Stores, Slave Island, are utterly different from that, and are devoted to the preparation and export of many of Ceylon's products. Tea, for instance, is there tasted, blended, and packed for shipment to many parts of the world. Cocoa, desiccated coconut, coconut-oil, citronella-oil, cinnamon-oil, etc., are also handled by Messrs. A. F. Jones and Co., whose business was started in 1918. The partners are Mr. A. F. Jones and Mr. H. W. Dainty.

The firm operate likewise as general commission agents, and are agents for the I.O.A. (Insurance of Australia). Their cable address is "Afjon," Colombo, and the codes used by them are Bentley's, Lieber's, A B C 5th edition, and private.

FENTONS, LTD., Electrical Engineers and Contractors, 46, Union Place.

In the wide range of electrical engineering and supplies, Messrs. Fentons, Ltd., operate with the specialised knowledge and skill that solve every problem by the most economical as well as the most effective and speedy methods. In electrical work it is the little things that count, the little errors avoided, the anticipation of the little weaknesses and flaws which, if neglected, lead to extensive and costly damages and repairs. Messrs. Fentons, Ltd., are particular about these little things, and nothing is too great for them to undertake. Their supplies of electrical fittings and accessories of all kinds provide object lessons in the multiplicity of things which electric science has evolved for the perfection of illumination and motive power. The exterior of their premises proclaims in arresting letters that they supply "Switchboards, telephones, turbines, lamps, radio apparatus, dynamos, motors, repair mechanics available night and day, transformers, voltmeters, switches and electric fans for hire from Rs.2.50 per month. Fentons for everything electrical," etc.

The business was established in 1919 by Mr. H. Fenton, A.M.I.E.E., the managing director of the present limited liability company, which took it over in 1921.

The telegraphic address of Messrs. Fentons, Ltd., is "Electric," and the codes used are the A B C 5th edition, Western Union, and Bentley's.

PREMISES OF FENTONS, LTD.

They are agents for:—

Philips' Glowlampworks, Ltd.
British Insulated Cables, Ltd.
The Century Electric Co.
Pritchett & Gold & Electrical Power Storage Co., Ltd.
Peto & Radford.
"Higgs Motors," Birmingham.
McDowell & Co., Ltd., Madras.
Marconi Wireless Telegraphy Co., Ltd.
F. W. Berk & Co., Ltd.
Burndept Wireless, Ltd.
Sir W. G. Armstrong-Whitworth & Co., Ltd.
Hydro-Electric Dept.

GALLE FACE HOTEL COMPANY, LTD.

The nucleus of the Galle Face Hotel was formed about 1885 by the construction of a building that had accommodation for about twenty persons, and was used chiefly as a resthouse by coffee planters. But the growth of Colombo led to a corresponding demand for first-class hotel accommodation, and accordingly the Galle Face Hotel was rebuilt on a large scale—sufficient, it was thought, to meet all possible future requirements. That was in 1894, and the metamorphosis which has since been effected in the hotel has been great indeed. The establishment, built in the Renaissance style, occupies about five acres of land, gives employment to about 350 persons, and has accommodation for 400 guests. The situation of the Galle Face Hotel is magnificent, and the warm, blue tropic sea comes up almost to its walls. The hotel is a little over a mile from the landing stage and about equidistant from the main railway station. In the lounge, or central hall, are to be seen, especially

GALLE FACE HOTEL.

during the tourist season, from November to April, people from every part of the world. For their comfort and convenience there are long and comfortably furnished verandahs, arranged so that they get the benefit of the breezes from the sea and land. The dining-room has seating capacity for 400 persons, and the kitchen and kindred sections are under the supervision of an experienced European chef.

The bedrooms of the hotel are comfortably and tastefully furnished, and range from single rooms to luxurious suites commanding views that will remain in the memory. A large number of the apartments have their own bathrooms, and all of them are fitted with electric lights and fans.

The spacious ballroom of the hotel presents a very gay and animated scene on the frequent dance evenings. The grounds and terraces of the hotel are exceedingly pleasant, especially in the evenings when Colombo's famous sunsets transform sea and coast with a chromatic glory that is never duplicated and never can be.

Not the least of the many attractions of the Galle Face is its sea-water swimming bath with dressing-rooms and fresh-water shower. The hotel has its own steam laundry, ladies' and gentlemen's hair-dressing saloons, tailors' shop, pharmacy, post-office, etc. It has also a fleet of 80 motor-cars, and experts are at the disposal of visitors for the purpose of mapping out comprehensive tours in Ceylon at moderate rates. The wireless address of the Galle Face Hotel is "Gallfacio," Colombo, and the codes used are the ABC 5th edition and Bentley's. Rooms at the hotel may be booked and deposit paid at any of the offices of Thomas Cook and Son.

BRODIE and CO., LTD., Wholesale Wine and Spirit Merchants, 19, Upper Chatham Street.

MOST of the commerce of Colombo is transacted by firms very much alike in the scope of their activities as general merchants and commission agents. Messrs. Brodie and Co., Ltd., however, have specialised exclusively in the wholesale wine and spirit trade since 1846, when their business was established. Their premises are admirably adapted for the purpose to which they are devoted; and the portion fronting Chatham Street is an interesting example of how the Dutch built when the island belonged to Holland. Behind that section, with its thick walls and welcome shade, are the commodious stores which were erected for the firm between thirty and forty years ago. The object aimed at in their construction, evenness of temperature, has been fully realised, which is an important and valuable asset in a climate like that of Colombo, where it is very difficult to keep wines in good condition without the facilities possessed by Messrs. Brodie and Co. In their cool recesses are the bottled reminiscences of long past days in sunny lands, sunbeams appropriated by grapes in famous vineyards, usquebaugh that restores the accent of the glens and moors of the Celts, malt brews for thin and feeble folk, liqueurs for fastidious connoisseurs, and all kinds of beverages for all kinds of people. They import a good deal of wine in bulk, and their bottling department is equipped with modern machinery.

The firm was formed in 1924 into the present limited liability company, and the managing director is Mr. W. C. Brodie, son of the founder of the business. The other directors are Messrs. R. Robinson, S. M. M. Mac, L. C. Queen, M. J. Carvalho, and L. F. Arnolda. Messrs. Brodie and Co., Ltd., are agents for Ainslie's Royal Edinburgh whisky; J. and F. Martell's brandies, Cognac; W. and A. Gilbey, Ltd., ports, gin, and whisky, London; Barclay Perkins, Ltd., London lager, London; and J. Wix and Sons, "Kensitas" cigarettes, London.

BROUGHAMS, LTD., Complete House Furnishers and Outfitters, York Arcade, Fort, and Front and Main Streets, Pettah.

SUITABILITY is one of the most important considerations for a business catering to public requirements. Consequently the new premises of Messrs. Broughams, Ltd., in York Arcade, are admirably located, and very convenient for passengers landing from the steamers for shopping purposes. Gentlemen will find there an excellent assortment of outfitting materials well calculated to meet every requirement; and special attention is devoted by the firm to the tailoring trade in all its branches. A very attractive selection is afforded in tropical suitings as well as in those for colder climes. Sartorial efficiency is primarily dependent upon accuracy of measurements and cut, and in that respect the facilities and resources of Messrs. Broughams, Ltd., are all that the most fastidious could desire. All orders are fulfilled on the premises, and a feature is made of rapidity as well as efficiency of execution; so that orders may be completed while the passenger remains in port.

Messrs. Broughams, Ltd., are importers of all kinds of general household goods, curtains, tapestries, upholstery materials, glassware, crockery, etc.; and at the corner of Front and Main Streets, Pettah, have an establishment devoted exclusively to furniture, which they manufacture in all designs, to suit all exchequers.

The business was established in 1923, and the present company was incorporated on November 1st, 1926, the directors being Messrs. J. Macdonald, H. H. Brougham, W. G. Beauchamp, and H. J. Adkins. The telegraphic address is "Smart," Colombo, and the code used is Bentley's.

CUMBERBATCH and CO., General Merchants and Commission Agents, Ambawatte House, Vauxhall Street, Slave Island.

The premises of Messrs. Cumberbatch and Co., occupying about three acres, have an appearance reminiscent of former times, when there were no great modern office buildings in Colombo, and the merchants arrived at and departed from their business places in horse-drawn vehicles, many with coachmen and footmen in gorgeous and distinctive liveries. If anyone connected with the business in its early years could visit the old premises now, much would be found as it used to be and very much that has altered considerably. The records of the concern go back to the 70's of last century, when it was founded under the name of Sabonadière and Co., and carried on as such until 1884, when the present designation was assumed. Coffee figured at first very largely amongst the firm's exports, and after the failure of that industry Messrs. Cumberbatch and Co. turned their attention to tea, with very gratifying results, for they became one of the leading houses in Ceylon in that connection. Accordingly to-day the testing and blending of tea for shipment abroad are carried out by Messrs. Cumberbatch and Co. with the minute understanding that comes from long experience of that work.

OFFICES OF CUMBERBATCH and CO.

The firm are also exporters of rubber, and for that branch of trade they have an office at Kuala Lumpur, in the Federated Malay States. They are likewise importers of general estates' supplies. The partners are Messrs. R. S. Templer, A. J. Denison, H. V. Hill, C. C. Durrant, R. Whittow, and J. A. Loram. Messrs. Cumberbatch and Co.'s telegraphic address is "Cumberbatch," Colombo, and the codes used by them are the A B C 5th and 6th editions, Lieber's, Bentley's, and Broomhall's rubber edition. They are agents for the following:—

Inglis, Ltd., Melbourne, Sydney, and Brisbane.
Crabbe & Co.; Dickson, Anderson & Co., Ltd., London agents for the Scottish Trust & Loan Co. of Ceylon.
Deltenne Ceylon Tea Estates, Ltd.
The St. George Rubber Estate, Ltd.
The Glendon Rubber Co., Ltd.
The Rubber Estates of Bentota, Ltd.
The Avon & Golconda Tea & Rubber Co., Ltd.
The Lowmont Estates Co., Ltd.
The Elmhurst (Ceylon) Tea & Rubber Estates, Ltd.
The Palatine Insurance Co., Ltd.
Stratheden Estate & Gautier de Ste Croix & Sons.

Agents and Secretaries for:

Shalimar (Malay) Estate Co., Ltd.
The Ceylon Planters' Rubber Syndicate, Ltd.
The Rubber Growers Co., Ltd.
Indo Malay Estates, Ltd.
The Bukit Darah (Selanger) Rubber Co., Ltd.
The Good Hope (Selanger) Rubber Co., Ltd.
The Gonagama Rubber Co. (Ceylon), Ltd.

CEYLON MOTOR TRANSIT COMPANY, Motor and General Engineers, Kanatte Road, Borella.

Human progress has always been indicated by its methods of transit, and probably the most momentous occurrence in that wonderful story was the advent of the first wheel, away back in the dim unrecorded past. Progress of every description generally meets at first with opposition. When Mr. T. W. Collette, founder of the Ceylon Motor Transit Co., began his enterprising activities as pioneer of motor traction in Ceylon with a Thorneycroft bus, the Government was against the scheme because of the damage it was feared would be done to the roads. Mr. Collette, however, overcame that opposition by importing the "Commer" vehicles made with wheels specially constructed to prevent any possibility of damage to the island's highways; and when he eventually won the Government's sanction, his efforts for the economic development of Ceylon proceeded apace. His business, in which he had been in partnership with his brother, Mr. H. H. Collette, now Mechanical Engineer of the Colombo Municipal Council, was in 1921 formed into the Ceylon Motor Transit Company, of which Mr. T. W. Collette is managing director; and it contributes an important part to the motor transit facilities in Ceylon. For that purpose it has a fleet of thirty powerful vehicles, including the celebrated "Brockway" motor lorries, for which it is agent, as well as the "Commer" and "Benz" omnibuses, which maintain the longest motor service in the island, extending from Borella to Batticola, on the eastern side of Ceylon.

The premises of the Ceylon Motor Transit Co. have an area of about 3½ acres, and give employment to about eighty workmen, who are engaged in everything associated with repairs to motor vehicles and engineering. The company devotes special attention to the building of all kinds of motor bodies, and its stock of spare parts and accessories is of the most comprehensive character. The company has branch offices at Bandarawela and Badulla. The telegraphic addresses are "Bonanza," Colombo; "Tranzor," Bandarawela; and "Omnibus," Badulla. The code used is the 5th edition of the A B C.

JOHN and CO., Photo Artists and Importers of Photographic Materials. Head Office: Maradana.

FORT BRANCH, COLOMBO.

HEADQUARTERS, MARADANA, COLOMBO.

NUWARA ELIYA BRANCH.

KANDY BRANCH.

PREMISES OF JOHN and CO.

No materials are more dependent on accuracy and suitability than those pertaining to photography, which has now developed a range of operation far exceeding its pristine demarcations. Very much has been contributed to that development by the Agfa and Ilford manufactures, which are in such popular use throughout the world. Year after year these celebrated goods have seemed to reach their maximum in general merit and adaptability; but every now and then they exemplify some new improvement, some clever enhancement of standard perfection; and now it appears impossible that anything further can be achieved which can add to the wonderful simplicity of modern photography and the results possible to even unskilled operators equipped with Agfa or Ilford outfits.

The agents in Ceylon for these goods are Messrs. John and Co., who are also dealers in and general importers of photographic materials of every description, which they obtain from firms of world-wide fame in London. They also operate in all branches of photography, and devote special attention to portraiture, for which they have a large variety of backgrounds and accessories. Their studio at Maradana has a floor space of 650 square feet, and is admirably equipped with everything for the production of the highest class of work. Messrs. John and Co. know by long study and experience the exact psychological moment when and how to secure the expressions and attitudes best suited to their customers, and the many charming examples of their ability in that connection on view in their premises testify much more eloquently to the firm's skill than columns of printed eulogy. Particularly noteworthy are their enlargements in black and white, sepia, and in colours, by clever artists.

Messrs. John and Co. are also manufacturers of all kinds of printing blocks. They have been established since 1919, and have branches at Kandy and Nuwara Eliya. They have also in the Fort, Colombo, another establishment devoted to the sale of photographic materials, book and general literature, stationery, curios and fancy goods, also view books and picture postcards of Ceylon reproduced from the firm's own photos, of which they have a very large selection. Messrs. John and Co. are engaged in wholesale as well as retail trade. Their telegraphic address is "Platino," and their codes are the A B C 5th edition and Bentley's.

G. ROBERT DE ZOYSA and CO., Successors to A. H. MARSHALL and CO., Merchants, Exporters and Importers, Balers, Brush Manufacturers, Owners of Estates, Fibre and Desiccating Coconut Mills, and the CEYLON BRUSH MANUFACTURING CO., Fairfield House, Union Place.

Messrs. G. Robert De Zoysa and Co. are amongst the largest employers of labour in Ceylon, and have between 3,000 and 4,000 persons on their pay rolls. At Madampe they have what are said to be the largest fibre mills in the island. They are also the proprietors of the Nagoda fibre mills and the desiccating factory at Kandana. Their estates throughout the island aggregate about 4,000 acres and are as follows:

Dromoland Tea Estates.
Maharappolla Rubber Estates.
Anganaketiya Rubber Estates.
Munnewa Rubber Estates.
Galduwa Coconut Estates.
Ganewatte Coconut Estates.
Pannalla Group Estates.
Kiniyama Group Estates.
Madampe Group Estates.
Siri Sumana Group Estates.
Pehebiakanda Cinnamon Estates.
Dickduwa Cinnamon Estates.

Messrs. G. Robert De Zoysa and Co. are also brush manufacturers, and operate in that connection under the name of the Ceylon Brush Manufacturing Co., which was established in 1918. They manufacture brushes of every description, and as the requisite materials are all obtained in Ceylon, it naturally follows that the firm are able to sell their excellent brushes much cheaper than similar imported articles. The Ceylon Brush Manufacturing Co. are contractors and suppliers to the Colombo Municipality, Kandy Municipality, Colonial Stores, Harbour Engineer, Walker Sons and Co., Ltd., Hunter and Co., Colombo Hotels Co., Ltd., etc.

Messrs. G. Robert De Zoysa and Co. are likewise exporters of Ceylon produce, and have agencies throughout the world. The chief commodities dealt in by them are rubber, copra, coconuts, desiccated coconut, fibre of all grades, coir, yarn, cinnamon and other spices, etc. The proprietor of the concern, Mr. G. Robert De Zoysa, is the present Chairman of the Ceylon Low Country Products Association, and the firm are in a position to transact a very competitive trade.

The business of Messrs. G. Robert De Zoysa and Co. was established in 1905, and carried on under the name of A. H. Marshall and Co. until 1920, when the partnership was dissolved, and the concern was continued under its present name by Mr. G. Robert De Zoysa, who had been one of the principals of the former firm. The telegraphic address is "Wick," Colombo, and the codes used are the A B C 5th and 6th editions, Lieber's, Bentley's, Kendall's, and private.

PARAKRAMA ENGINEERING WORKS, Skinner's Road (South).

There is always room at the top for ability, always plenty of scope for the effort directed towards perfection in ways and means. That fact is proved everywhere in all branches of business activity by the attaining of success in the face of powerful and long established competition. An excellent example of it is manifested by the development which has taken place in the Parakrama Engineering Works. That undertaking was started in 1925 with one engineer, a clerk, and two workmen, and the monthly turnover amounted to Rs. 400. Sixteen months later its staff comprised upwards of 100 workmen, supervised by highly skilled European engineers, and the turnover had risen to more than Rs. 60,000 a month. By the time this volume is published these figures will probably be doubled, for when the writer inspected the works the firm were making arrangements for transforming their premises into a very large

PARAKRAMA ENGINEERING WORKS.

general engineering establishment, equipped with a powerful plant of up-to-date machinery that would be able to meet every demand likely to be made upon it. As was stated in the local press,

"The success of the Parakrama Engineering Works is due to accurate workmanship, expert design, low rates and straightforward dealing. Repeated orders are its testimony."

The Parakrama Engineering Works undertake complete installations of all kinds of industrial buildings, factories, mills, aerial ropeways, hydro-electric plants, etc. They have attained particular fame for the supply and erection of bungalows of every description, in which they specialise with marked ability, and have erected these and other structures on very many estates throughout Ceylon. Besides their engineering activities they are also importers of hardware, building materials, and bungalow fittings, galvanised corrugated and ceiling sheets, iron joists and steel sections, bolts, nuts and rivets, steam, gas, and water piping, English and Continental cement, paints and oils, motor accessories, electrical bulbs and fittings. The firm are sole agents for Tip-top tiles, Dominion case hardening powder, Himalaya roller composition, Heenen and Froude, Ltd., Manchester; Boulton and Paul, Ltd., Norwich; Armstrong and Co., Ltd., Vancouver; Condor Lamp Manufacturing Co., Venlo; and Anderson Gibb and Wilson, Edinburgh.

The founder and proprietor of the business is Mr. J. S. Parakrama, M.I.M.E., A.M.I., Min. E., who gained his engineering qualifications in England, where he had very extensive experience, including seven years with Armstrong, Whitworth and Co., Newcastle-on-Tyne.

A. P. CASIE CHITTY, General Import and Export Merchant and Commission Agent, 3a and 4, Fourth Cross Street, Pettah.

There is probably no Tamil family in Ceylon better known nor longer established in the island than that of Casie Chitty, who, hailing originally from Benares, India, are particularly noted for their mercantile ability. A well-known member of that family is Mr. A. P. Casie Chitty, who traces his ancestors in Ceylon back for fifteen generations, and is one of the most successful business men there. Established since 1906, he is a large importer of groceries and provisions, wine and spirits, and his name in that connection is highly appreciated amongst manufacturers of such things in Great Britain, Germany, France, Belgium, Italy, etc.

His imports of rice from India and Burma supply the requirements of estates throughout the island. From Java reach him big quantities of sugar, and in the Jampettah suburb of Colombo he has an excellently equipped factory where he manufactures all kinds of boiled sweets from the finest cane-sugar. Contiguous to that factory, Mr. Casie Chitty owns a series of warehouses known as Mervyn's Stores, built in 1924 on the latest scientific principles for the storage of merchandise, and let out to various prominent European firms. The land occupied by him there covers an area of ten acres and is of an estimated value of ten lakhs of rupees.

Mr. Casie Chitty controls very much of the local liquor trade. He imports in bulk and his total operations are naturally on an extensive scale, including all the bottling of arrack for the Government.

Mr. Casie Chitty is the financial partner in the Central Medical Stores described in the following article, and is also a partner in the firm of Sand and Co., exporters of rubber and other produce. In the Kotehena suburb of Colombo Mr. Casie Chitty owns a large area of land which he is developing into a model settlement. At the time of writing he has built 40 houses there for the accommodation of some of the many people employed by him. Mr. Casie Chitty's cable address is "Gemini," Colombo, and the codes used by him are the A B C 5th editions, Lieber's, Bentley's, and private.

C. GOMEZ and CO., Central Medical Stores, Main Street.

In all English-speaking countries the name most frequently given to the principal thoroughfare in town and village is Main Street. Such is the designation of the chief shopping thoroughfare in the busy Pettah district of Colombo, and prominent amongst the names there is that of Gomez. Prior to 1914 Messrs. Gomez and Co. operated as general importers and had their connections near and far. In that year, however, the concern was dissolved and one of the former partners, Mr. C. Gomez, continued business by opening the well-known establishment entitled the Central Medical Stores, where are obtainable, as might be inferred from its name, pharmaceutical requirements of every description. A considerable wholesale trade is transacted at the Central Medical Stores, and through the firm's connections at Kandy and Negombo retail chemists and druggists in Ceylon are provided with the means of keeping their stocks fresh and pure. The establishment is a reliable place for the compounding of doctors' prescriptions, and for that important work qualified assistants are employed. In partnership with Mr. Gomez is Mr. A. P. Casie Chitty, referred to in the preceding article. The business has undergone very successful development, and now gives employment to upwards of 36 persons. From the firm's excellently got up catalogue is the following quotation which is significant of the policy by which the concern is conducted:—"The man who stands behind the counter at the Central Medical Stores is willing to stand behind the reputation of the groceries he sells. He knows that every article measures up to the highest standard of quality at low prices."

NORMAN BLANDE and CO., Brokers and Advertising Contractors to the Ceylon Government Railway, 34, Baillie Street.

Mr. Norman Blande is a gentleman of many activities, for which he is well qualified by his long residence at Colombo and his extensive experience of local trade. He was for nearly nineteen years connected with the firm of Tarrant and Co., in which he eventually became a partner and was manager of its import department. In 1926 he severed his connection with that concern and, starting in business on his own account, has made excellent progress.

Mr. Blande operates as a share, exchange, freight and general produce broker, and is advertising contractor to the Ceylon Government Railway, controlling all the advertising space at 170 stations throughout the island. His service and supplies in the latter connection include permanent enamelled iron plates of all sizes and styles; and inquiries regarding the rates for these excellent publicity mediums should be addressed to him.

Mr. Blande is furthermore Member for the Fort district in the Colombo Municipal Council. His telegraphic address is "Norbla," and the codes used by him are Bentley's and Western Union.

WALKER, SONS and CO., LTD., Engineers, Prince Street, Fort.

Colombo is noteworthy for its excellent engineering establishments. The works of Messrs. Walker, Sons and Co., Ltd., for instance, cover an area of eleven acres and, under normal conditions, employ about two thousand men, who are engaged in the production of tea, rubber, coffee and water-power machinery, factory ironwork, roof trusses, girder bridges, steel barges, tanks, etc. The works are in direct railway communication with all parts of Ceylon, and have their own jetty to facilitate imports and exports of materials.

The business was founded at Kandy in 1854 under the name of John Walker and Co., and during the next twenty years the firm specialised in the manufacture of coffee machinery for Ceylon, Java, Southern India, and Brazil. In 1870 the coffee industry of Ceylon reached its greatest development with the exportation of more than 1,000,000 cwts. of coffee; but from that date there was a rapid decline until leaf disease finally extinguished all the coffee plantations on the island.

Whilst the planters were occupied with fresh products Messrs. John Walker and Co. were busy preparing for the removal of their workshops to Colombo, for it was recognised that with the completion of the southern arm of the breakwater, the harbour was bound to increase rapidly in importance. It was also realised that the increasing tonnage entering it would mean corresponding increase of work in connection with steamer repairs, docking, etc., and hopes in these directions were amply justified. In this way the marine engineering side of their business helped to compensate the firm for the loss of work up country through the failure of coffee. The transfer of the workshops from Kandy to Colombo took place in 1880, and the new premises in Prince Street, Fort, were opened in 1881.

In 1890 the firm was formed into a limited liability company.

Owing to the continuous expansion of the business, the company was forced to consider the question of removing the workshops out of the Fort altogether and ultimately obtained from Government a lease of a suitable site adjoining the Graving Dock. On this site, in extent about nine acres, entirely new workshops were erected. They were formally opened on March 22, 1912.

Messrs. Walker, Sons and Co., Ltd., have branches at Kandy, Talawakelle, Galle, Ratnapura, and Bandarawela.

F. X. PEREIRA and SONS, General Importers, Indent Agents, Manufacturers' Representatives, Steamship and Insurance Agents, Ridgeway Building, Pettah.

Very many of the great number of people who pass through Colombo are only familiar with the shopping emporiums of the Fort, and are unaware of the attractions and advantages that await the discerning in the busy Pettah district that is only a short distance away by the first road to the left from the landing jetty. That district is full of stores, meeting requirements of every description, but none of them is more worthy of notice than Messrs. F. X. Pereira and Sons', who have been established since 1889 and are very well known among the permanent residents of Colombo and throughout the island. Their attractive establishment, which gives employment to about sixty persons, is an excellent place for the supply of everything associated with a general department store, but more especially for ladies' and gentlemen's outfitting, in which the firm have always specialised with marked success. Indeed, in that connection it is difficult to say to which sex they cater best. In their tailoring departments, giving employment to a large staff of expert workmen, the sartorial trade is administered with ability equal to that associated with the most noteworthy centres of fashionable decree.

In the old records of the business is found the interesting fact that Messrs. F. X. Pereira and Sons were specially appointed drapers to Sir West and Lady Ridgeway, when the former was Governor of the island. Lady Ridgeway was a regular customer of theirs during her husband's six years term of Governorship, and on leaving Ceylon she gave a testimonial to them, expressing her entire satisfaction with her dealings at their establishment. The title of the latter, Ridgeway Building, commemorates that pleasant association.

At Tuticorin Messrs. F. X. Pereira and Sons are manufacturers of iron safes and cash chests, and also are general motor engineers handling the Dodge and Overland cars, spare parts and accessories, etc. They are likewise at that place exporters of coconut fibre, senna and other products, and importers of cement and building materials. During recent years they have developed their activities very considerably as indent merchants for all classes of merchandise, manufacturers' representatives, and general commission agents, and are agents for the following:

The Scindia Steam Navigation Co., Ltd.
Sissons Brothers and Co., Ltd., Hull.
John Shaw & Sons (Wolverhampton), Ltd., Wolverhampton.
Goodwin & Co., Birmingham.
British Manufacturers' Agency, Ltd., Manchester.
Lewis Banks & Co., Ltd., London.
Deutsche Einkaufsgesellschaft, m.b. H. Hannover.
Plate and Van Heusde, A. sterda.
Iida & Co., Ltd., Takashimaya, Yokohama.
H. E. Travis & Co., Manchester.
Evans and Weale, Ltd., London.
Franz Gahlert & Sohne, Barenstein.
The Universal Fire and General Insurance Co., Ltd.
The Burma Fire and Marine Insurance Co., Ltd.

The founder of the business, Mr. Francis X. Pereira, died in 1906, and since that date it has been carried on by his sons, the present partners being the Hon. I. X. Pereira, M.L.C.; R. G. Pereira; J. E. A. Pereira; J. L. Pereira; and J. R. T. Pereira.

GEORGE STEUART and CO., Private Attorneys, Estate, Commission and Banking Agents, 14, Queen Street.

If it were possible for any of the Dutch colonists who lived at Colombo before its capitulation to the British in 1796 to return to it now, the name of Steuart would be familiar to them, for that was the name of the gallant Colonel who commanded the victorious British force to which the island was surrendered and became part of the British Empire.

The name of Steuart has long been and is prominent and influential in local commerce. The firm so designated — George Steuart and Co. — dates its history back to 1837, and was founded by Mr. James Steuart, formerly Port Attendant at Colombo. The book written by that gentleman, *Notes on Ceylon (and its affairs during a period of* 38 *years ending in* 1855), was printed in 1862 for private circulation, and contains very interesting and instructive information regarding the colony as it was in Mr. Steuart's lifetime.

The offices of Messrs. George Steuart and Co. form part of a block of buildings erected during the Dutch occupation of Colombo, and are among the few business structures that still remain as mementoes of the past.

The firm are agents for the following:—

Arbuthnot, Latham & Co., Ltd., London.
Colombo Commercial Co., Ltd., London.
Dickson, Anderson & Co., Ltd., London.
M. P. Evans & Co., London.
George Williamson & Co., London.
James A. Hadden & Co., London.
Shand, Haldane & Co., London.
Taylor, Noble & Co., Ltd., London.
William Nevett & Co., London.
Rowe, White & Co., Ltd., London.
Gillanders, Arbuthnot & Co., Calcutta and Rangoon.

For Insurance:

The Alliance Assurance Co., Ltd.
The North British & Mercantile Insurance Co.

For Bankers:

Coutts & Co.
Bank of Liverpool & Martins, Ltd.
The Westminster Bank, Ltd.
Chas. Hoare & Co.
Ulster Bank, Ltd.
Bank of Montreal.
National Provincial Bank, Ltd.

For Sterling Companies:

The Consolidated Estates Co., Ltd.
The Ceylon (Para) Rubber Co., Ltd.
The Duff Estates Co., Ltd.
The Deviturai Rubber and Tea Estates Co., Ltd.
The Doranakande Rubber Estates, Ltd.
The Elston Estate Co. of Ceylon, Ltd.
The Gibson Estates, Ltd.
The Glen Rubber and Tea Co., Ltd.
The Hanipha (Ceylon) Tea & Rubber Co., Ltd.
The Hardford Estate, Ltd.
The Hattangalla Tea & Rubber Estates Co., Ltd.
The Kurugama Tea Estate, Ltd.
The Kintyre Tea Estates Co., Ltd.
The Nayabedde Estate Co., Ltd.
The Standard Tea Co., Ltd.
The Sumtravalle Estates, Ltd.
The Sunnygama Co., Ltd.
The Talawakelle Estates Co., Ltd.
The Tea Estates Control Co., Ltd.

Agents and Secretaries for Rupee Companies:

The Albion Tea Estates Co., Ltd.
The Arawakumbra Rubber Co., Ltd.
The Ceylon Provincial Estates Co., Ltd.
The Ceylon Rubber Co., Ltd.
The Dickapitiya Tea & Rubber Co., Ltd.
The Dickoya Tea Co., Ltd.
The Doone Vale (Ceylon) Rubber Co., Ltd.
The Easter Seaton Cocoanut Estates Co., Ltd.
The Gangawatta Estates Co. of Ceylon, Ltd.
The Glenanore Tea Co., Ltd.
The Govinna Rubber Co., Ltd.
The Hantane and Bollagalla Estates Co., Ltd.
The Holbrook Co., Ltd.
The Karandagama Tea Co., Ltd.
The Kataboola Co., Ltd.
The Kirklees Estate Co., Ltd.
The Knavesmire Estates Co., Ltd.
The Lucky Land Tea Co., Ltd.
The Mahanilu Tea Co., Ltd.
The Moolgama Estate Co., Ltd.
The Nahavilla Estates Co., Ltd.
The Narangoda Rubber Co., Ltd.
The Rahatungoda Tea Co., Ltd.
The Ratwatta Cocoa Co., Ltd.
The Remuna Rubber Co., Ltd.
The Ryans Estates (of Ceylon), Ltd.
The Shawlands Tea Co., Ltd.
The Stratnspey Tea Co., Ltd.
The Syston Estates Co. of Ceylon, Ltd.
The Tempo Tea & Rubber Co., Ltd.
The Troup Tea Co., Ltd.
The Udagoda Tea & Rubber Co., Ltd.

ARISTON GARAGE, 240a, Steuart Place, Colpetty.

THE owner of a motor-car in Colombo is, in many respects, better off regarding service and supplies than people who live in many of the provincial towns in Great Britain and other countries. As Colombo is so far away from the chief centres of industrial production, the Ariston Garage, like its competitors, is obliged to meet the most diverse requirements, many of which, in the smaller towns in the British Isles, for instance, would be referred to the manufacturers of the cars. That necessity is the mother of invention is demonstrated in the Ariston Garage, where a plant of machinery is in operation that covers every phase of skilled workmanship in connection with automobile repairs. It is, of course, impossible here to describe the work in the various departments, and the appliances with which that work is skilfully accomplished. To do so would necessitate much space devoted to various machine tools, electric utilities, and manipulative adaptability only possible through long specialisation in distinctive operations, which in less up-to-date garages are often bungled over by workmen with limited knowledge and experience of their trade.

Although the business has been only established since 1923, the proprietors, Messrs. A. J. van der Poorten and F. Guillain, are motor engineering and electrical experts of extensive experience. Mr. Guillain, for instance, is a specialist in the supply and erection of distillery plants, and at the time of writing the firm are making arrangements for launching out very largely in that connection. Their telegraphic address is "Selecmotor," and the codes used by them are the A B C 5th edition and private. They are agents for Hotchkiss, Peugeot, Sizaire Freres, Amilcar, and Unic motor-cars; Unic lorries; Ariel, Monet and Goyen motor-cycles; Marchal and Ducelliers electric equipments; L'Aster lighting sets; Tudor batteries; Marvel mascots; Wanguier electric motor pumps; Universal wood machine, " Balleydier " and crude oil engines. The Ariston Garage is also service station for the Jowett, Paige, Bean, Adler, Opel, Benz, Swift, Maccar, Fafnir, and Lalicorne cars.

CARGO BOAT DESPATCH COMPANY.

THE business of the Cargo Boat Despatch Co. was established in 1866, and was taken over in 1915 by the late Mr. P. Cosmas, who amalgamated with it the undertakings of the Colombo Water Boat Co. and Passe and Co. The Cargo Boat Despatch Co. has a fleet of 150 boats of all tonnages, the average capacity being 40 tons each, also 3 steam tugs and a large fleet of motor lorries for transport work. It has its own boat-building yard at Peliyagoda, near the mouth of the Kelani River, and repairing yards at Kochchikade.

The company operates as water suppliers, coal contractors, and stevedores, and lands cargo for various steamship lines. It also ships cargo to every line of steamers calling at the port of Colombo. There is also a forwarding branch attached to the business. The office premises of the company are leased from the Government. The partners in the company are Messrs. H. P. Cosmas, A. Zarephe, and John Cosmas. The manager is Mr. P. Muller. The telegraphic address is "Despatchco," Colombo, and the code used is the A B C 5th edition.

JOHN COSMAS, Importer, Exporter, and General Commission Agent, 17, Baillie Street.

THE name of Cosmas has long been associated with business activity in Colombo. The gentleman indicated at the head of this brief reference, Mr. John Cosmas, is a co-proprietor of the Cargo Boat Despatch Co. referred to in the preceding article. In 1918 he established a general merchandising business which is making excellent progress. Mr. Cosmas is an importer of piece-goods, sugar, hardware, and the infinity of things that come under the term of general sundries. As an exporter of Ceylon produce Mr. Cosmas handles chiefly rubber, copra, desiccated coconut, and cinnamon. He is agent for Cussons and Sons, manufacturers of soap and perfumery, London, and Bontwevirij Insulinde, manufacturers of sarongs and comboys, Hengelo, Holland. The joint managers are Messrs. Chr. Christodoulis and S. Tiverios. His telegraphic address is " Johncos," and the codes used by him are the A B C 5th and 6th editions and Bentley's.

H. P. COSMAS and CO., General Merchants and Commission Agents, 2, Canal Row.

MESSRS. H. P. COSMAS AND CO. are exporters of all kinds of Ceylon produce, but chiefly cinnamon, copra, desiccated coconut, coconut oil, and cocoa, while as importers their principal lines are hardware, tools, and motor accessories. The founder and proprietor of the business is Mr. H. P. Cosmas, who is one of the directors of the Cargo Boat Despatch Co. The firm's cable address is " Apollo," and the codes used by them are Bentley's and the A B C 5th and 6th editions.

E. G. NEGRIS and CO., Ship-chandlers, Import and Export Merchants, York Street.

ONE of the most recent of the commercial buildings in Colombo is that of Messrs. E. G. Negris and Co., which was completed in July, 1927. That firm are amongst the most notable of the local ship-chandlers, and supply fresh meat, vegetables, and everything pertaining to the commissariat of a steamer. They are also importers of piece-goods from England, Germany, Switzerland, and France, and also of the French "Lalicorne" motor cars. The business was founded about a quarter of a century ago by its present proprietor, Mr. E. G. Negris, who is ably assisted in its management by Mr. A. C. Jordanidis. Messrs. E. G. Negris and Co.'s telegraphic address is "Negrisco," Colombo, and the codes used by them are the A B C 5th edition and Bentley's.

W. E. BASTIAN and CO., Paper Merchants, Stationers, Printers, etc., 13, Norris Road, Pettah.

THE great range in the qualities of paper supplied by Messrs. W. E. Bastian and Co. gives an idea of the remarkable development which has been attained in the paper-making industry, especially since 1862. Prior to that date paper was made from rags. Thereafter experiments began to

PREMISES OF W. E. BASTIAN and CO.

develop the use of fibrous materials in the form of chemical pulp. To-day raw materials of that character are prepared in enormous quantities, and the evolution of the paper-making industry has been accompanied by the invention of ingenious machinery that contributes very greatly to the many different qualities and varieties of paper now in use, as exemplified by the supplies of Messrs. W. E. Bastian and Co. That firm's assortments of general stationery and writing materials of every description are equally impressive, and are imported by them from the leading manufacturers in Europe and America. Messrs. W. E. Bastian and Co. are also dealers in all kinds of fancy goods, gramophones, perfumery, etc.

They operate very commendably as printers, and in their works in Fourth Cross Street is executed printing of every kind in Sinhalese and Tamil as well as in English, including beautiful colour work. An excellent example of their ability in that direction is afforded by the *Buddhist Annual of Ceylon*, which is always printed and published by Messrs. W. E. Bastian and Co. The firm are likewise noteworthy for their operations as manufacturing stationers, bookbinders, and machine rulers.

The business was started in 1904 in a very small way by Mr. W. E. Bastian, who had been for some years previously manager of a similar concern in Colombo. As time passed his undertaking developed very successfully, and now gives employment to about 150 persons. The two-storey building, in Norris Road, forming his retail store and offices, is his own property. It was erected for him in 1924, and is larger than might be inferred by its external appearance in the accompanying photographic reproduction.

Messrs. W. E. Bastian and Co.'s telegraphic address is "Paper," Colombo, and they are sole agents in Ceylon for the celebrated Carter's inks and adhesives, and the "Webco" gramophones They are sole importers into the island of the well-known "Three Star" notarial paper, Charles Walter and "Lion" ledger account book papers and "Sri," "Lanka," and "Webco" writing and printing papers."

THE COLOMBO SHIP SUPPLY CO., Ship-chandlers, Provision Dealers, 44, Baillie Street.

IT is but natural that at a great port like Colombo the trade of the ship-chandler should be well represented. Amongst the firms there engaged in that connection is The Colombo Ship Supply Co., whose services embrace everything associated with their vocation—provisions, water, etc. Their business was established in 1912 under the name of F. E. Porritt and Co., and carried on as such until 1925, when it assumed its present designation. The proprietor is Mr. F. E. Porritt, who is the only European operating exclusively a ship-supply concern at Colombo. The telegraphic address is "Colsupco," and the codes used are Scott's 10th edition, A B C 5th edition, Bentley's, and Standard. The company are agents for the Imperial Merchant Service Guild.

HILLMAN, BECK and CO., Importers of Musical Merchandise; Tuners, etc., Union Place.

The handsome building in which Messrs. Hillman, Beck and Co. are located was formerly a private residence, and when they removed there from their original quarters in the Consistory Buildings, Front Street, they converted it into an admirable place for the activities of a business devoted in a very special manner to the attraction and enhancement of home life. A home without music, for instance, falls short of the ideal; and as music is the most spiritual of all the arts, its effects on the character and happiness of people are not to be measured in terms of material things. In that connection it would be very interesting, were it possible, to know the things that have resulted through their pianos, organs, and other instruments in homes throughout Colombo and, indeed, in all parts of the island. Messrs. Hillman, Beck and Co. are importers of musical merchandise of every description, and their supplies include, therefore, the most comprehensive selection of all the means for the creation of sweet sounds by the breath or the fingers, the two ways by which the intangible infinity of music is rendered discernible to the physical sense. They are as ready to equip a complete orchestra as to meet any specialised requirements in pianos and organs, and are agents for the "Rogers," "Hopkinson," and "Brasted" pianos, all of English manufacture.

They are the only firm in Ceylon operating in connection with church organs, and devote special attention to the skilful execution of repairs of all kinds and also to tuning.

Each of the partners is a Member of the Pianoforte Tuners' Association of London. They comprise Messrs. H. L. Hillman and R. C. P. Beck, who learned their trade with Chappell, of London, and P. Silverman, who was trained with Collard and Collard, London. They all went to Ceylon in the employ of Messrs. H. W. Cave and Co., and left that firm in 1922 in order to start in business for themselves.

It may be mentioned that the firm's premises are very frequently used for musical recitals and concerts, which are much appreciated by the local musical community.

H. DON CAROLIS and SONS, Furniture Manufacturers and Complete House Furnishers, General Importers and Commission Agents, 52-55, First Cross Street, Pettah.

The business of Messrs. H. Don Carolis and Sons has the distinction of being the largest of its kind in Ceylon, if not in the entire Orient, and their enterprising specialisation in the manufacture of furniture and the supply of household equipments has gained for them the term of the "Maple" of the East. In the firm's showrooms in First Cross Street and Keyzer Street, Pettah, covering an area of about an acre, with a window display on the ground floor of about 300 feet, are furniture and general household requirements of the most comprehensive description, from the cheapest equipment for the humblest homes to the rich and exquisite woodwork, upholstery, and objects of art for the largest of mansions. Besides the firm's own manufactures, chiefly in native woods like nadun (Ceylon walnut), satin, ebony, calamander, and jak—the latter assuming with age a rich mahogany colour—Messrs. H. Don Carolis and Sons are large importers of rosewood and bentwood furniture, lamps, crockery, bedsteads, spring mattresses, clocks, hardware, carpets, plated ware, pianos, gramophones, etc., being in fact universal providers in all that relates to domestic and office equipment. Their productions are made at their excellent steam furniture works in Slave Island, which are equipped with the latest Western machinery.

The manufacture and sale of furniture formed the initial activities of Messrs. H. Don Carolis and Sons; and while they are still so largely engaged therein, their business has at the same time developed very considerably in other directions. Thus, they are extensive importers of cycles, tools, agricultural implements, cement, galvanised iron, general hardware and building materials. They have also in Pettah a motor garage, where repairs of all kinds to cars are promptly and skilfully executed, and are agents for the American "Gardner" and "Elcar" cars. The motor department is being developed considerably, and is in charge of one of the founder's grandsons, Mr. Rajasinghe Hewavitarne, who followed his long college career in England by a course of study in the celebrated Humber works, Coventry.

Messrs. H. Don Carolis and sons are agents and secretaries for the Ceylon Safety Matches Manufacturing Co., whose works in Bambalapitiya, giving employment to about 200 persons, produce on an average about 15,000 gross boxes of matches per month. They are also agents and secretaries for the Low Country Food Products, Ltd., and agents for the famous Rudge-Whitworth cycles.

The business of Messrs. H. Don Carolis and Sons gives employment altogether to upwards of 750 persons, and was started in 1860 by Mudaliyar Don Carolis Hewavitarne, who died in 1906 at the age of 73. He was a gentleman of pure Sinhalese and Buddhist origin and culture, having received his education at the Buddhist Monastery of Raja Maha Vihare, near Matara, in the south of the island. He was an expert in astrological mathematics, and was the first to print the Sinhalese *Astronomical Year*

Book. A student of Brahminical and Buddhist spiritual literature, he was one of the founders of the Vidyodaya College—an institution for training Buddhist monks—which he supported throughout his life. He was also a large-hearted, open-handed man, and his munificence to the poor, the sick, and the needy eventually came to the notice of the Ceylon Government, which honoured him with the rank of Mudaliyar. The last act of his life was the setting apart of Rs. 30,000 for the spread of industrial education in Ceylon among Buddhists by sending suitable Buddhist young men to Japan to learn Japanese industrial methods, from which resulted the establishment of the Ceylon Safety Matches Manufacturing Co., already referred to, the Hewavitarne Weaving School at Rajagiriya, where weaving and kindred subjects are taught, and the Hewavitarne Dyeing School at Peliyagoda. Both the latter institutions are managed by past scholars of the scholarship founded by the Mudaliyar, who thus revived in the island the arts of weaving and dyeing that had been in decadence for many years.

After the Mudaliyar's death the business was carried on by his two sons, the late Edmund and Simon Hewavitarne. The latter, Mr. Simon Hewavitarne, left a bequest for the printing and free distribution abroad of a series of Buddhist literature, and that series has, in the opinion of Western scholars, contributed very largely to the satisfactory state of orthodox Buddhism. The business is now managed by the last surviving son, Dr. C. A. Hewavitarne (ably assisted by his brother-in-law, Mr. J. Moonesinghe) in partnership with Messrs. Neil Hewavitarne, R. Hewavitarne, Sanath Moonesinghe, Kumaradasa Moonesinghe, Piyadasa Moonesinghe, and Daya Hewavitarne.

P. C. FERNANDO and CO., Contractors, Stevedores, Ship-chandlers, 24, Upper Chatham Street.

When the business of Messrs. P. C. Fernando and Co. was started under the name of H. P. Fernando and Co., about half a century ago, the sailing ship still retained the romance and glamour of the sea, and the premises of the firms who then specialised in meeting ships' requirements were certainly very interesting, for their stocks were much more individualistic and suggestive of the ocean than those which pertain to the ship-chandlery trade in these greatly changed times. Some of the old establishments in question, which the writer remembers, included in their wonderful assortments articles that were always associated with life on the ocean wave—shapely figureheads, guns, cutlasses, masts, cordage, sails, compasses, canned goods, fruits, etc. Many changes have, therefore, taken place in Messrs. P. C. Fernando and Co.'s vocation since the "White Wings of the Sea" still carried much of the world's merchandise, and had not been ousted by the prosaic but more utilitarian steamers. Their business, however, has always kept in line with changing conditions, and they are ever ready, as they have always been, to supply at the shortest notice, canvas, rope, deck and engine stores, water, fresh meat, provisions, etc. The firm are contractors to the Orient Line, Glen Line, Clan Line, Dollar Steamship Co., Osaka Shosen Kaisha, Furness, Withy and Co., etc., and reference may be made to Messrs. Whittall and Co. and James Finlay and Co., Ltd., Colombo, in respect of the firm's steamship connections. The partners are Messrs. P. Charles Fernando and A. R. Fernando. Their telegraphic address is "Stebash," and their codes Scott's 10th edition and the A B C 5th edition. Messrs. P. C. Fernando and Co.'s agents in England are Ross, Schoefield and Co., Ltd., 15, Brunswick Square, Liverpool.

THE COLONIAL MOTOR AND ENGINEERING CO., LTD., 91 and 93, Union Place.

In 1909 the motor vehicle was only in its infancy in comparison with its present condition and vast trade, and the motor cars of that period in Ceylon, amusing in their crude capacity and appearance when contrasted with those of the present day, gave little indication of the great development which was to be effected in their manufacture. In the year mentioned the nucleus of The Colonial Motor and Engineering Co.'s business was formed as a small concern devoted more especially to the repair of cycles, which at that time were still triumphant on the roads of the world. Soon after it was established, the company imported one of the Fiat motor cars, and with the advent of that 40 h.p. vehicle, the character of the undertaking was altered into harmony with the growing demands of the new transportation that was doing and has done so much for the development of the industries of Ceylon.

The story of the phenomenal expansion of the motor industry has no more interesting and impressive example of the universal recognition of fine workmanship in that connection than the story of the Fiat factory at Turin. That great establishment was started in 1900, and the cars produced there soon won such remarkable successes in racing competitions, and proved so eminently efficient under tests of every description, that they became in great demand in all parts of the world. So much indeed has their popularity grown that the Fiat factory has the distinction of possessing the largest building in the world devoted exclusively to the manufacture of motor cars. That establishment, one of the series comprising the Fiat works, gives employment to close on 20,000 workmen, and has on its roof a testing track three-quarters of a mile long. The Fiat cars are to be found wherever there exists the desire for superiority in all the details that contribute to comfort, speed, durability and appearance in the construction of motor vehicles. In Ceylon, as in all other countries, the Fiat cars have demonstrated their wonderful adaptability to every road and climatic condition. The exclusive agents for them in the island have alwavs been and are The Colonial Motor and Engineering Co., Ltd., whose works in Union Place, employing about 100 persons, are popular for the skilful manner in which all the work there is performed, including repairs and the building of motor bodies of every description. At the time of writing, arrangements are being made for the transformation of the entire premises into motor works on a scale of very considerable magnitude. This will include a two-storeyed workshop which will be one of the largest of its kind in Ceylon. Besides the works in Union Place, the company has in Cotta, on the outskirts of the city, another establishment devoted chiefly to the supply of petrol and service to the 'bus traffic of that district.

The Colonial Motor and Engineering Co., Ltd., is the special service depot for the Essex and Singer cars, the sales of which are handled by the Essex and Singer Agency, and for these, as well as for the Fiat cars, it keeps a very comprehensive stock of spare parts and accessories. The managing director of the company is Mr. F. J. de Saram, who has been associated with it since 1919, and to whose able control is due the successful development which the concern has since attained.

The company's telegraphic address is "Menco," Colombo, and the code used is Bentley's.

KENNEDY and CO., Importers of Boots and Shoes, "Times" Building.

The name of Kennedy in Colombo is a popular association of footwear, and it has become so because of the exclusive specialisation devoted in the Kennedy store to boots and shoes and hosiery to match. In that respect the establishment differs from all other stores in Ceylon, and is one of the most noteworthy concerns of the kind in the Orient. Specialisation makes for increased knowledge and skill in any direction, and in Messrs. Kennedy and Co.'s establishment it is very apparent to people able to appreciate the difference between merchandise collected without discrimination for sale at the greatest profit and that which is the result of continual attention directed to everything pertaining to comfortable fit, elegant appearance, and durability in footwear. It is that knowledge which is at the back of Messrs. Kennedy and Co.'s importations from the leading sources of supply in England, France, Switzerland, America, etc., for the firm know footwear better than anything else, and Mr. Alexander Kennedy, the principal, has spent his career in all branches of the trade. Mr. Kennedy opened his present store in 1920, and its trade has developed considerably.

C. S. ANTONY and CO., Exporters and Importers, Chartered Bank Building.

The influence of Messrs. C. S. Antony and Co. in local trade is far reaching, and their warehouses and mills, occupying an area of about seven acres and giving employment to about 500 persons, are amongst the largest establishments of the kind in Colombo. At these impressive premises are handled all the products of Ceylon; but special attention is paid by the firm to tea, which they bulk and packet and ship on an extensive scale under their own labels registered in Europe and elsewhere. Each of the large tea exporting houses has some characteristic in its activities peculiarly its own. Thus while Messrs. C. S. Antony and Co. supply many markets, they are exceptionally prominent in the tea trade of Egypt, and to that country as well as to the Levant and South America they ship most of their tea.

Messrs. C. S. Antony and Co. are likewise large exporters of coconut oil, copra, plumbago, etc.; while as importers their chief commodities are liquor, piece-goods, momi tea chests, hardware, and building materials.

The business is an eloquent testimony to the enterprise and ability of its founder and proprietor, Mr. C. S. Antony, J.P., who started it in 1886 in a small way. To-day the firm are known throughout the world and have agencies in London, Marseilles, Hamburg, Barcelona, Bilbao, Genoa, Cyprus, Port Said, Suez, Alexandria, Cairo, Malta, Suakim, Abyssinia, Zanzibar, Mombassa, Lama, Djibouti, Aden, Bombay, Karachi, Penang, Singapore, Shanghai, Tokyo, Osaka, Yokohama, Sechelles, Madagascar, Persian Gulf, Honolulu, San Francisco, Chicago, New York, Boston, Seattle, St. John's, Buenos Ayres, Wellington, Melbourne, Valparaiso, and other parts of the world. Their telegraphic address is "Elephant," Colombo, and the codes used by them are the A B C 4th and 5th editions, Lieber's, and Bentley's.

ARMSTRONG'S TOURIST AGENCY, Church Street and York Arcade, Fort.

No country offers greater diversity of beautiful scenery than Ceylon, and for the many thousands of people who visit Colombo every year, but only make a brief stay at the port, Armstrong's Tourist Agency provides a service worthy of the highest commendation. Established in 1920, this excellent business, under the personal direction of its founder and proprietor, Mr. C. D. Armstrong, is utilised by Government House when occasions arise for guests of that establishment to tour the island. Accordingly Armstrong's Minerva Service has conveyed many celebrities about Ceylon, including the King and Queen of the Belgians, the Crown Prince and Princess of Sweden, Prince George, etc.

It is very important that visitors to Colombo should avoid the unreliable cars and drivers with whom they may be pestered on landing. The roads throughout Ceylon are uniformly good, but the enjoyment of travelling over them in the Armstrong Tourist Agency's cars is greatly enhanced by the comfort of the vehicles and the absolute reliability of the chauffeurs. Moreover, the latter all speak English, and are by years of service competent to act as guides to the island. The fleet consists of 80 modern cars—five and seven seaters—and is utilised by most of the shipping lines, as it is recognised by the passenger agents that only thoroughly reliable service must be provided for local excursions and day trips to Kandy.

If the steamer remains at Colombo for nine hours or more, the opportunity should not be missed of visiting Kandy. Situated 1,600 feet above sea level, amid scenery of indescribable beauty, the capital of the last of the Kandyan kings offers attractions to the tourist elsewhere unequalled. The motor drive of 3½ hours, at small expense, begins with the low country, where the scenes of Ceylon village life are very interesting and in many respects unique. Entering the mountains from the fiftieth mile, the air becomes cooler, while the scenery during the last part of the journey is beyond description. Other longer or shorter tours can be arranged, notably the one to Mount Lavinia for the delightful bathing at that popular place.

The cable address of Armstrong's Tourist Agency is "Awake," and the codes used are Bentley's and private. The firm is agent and correspondent in Ceylon for the following:

Raymond & Whitcomb Co., U.S.A., Tours and Cruises.
Frank Clark, U.S.A., Tours and Cruises.
Edward Grey's World Tours.
Hudson Motor Car Co.
Burns, Philp & Co., Ltd., Australia, Tours.

PART OF FLEET OF 80 MOTOR CARS OWNED BY ARMSTRONG'S TOURIST AGENCY.

Macdonald, Hamilton & Co., India-Ceylon Tours.
H. Middlebrook, Ltd., U.S.A.
John Hamilton & Co., Tours.
William Allison & Co., Tours.
Australia Travel Service.
Frame's Tours.
International Tours.
Gillespie, Kinports & Beard's World Tours.
Northern Assurance Co., Ltd.
Dean & Dawson, Ltd.
Geo. Lunn's Tours.

T. S. SABAR and CO., Import and Export Merchants and Commission Agents, 45, Keyzer Street.

Like many other important things tersely expressed in popular phraseology and conception, the term "piece-goods" covers one of the greatest departments of commerce and industry. Textiles, or woven materials! Consideration of the vast range of goods embraced therein, and also of the overwhelming variety of designs in which they are made, the infinite variety of their chromatic effects, the endless difference in quality and texture, and the continual multiplicity of standard pattern and idiosyncrasy throughout all the wide field presented by such necessitous materials, gives appreciation of the knowledge and experience necessary for the successful management of a business like that of Messrs. T. S. Sabar and Co., who are amongst the leading importers of piece-goods in Ceylon, and through them many retail merchants throughout the island obtain their supplies.

Messrs. T. S. Sabar and Co. are also importers of hardware, fancy goods, and general sundries. Another important section of their business is represented by their fibre mills, St. Joseph's Stores, Grand Pass, Colombo, where they employ a large number of persons. They are exporters of fibre, desiccated coconut, copra, coconut-oil, tea, cocoa, cinnamon, papaine, citronella-oil, etc., and are agents for Atkinson's celebrated perfumery, the Bata shoes of Zecho Slovakia, and Muller, McLean, and Co., shippers of American goods, New York.

The proprietor of the business, Mr. T. S. Sabar, established it in 1917, but had been, during the preceding quarter of a century, engaged with various other local firms, so that he has had a long and varied experience of commercial conditions and potentialities in Colombo.

THE CEYLON MOTOR COMPANY, No. 23, Colpetty.

THE company in Belgium manufacturing the celebrated Minerva motor cars began their operations at the commencement of the automobile industry in 1897, and their various models have always been an epitome of the latest advances in scientific invention and quality of workmanship. That is why every Minerva owner is proud of his possession. He appreciates its easy handling; he likes the smooth and silent power output of the engine; and he delights in its safe docility and robustness. If some competition should be held amongst motor experts as to the car most nearly approaching perfection, it is certain that the Minerva would be well to the forefront amongst the choice of such experts. Eloquent testimony as to the high esteem in which the Minerva cars are held may be indicated by the fact that several sovereigns, high Government officials and other persons of exceptional status utilise them year after year. In Ceylon they are sold by The Ceylon Motor Co., who have also happily combined with them the sale of the British Vulcan lorries, busses, and other heavy transport vehicles.

The business of the Ceylon Motor Co. was established in 1907 under its present name, which was subsequently changed to Ceylon Motor Co. (Lover Bros.), chiefly in connection with the letting out of cars on hire; but with the development of its sales and other departments, the hiring section was sold and is now operated by another firm. Thereafter the original designation was resumed.

The company's present handsome premises in Colpetty were built in 1925, and are admirably adapted for their purpose, which includes repairs of all kinds to all makes of cars. The partners are Messrs. R. R. B., A. E. B., and F. B. B. Lover, and the telegraphic address is "Lover," Colombo.

A. SANKAR IYER, Manufacturers' Representative and Agent, 5, Main Street.

THE ramifications of modern commerce have developed enormously, and all the markets of the world are intimately related and upheld very influentially by manufacturers' representatives and agents, such as Mr. A. Sankar Iyer, through whose services merchants in Ceylon obtain their supplies of goods famous everywhere, as, for instance, Peak, Frean and Co.'s biscuits, Pears' soap, and C. and E. Morton's groceries and preserved foods, for which he is agent. Mr. A. Sankar Iyer is very well known and esteemed in business circles in Colombo, where he has been engaged in commerce for a quarter of a century. From 1908 to 1927 he was manager of the business of A. V. R. A. Adycappa Chetty, referred to on page 486. He is, therefore, thoroughly well versed in local mercantile conditions and potentialities and excellently qualified to look after the interests of the firms whose affairs in the island are entrusted to him. Mr. Sankar Iyer's telegraphic address is "Watch," Colombo, and the codes used by him are the A B C 5th and 6th editions, Bentley's, and private.

CEYLON AUTO CARRIERS COMPANY, Hyde Park Corner.

AT Hyde Park Corner, opposite to the magnificent old banyan tree which is one of the sights of Colombo, are the premises of the Ceylon Auto Carriers Co., covering an area of about an acre and a half, and giving employment to about 230 persons. That important establishment is an excellent illustration of the great development which has taken place in the local motor car trade, and the facilities and resources which have been evolved to meet its requirements.

Garages in the United Kingdom are usually of small dimensions, with simple equipment and minimum stock, because of their comparative proximity to the great centres of actual production. In Great Britain, therefore, similar necessity does not exist as in Ceylon for establishments so comprehensive in their service and supplies as that of the Ceylon Auto Carriers Co., where work is done that embraces the whole range of motor engineering. The thorough manner in which repairs of every description are performed there testifies eloquently to the efficiency with which the business is conducted.

The premises have recently undergone complete remodelling and transformation, and the many visitors who go to Hyde Park Corner to see the famous tree there are, after their inspection of it, provided with a very interesting motor exhibition in the company's large and handsome new showroom, which has a frontage of 210 feet. The magnificent plate-glass windows and other appointments were imported from England. The cars displayed in their glory of shining enamel and electro-plate provide interesting comparisons in appearance and capacity, and include the Rugby, Flint, Locomobile Junior 8, Reo, Darracq, Clement Talbot, Panhard, and Swift vehicles and the Stewart motor trucks, for which the firm are agents.

The Ceylon Auto Carriers Co. operate also as transporters of goods of every description, and are Government mail carriers. Although only established in 1924 the business has grown very considerably, thanks to the ability brought to bear on all the details of its administrative and executive departments. There are branches of it at Haputale and Hatton. The company's cable address is "Dandico," and the codes used are Bentley's and the A B C 6th edition.

A. Y. DANIEL and SON, Auctioneers, Brokers, Appraisers, and Commission Agents, 19, Baillie Street.

THE large and handsome office buildings which have been erected during recent years in Colombo, especially in the principal European business district called the Fort, have entirely changed the appearance of that place from what it was when the business of Messrs. A. Y. Daniel and Son was founded in 1880. At that time the local thoroughfares still retained the quaint and picturesque aspects of the past, and life in the then little capital of Ceylon was more leisurely and enjoyable than it is in these days of vast development and competition in every department of human activity. Nevertheless, Baillie Street, where Messrs. A. Y. Daniel and Son have been located since the commencement of their business, is still reminiscent of Colombo as it was, and through the doors of that firm's premises, formerly the local branch of the National Bank of India, Ltd., come and go goods and chattels of the most varied description, ranging from the latest productions of the world's chief sources of supply to rare and interesting articles that were prized possessions when the flag of Holland fluttered on the ramparts of the Fort in the eighteenth century. An establishment like that of Messrs. A. Y. Daniel and Son is always interesting to the discerning eye and understanding mind, and many excellent bargains may be obtained at their auction sales, when are disposed of, to the advantage of everyone concerned, anything that can be regarded as collateral for cash.

Messrs. A. Y. Daniel and Son make valuations of landed estates, etc., for appraisement, undertake all kinds of inventories, and furniture and other moveables are purchased by them on valuation. They negotiate loans, make advances on goods entrusted to them for absolute sale, and also act as general house and estate agents. A noteworthy department of their many activities is their importation of milch cattle from India and elsewhere.

Mr. A. Y. Daniel, the founder of the business, is a Fellow of the Auctioneers' and Estates Agents' Institute of the United Kingdom, and well known amongst all classes of the community. His eldest son, formerly in partnership with him, Capt. A. R. Daniel, is now blind through the effects of the wounds he got in Mesopotamia in the Great War. His second son, Lieut. R. Y. Daniel, served in the battalion from Oxford University, was wounded four times, and is now Police Magistrate at Kalutara, Ceylon. His youngest son, Mr. E. M. Daniel, also served in the Public School Battalion, lost both legs at Kut, and is at present employed in the Home Office, London.

In partnership with Mr. Daniel is Major J. G. Vandersmaght, of the Ceylon Rifles, who served in England and France.

The firm's telegraphic address is "Lions," Colombo.

M. E. OTHMAN and SONS, Wholesale and Retail Grocers and Provision Merchants, etc., Adjoining Belfry, Pettah.

THE grocery and provision trade differs from many other departments of service and supply by reason of the fact that the goods by which it is sustained are prime necessities of life, and must, therefore, be provided despite all commercial depressions,

PREMISES OF M. E. OTHMAN and SONS.

strikes, wars, and other happenings. That fact is eloquently demonstrated by the business activities of the firm operating under the name of M. E. Othman and Sons, the well-known wholesale and retail provision merchants, whose premises, adjoining the Belfry, in Pettah, are the source whence are obtained the supplies for innumerable homes throughout Colombo and Ceylon. This alert firm reach out to the world's best sources of production, and place before their numerous customers very many dainties that a few years ago were unknown, or had not evolved into their present character and get-up. Many famous names and trade-marks are to be seen on the boxes and canisters of preserved foods with which the Othman stores are so well filled; and amongst them are those of Rowntree's chocolate, Gray, Dunn and Co.'s biscuits, and the commodities of J. H. Newbaur and Co., San Francisco, for whom, as well as for Nugget polish, Messrs. Othman are agents.

The firm are also importers of all kinds of patent medicines, toilet articles, etc.; and besides their premises at the Belfry they have other stores in 4th Cross Street.

The business was started in 1908 by the gentleman whose name it bears, and in partnership with him is his son, Mr. M. A. Othman. The manager is Mr. S. M. Pillay, who has been connected with the concern for many years. The firm's telegraphic address is "Aduam," and the codes used are Bentley's, A B C 5th edition, and private.

N. D. H. ABDUL GAFFOOR,
Dealer in Precious Stones, Manufacturing Jeweller, etc., Gaffoor's Building.

ONE of the largest and finest commercial structures in Colombo is known as Gaffoor's Building. It was completed in 1915, and is owned by Mr. N. D. H. Abdul Gaffoor, whose splendid jewellery emporium is located there. Ceylon is famous for its precious stones, and these are displayed in Mr. Gaffoor's premises in great variety, ranging from raw, uncut jewels as they are found in the earth to polished gems worth a king's ransom. Mr. Gaffoor has supplied gems and jewellery to Royalties and celebrities throughout the world, including Their Majesties King George and Queen Mary, King of the Belgians, Queen of Spain, Queen of Rumania, Prince of Wales, Duke and Duchess of York, etc. He has been established since 1895, and the development of his business is indicated by the following copies of testimonials received by him :—

Colonial Secretary's Office, Colombo, Sept., 1924.

"I am directed to inform you that it has been brought to the notice of the Government that the exhibit of gems and jewellery displayed by you in the Ceylon Pavilion at Wembley has been the finest of the kind in the British Empire Exhibition, and that you spared no expense and trouble in collecting your specimens of gems and jewellery from your establishments in Colombo, Paris, New York, and London, and in achieving such signal success.

"I am to convey to you a resolution of His Excellency the Governor's high appreciation of the service rendered by you to Ceylon in arranging, at your own great expense, risk, and personal inconvenience, to display on this important occasion the exhibit of gems and jewellery which has redounded greatly to the credit of this colony."

(Signed) FOR COLONIAL SECRETARY.

"The Sesquicentennial International Exposition held in Philadelphia in the year 1926 for the purpose of celebrating the 150th Anniversary of the Signing of the Declaration of Independence, establishing this nation as a free and independent one, contained many interesting and instructive exhibits.

"The exhibits from foreign countries were most representative. Included in this group was your own exhibit of gems and jewellery, which have been pronounced by many who viewed them as 'one of the greatest collections ever brought to, or assembled in, America.' You are to be congratulated on your wonderful display and the part which you played in this great event.

GAFFOOR'S BUILDING.

"I wish to express to you my personal appreciation and gratitude for the hearty co-operation which you gave us, and assure you that when the history of our Exposition is written your exhibit will have its proper place therein."

(Signed) DIRECTOR-IN-CHIEF.

"This is to notify to you that the International Jury of Awards of the Sesquicentennial International Exposition has awarded to you a Grand Prize for quality, display value, for the gems and jewellery exhibited.

(Signed) SECRETARY, EXECUTIVE JURY OF AWARDS.

M. P. GOMEZ and CO., The British Pharmacy, 7, Main Street.

THERE are many degrees of importance in the supply of modern merchandise, but there is no disputing the fact that foodstuffs must be placed in the forefront of universal necessity. Next to them doubtless in the order of indispensability are medical requirements, or the infinity of things coming under the scope of the pharmaceutical trade. In these two great branches of supply, Messrs. M. P. Gomez and Co., established since 1888, have built up an extensive business throughout Ceylon, and have branches at Avisawella, Balangoda, Galle and Yatiyantota. These branches are concerned chiefly with everything for the commissariat of planters, with special regard to eatables and drinkables; but at Colombo, where Messrs. M. P. Gomez and Co. have their headquarters, the firm confine themselves to provisions and pharmaceutical goods. Their commodious establishment at 7, Main Street well substantiates its title of The British Pharmacy by its comprehensive assortment of all the commodities associated with the British pharmacopœia. The dispensing department is under careful management, and the onerous work there is performed by duly qualified assistants.

Similar completeness is observable in the firm's assortment of groceries and provisions, which include all the best known brands of condiments and preserved foods on the market. Among the agencies held by the firm are the following:—Mariani Wine, Yeast Vite tablets, Sarony and Grey's cigarettes, Sen Sen breath perfumes, Grimault's Hæmoglobin (blood purifying syrup), Dr. Ross' life pills and the pharmaceutical preparations of Perry Davies and Co. of America, and Ayrton, Saunders and Co., Ltd., of England.

Mr. M. P. Gomez, the founder of the business, died in 1922. The general manager of the Colombo establishment is his son, Mr. Gaspar Gomez, who has been connected with it all his career. The firm's telegraphic address is "Medicines," Colombo, and the code used is the A B C 5th edition.

C. JINASENA and CO., Wijaya Engineering Works, 41-45, Hunupitiya Road.

Messrs. C. Jinasena and Co. are concerned with making things new, which covers a very great range of sins of omission and commission by people who forget, or are negligent, or are given to lines of least resistance or the postponement of necessities indefinitely until breakdowns occur that result in much inconvenience and loss of time and money and opportunity. The mechanical repairs which Messrs. C. Jinasena and Co. are called upon to execute are exceedingly varied; but by long experience they are well qualified to carry through everything in that connection committed to their trust. They know with minute understanding what it is that makes, or does not make, the wheels go round, and hold themselves in readiness at all times to undertake contracts pertaining to the production and erection of factory plants of all kinds. The firm are specialists in mining machinery, and are noteworthy also in the manufacture of everything associated with waterworks and accommodation requirements for coolies on estates, etc. Their premises, entitled the Wijaya Engineering Works, are excellently equipped for the rapid as well as accurate manipulation of metals; and the articles produced in their iron and brass foundry are very comprehensive.

The business was established in 1905 by its sole proprietor, Mr. C. Jinasena, A.M.I.Mech.E., and has developed well. There is a motor department of it at 2, Park Street and Hunupitiya Road, and a London office at 194-200, Bishopsgate, E.C. The firm's telegraphic address is "Sinha." Cin-Gardens, and their codes are the A B C 5th edition, Bentley's, and private.

J. LAZARUS ROCHE and BROS., "Silk Palace," 104, Main Street, Pettah.

Main Street, Pettah, is one of the busiest thoroughfares in the Orient, and one of its most noteworthy establishments is the "Silk Palace" of Messrs. J. Lazarus Roche and Bros., which is ever a source of attraction to people desirous of goods that are not likely to be found duplicated anywhere else. While operating as general drapers and milliners, Messrs. J. Lazarus Roche and Bros. have become famous for their specialisation in silk, and the stock of that material to be found in their premises is well calculated to meet the most fastidious requirements—silk in every shade and texture for purposes innumerable. There it is, waiting the discerning—those who know exactly what they want, and will not be put off with inferior substitutes. The very large range of silk kept by Messrs. J. Lazarus Roche and Bros. provides an interesting and instructive demonstration of the many varieties of that material now on the market.

The firm have been established since 1894, and the partners are Messrs. M. Roche and Bonjean Roche. At Kandy they have a branch which should be inspected by visitors to that town, who will doubtless find something specially attractive and appealing amongst the allurements of its stock. The firm's telegraphic address is "Lazaru," and they use the 5th edition of the A B C code.

Mr. Bonjean Roche operates also as an importer of cotton and silk goods and sundries as well as an exporter. He is desirous of representing first-class firms, and inquiries in that connection should, therefore, be addressed to him.

THE NATIONAL MOTOR ENGINEERING WORKS, 107, Union Place.

There are so very many excellent cars now on the market that it is very difficult to select one with the absolute assurance that it is the best outlay for the money expended. Amongst the most famous are the Bianchi and Citroen cars, for which the sole agents in Ceylon are The National Motor Engineering Works. The Bianchi factory was established in 1885, and since 1890 has been engaged in the production of motor vehicles of only the highest grade, which is substantiated by the character of the cars bearing that celebrated name. The fact that His Holiness Pope Pius XI selected one of them for his personal use, after careful consideration of the merits of the many other makes of cars, is a lead that others can follow very advantageously.

The Citroen cars are rapidly increasing in popularity throughout the world, which is not surprising in view of their brilliant record under the severest tests. To the Citroen car belongs the distinction of being the first motor vehicle to cross the Sahara Desert. Models of these two celebrated makes may be seen in the premises of The National Motor Engineering Works, where every facility exists in men and machinery for the rapid execution of repairs, as well as a full assortment of Bianchi and Citroen spare parts.

The National Motor Engineering Works was started in 1911 by Mr. V. Tradigo, the present proprietor, under whose able direction it has undergone very successful development. Mr. Tradigo is an Italian motor engineer, of great ability, and has been engaged throughout his career in the motor trade.

The firm's telegraphic address is "Aero," Colombo, and the codes used are A B C 5th edition, Bentley's, and private.

MARTINUS C. PERERA and SON,
Scientific Instrument Repairers, Electro-platers, Vulcanisers, etc., 20, Union Place.

NOWHERE in Colombo is more wonderful and intricate work performed than in the premises of Messrs. Martinus C. Perera and Son, who repair all kinds of scientific instruments, such as barometers, aneroids, chronometers, surveyors' apparatus, etc. Much could be written of the minute precision with which their highly skilled operations are conducted, and the extraordinary variety over which they extend; indeed, the entire gamut of modern achievement in delicate and complicated mechanisms of every description is covered by them. The ordinary person inspecting the astonishing things done by this enterprising firm feels how great the gulf is between the keen specialisation that is intimately acquainted with cause and effect in microscopic appliances and adjustments in wheels and springs, etc., and the ignorance of the lay mind in the same connection.

Messrs. Martinus C. Perera and Son have also attained well-deserved recognition as platers in gold, silver, nickel, brass, and copper, and for their enamel, bronze, and lacquer work. The articles brought to them for attention are exceedingly varied—jewellery, domestic utensils, swords and military accoutrements, cycle and motor-car fittings, etc. These reach the firm in every degree of dilapidation, some apparently quite beyond redemption; but after they undergo the magic Perera process, they are returned to the owners as bright and attractive as they were when new, if not, in some instances, very much better.

Messrs. Martinus C. Perera and Son are holders of the Harvey Frost certificate of proficiency in motor-tyre vulcanising, and devote special attention to that class of work.

The business was established in 1884 by the senior partner, Mr. Martinus C. Perera, who has been engaged for upwards of fifty years in all kinds of work relating to delicate mechanisms. He was born in Ceylon and was trained in various colleges there, winning prizes in optics, physics, acoustics, electricity, etc. After serving for many years in the Survey Office, he started business for himself, as already indicated, in 1884, and soon built up a very appreciative clientele amongst whom he won high praise for the quality of his workmanship. Mr. Perera was the first to introduce electroplating and its kindred processes into Ceylon. He it was also who introduced there the Underwood typewriters, and acted as agents for them for many years. Cycling in Ceylon owes much to Mr. Perera, who has taken a prominent part in connection with the various cycling clubs of the island, and has had no fewer than 36 cycles.

Mr. Perera has long been a district visitor of the Social Service League and Friend-in-Need Society and has done much good work in that connection, as well as a member of the Discharged Prisoners' Aid Association of Ceylon. He is Vice-President of the Ceylon Workers' Federation. His eldest son, Cecil, has been in partnership with him since 1915.

JOSEPH COSTA and BROS., General Merchants, Main Street, Pettah.

THE stock of things eatable in the premises of Messrs. Joseph Costa and Bros. embraces innumerable *bon mots* well adapted for the solution of culinary problems for special occasions when a departure is required from the stereotyped menus that arouse no gastronomic enthusiasm.

Equal attention is paid by the firm to their importations of wines and spirits, which include many of the best brands on the market. They have branches at Kandy, Nuwara Eliya, Matale, and Maskeliya, supplying, in addition to groceries and provisions, all kinds of drapery and ladies' and gentlemen's outfitting goods. The firm have an extensive connection throughout Ceylon with planters and hotels, and own 500 acres of rubber plantations.

The business was started in 1881 at Matale, whence it developed to its present proportions. The partners are Messrs. P. Peries and S., M. F., and J. Costa. The firm's telegraphic address is "Costas," Colombo, and the codes used by them are the A B C 6th edition and Bentley's.

O. L. M. MACAN MARKAR, Jewellers, Pearl and Gem Merchants, G. O. H. Building.

ADMIRABLY situated in the G. O. H. Building, and opening into the entrance hall of that establishment, is the emporium of the well-known firm of jewellers, pearl and gem merchants, Messrs. O. L. M. Macan Markar, who have done, and are doing, very much in sustaining the fame of Ceylon for its precious stones. The first acquaintance of the compiler of this volume with the store in question was made some years ago, when he succumbed to its wonderful display of jewels, and invested in some of them to an extent which, after the initial glamour was over, seemed more than the state of his exchequer at that time warranted. On reaching London, however, the gems purchased from Messrs. O. L. M. Macan Markar were sold by him at a very handsome profit to the best known jewellery firm there, if not in the world. So on returning to Colombo for the purposes of "Seaports of India and Ceylon," Messrs. O. L. M. Macan Markar's establishment was regarded with the appreciation of a friend that had been tried and found worthy of the utmost confidence and encomiums.

When precious stones are about to be purchased, the most important essential to be considered is the probity of the seller. In that connection the reputation of Messrs. O. L. M. Macan Markar, who have branches at Shepheard's Hotel and the Continental-Savoy Hotel, Cairo, is world wide, and as a firm who are honoured and appreciated by Royalties, including H.M. King George and H.R.H. the Prince of Wales, they may well be regarded as in the category of those standards of rectitude that are accepted as beyond all controversy or refutation. The stock of gems and jewellery of all kinds kept by Messrs. O. L. M. Macan Markar is exceedingly varied and includes exquisite designs in platinum and diamond, sapphire, and emerald bracelets and necklaces of Ceylon pearls running into thousands of pounds each. Amongst their wonderful collection of precious stones is what is said to be the largest sapphire in the world. It is valued at £50,000, was discovered in 1926 at Pelmadula, Ratnapura ("City of Gems"), Ceylon, and weighs over 400 carats after having been cut and polished. Another of their treasures is the largest cat's eye extant, which they do not wish to sell; and it was exhibited to King Edward when, as Prince of Wales, he visited Ceylon in 1870. H.M. King George and H.R.H. the Prince of Wales also inspected that remarkable cat's eye when they passed through Colombo.

The most unique sight in the island, so far as gold and jewels are concerned, is the magnificent and unique private collection of antique heirloom jewellery of ancient Ceylon, which is exhibited free in the firm's attractive establishment, and should be seen by every visitor to Colombo able to appreciate the wonderful beauty and wealth of the display.

The business was established in 1860 by the gentleman whose name it bears, and who died in 1901. It is now directed by his sons, who are as follows: The Hon. Mr. H. M. Macan Markar, M.L.C.; and Messrs. S. D., A. V., and M. S. Macan Markar. The firm's cable address is "Macan," Colombo, and their codes are the A B C 5th edition and Bentley's.

D. C. JAYESINGHE and CO., Exporters, Importers, and Commission Agents, 39, Keyzer Street.

None of the many avocations sustained by the complexity of modern commerce is more useful and ubiquitous than that of the commission agent, who acts as medium between buyers and sellers, and negotiates between them on terms favourable to both, bringing to merchants and others in places remote from the sources of production the best that the world can offer for their particular requirements. Such is the character of the business of Messrs. D. C. Jayesinghe and Co., who may be said to be resident commercial travellers in Colombo, where, as well as throughout Ceylon, they have an extensive connection, and are representatives of many famous concerns in Europe and America, including the following:—

Muller & Phipps (Asia), Ltd.; Dayton, Price & Co., Ltd., New York.
Twentsche Overseas Trading Co., Ltd., Holland.
A. W. Price Bros. & Co., Birmingham.
Wirth & Co., London and Buhler.
E. Mercier & Co., France.
Creighton & Lynam, London.
A. Frisof & Cie., Belgium.
Hans W. M. Meyer, Hamburg.
Fairbanks Co. (Europe), Ltd., London.

The goods handled by Messrs. D. C. Jayesinghe and Co. embrace merchandise of every description, but chiefly piece-goods, hardware, provisions, wines and spirits, pharmaceutical articles, etc. They have been established since 1907, and the growth of their business has necessitated various changes of premises, the last being recently into the present quarters at 39, Keyzer Street. The partners are Messrs. D. T. Jayesinghe and P. V. Gunesekara. The firm's cable address is "Singjaye," Colombo, and their codes are the A B C 5th edition, Bentley's, Voller's, and private.

WILLIAM PEDRIS and CO.,
Manufacturing Opticians and General Merchants, Kayman's Gate, Pettah.

When it is remembered that 85 per cent. of all knowledge comes through the eyes, and when it is borne in mind also how easily the sight can be irremediably impaired through inattention or defective glasses, there is no refutation of the importance of the business of Messrs. William Pedris and Co., who are the only manufacturing opticians in Ceylon. Since the commencement of their optical activities in 1912 Messrs. William Pedris and Co. have been missionaries in Ceylon in everything pertaining to the welfare of the eyes, and thousands of persons all over the island owe to them the preservation of that priceless possession, the sight, and, therefore, all that is entailed thereby. The machinery and other equipment in Messrs. William Pedris and Co.'s premises embrace the most modern inventions for sight testing, the remedying of imperfect vision, and the preservation of the sight. The grinding of lenses and all the manufacturing operations range from the raw materials up to the gold finished articles. Every individual case is treated with minute understanding, and every prescription is fulfilled with scientific exactitude.

It may be mentioned that at the All Ceylon Industries Exhibition a gold medal was awarded to the firm for the high quality of their lenses.

Messrs. William Pedris and Co. are also general merchants and importers of hardware, crockery, glassware, household utensils, building materials, estates supplies, etc. They have been established since 1898, and the proprietor of the business is its founder, Mr. D. William Pedris. The general manager is Mr. K. D. Pedris. The telegraphic address is "Pedrico," Colombo.

THE IMPERIAL MOTOR WORKS, Braybrooke Place, Slave Island.

MOTOR garages, like the vehicles which support them, differ very greatly in character and scope. Most of them are agencies of famous cars, and each has thereby an individuality entirely its own. The Imperial Motor Works, for instance, have been since 1925 sole agents in Colombo for the French Donnet-Zedel and De Dion Bouton cars, which are growing in popularity for their many high-class qualities and eminent suitability to the climate and road conditions of Ceylon.

The Imperial Motor Works are noted for the excellence of their work in connection with repairs of every description, and for the building of bodies of trucks. Indeed, in the latter direction, they are specialists equal to the swift and skilful solution of every problem that may arise for uncommon requirements in vehicles for road transportation. About 65 workmen are employed.

The business has been established since 1908, and is under the personal supervision of its proprietor, Mr. P. V. J. Weerappah, who is a practical expert in all that relates to motor engineering. The firm's telegraphic address is "Imperial."

COLOMBO CRYSTAL PALACE, Keyzer Street.

THE Colombo Crystal Palace is a name that immediately arrests the attention and is not readily forgotten. The business so designated was started in 1889, and has become well known throughout

COLOMBO CRYSTAL PALACE.

Ceylon. The origin of the title lay in the firm's initial specialisation in glassware and crockery.

As the business developed other departments were added from time to time, and now the concern, giving employment to about 125 persons, is devoted to merchandise of the most comprehensive description, including cutlery, electro-plated lamps, picture frames, drapery and millinery, gentlemen's outfitting, etc.

The exterior of the Colombo Crystal Palace is misleading so far as its size is concerned. From the street it looks a negligible sort of place, with little indication of its popularity and the reasons thereof. But an inspection of its ramifications and also of the firm's other establishment for general hardware, estate supplies, and building materials in Prince Street, facing Third Cross Street, reveals an extensive business. The Colombo Crystal Palace firm have recently been devoting special attention to indenting on behalf of others, and while their retail trade is considerable, they are, however, chiefly general wholesale merchants. Mr. W. M. Mohamado Usooff, who founded the business in 1889, is still actively engaged in its control, and in partnership with him are his brothers, Messrs. W. M. H. M. Haniffa and W. M. Abdul Jabbar. The general manager is Mr. M. I. L. Mohamed Nuhman, F.C.I., Birmingham.

The firm's telegraphic address is "Crystal," Colombo, and the codes used by them are A B C 5th and 6th editions, Bentley's, Western Union, Lieber's, and private.

ABDULHUSSAN DAVOODBHOY, Merchants and Exporters, 130, Dam Street, Pettah.

THE premises of Messrs. Abdulhussan Davoodbhoy at 130, Dam Street, Pettah, are not much to look at, and the uninitiated reviewer of local commerce and industry, searching for facts, figures, and impressions, would be quite justified in passing them by. But the aspect of a business place is not always an accurate index to its status and resources. Everyone acquainted with the ramifications of Colombo's trade must know Messrs. Abdulhussan Davoodbhoy, whose operations as merchants and exporters are on an extensive scale, and quite at variance with the erroneous conceptions which might be deduced from the somewhat negligible appearance of their establishment. In the Pettah district especially the name of Abdulhussan Davoodbhoy is familiar to the man in the street, and commands the respect of all classes of the community. The firm are importers of general hardware, enamelled ware, domestic utensils, paints and oils, building materials, and estate supplies of every description, explosives, etc., etc. They have branches at Bombay and Calicut, and connections in England, America, China, Germany, and Japan.

The business was established in 1906 by the gentleman whose name it bears, and who died in 1909. The present proprietors are his sons, Messrs. Ackberally, Caderbhoy, Mohmedally, Alibhoy and Abbasbhoy Abdulhussan Davoodbhoy. The firm's telegraphic address is "Morbiwala," Colombo.

THE TOGO COMPANY, Importers, Exporters, and Commission Agents, 57, Keyzer Street.

THERE are not many Japanese in Colombo, and the leading firm of that nationality there is The Togo Co., which was established in 1914. Through it the people of Ceylon are provided with porcelain, glassware, enamelled ware, cotton goods, and the great variety of articles embraced by the term sundries, manufactured in Japan, together with the celebrated Sapporo Beer of that country for which The Togo Co. are agents. The firm are also exporters, and their principal commodity in that connection is tea.

MARKET GARDENS OF THE TOGO CO. AT NUWARA ELIYA.

No people are more enterprising and resourceful than the Japanese in market gardening, and accordingly it is not surprising to find that The Togo Co. have attained very noteworthy achievements in relation thereto. In 1925 they began at Nuwara Eliya the cultivation of fruit and vegetables, and so well have they developed that undertaking that they now transact a flourishing business as contractors for the supply of fresh fruit and vegetables to the Japanese lines of steamers visiting Colombo. The firm's cable address is " Togo," Colombo.

M. D. and A. D. SILVA, Stationers and General Merchants, 26, Norris Road.

IT is not very often that one comes across in the Orient a business like the one indicated above, and its specialisation in paper, general stationery, and educational books is more akin to the procedure of Western exponents of those branches of trade, who, because of their proximity to the actual sources of production, are in possession of advantages which their less fortunate Eastern contemporaries lack. However, there is no gainsaying the fact that Messrs. M. D. and A. D. Silva's business, operated with enterprise and ability, is well calculated to meet the most diverse requirements in all that relates to its supplies. An inspection of their stock of general stationery and educational literature affords an object lesson in the comprehensive character of modern necessities in such things.

The business was established in 1890, and was taken over in 1919 by Mr. J. D. S. Rupasingh (general manager) in partnership with Mr. A. D. Silva and Mr. C. E. D. S. Rupasingh. The firm's telegraphic address is " Martinus," and the codes used by them are the A B C 4th and 5th editions and Bentley's.

P. F. GOONESEKERE and CO.,
Importers of Sewing Machines and General Merchandise. Head Office: 36, Main Street.

ONE of the most useful inventions of modern times is undoubtedly the sewing machine, and it is difficult now to realise the restrictions and limitations that must have obtained before the introduction of that invaluable contrivance, which has revolutionised all the operations associated with the production of clothes and many other things.

Reference to sewing machines in Ceylon calls for reference to Messrs. P. F. Goonesekere and Co., whose influence in that connection extends throughout the island. They are importers of many kinds of sewing machines, and are sole agents in Ceylon for The Pfaff Sewing Machine Co., of Kaiserslautern and The Gritzner Sewing Machine Co., of Durlach, Germany. They are also representatives of The Jones Sewing Machine Co. of England and The New Howe Sewing Machine Co. of New York.

While sewing machines bulk so largely in the firm's activities, they form, however, only one department of the business, for Messrs. P. F. Goonesekere and Co. are also importers of chinaware, enamel and aluminium wares, glassware, trays, vases, clocks, tableware, fancy goods, etc.

Messrs. P. F. Goonesekere and Co. have been established since 1917. Their initial establishment was at No. 11, Keyzer Street, which is still maintained, but which soon became inadequate for their trade. In April, 1925, they opened a branch at Kandy, and in the following September another in China Street, Pettah, Colombo. In July, 1926, they moved into their present commodious headquarters at 36, Main Street, Pettah.

The sole proprietor of the business is Mr. P. F. Goonesekere, to whose ability and enterprise is due the noteworthy expansion it has attained in so comparatively short a period.

The firm's telegraphic address is " Dove," and they use Bentley's code. Their agents in London are Messrs. J. R. Martin and Co., Ltd., 31, Budge Row, Cannon Street, E.C.4, and in Germany Messrs. Mather, Iken, and Co., South Sea Buildings, 9, Lange Muhren, Hamburg.

A. F. RAYMOND and CO., Undertakers, " Raymond House," Kanatta.

Messrs. A. F. Raymond and Co., members of the British Undertakers' Association and Undertakers to His Majesty's Army and Navy, have been established since 1885, and their business is the principal one of its kind in Ceylon. The firm's premises are conveniently situated close to Kanatta Cemetery, and are equipped with everything conducive to the speedy and perfect execution of orders. A business such as this is different from any others, and requires discretion and tact in the sad necessity that brings it customers. Messrs. A. F. Raymond and Co.'s long experience of their trade and the efficient and sympathetic way in which they carry out everything committed to their trust has won for them the highest reputation amongst all classes of people. They do embalming and exhumations for shipment abroad and supply coffins and caskets of every description, from the cheapest up to productions of the richest and costliest materials. Messrs. A. F. Raymond and Co. are the only undertaking firm in Ceylon who have motor as well as horse hearses, and these are appointed in keeping with their solemn and dignified purpose. The firm also undertake cremations and make arrangements for that work to be performed at any of the local cemeteries.

The completeness of Messrs. A. F. Raymond and Co.'s activities is further demonstrated by their operations in the production of all kinds of marble monuments of choice designs. They obtain their marble from the world's chief source of supply, Carara, Italy, and the lettering they do on the grave stones is of imperishable black lead, hammered into the excavations in the marble. The founder of the business, Mr. A. F. Raymond, died in 1910, and the partners in it now are his sons, Messrs. Arthur Arion, S. R., L. L., C. E., H. L., and M. F. Raymond, each of whom takes an active part in its management.

IN MEMORY OF CEYLONESE FALLEN IN THE WAR 1914-1918.
(Memorial supplied and erected by A. F. Raymond and Co.)

P. N. KAPADIA,
General Merchant, Fourth Cross Street, Pettah, and " Pettah Commercial Stores," Dam Street.

Fourth Cross Street is an exceedingly busy thoroughfare and typical of the many other similar streets in the Pettah district, where so many of the native merchants have their premises. Amongst the largest of these merchandising concerns is the business founded in 1887 by the late Mr. P. N. Kapadia, and now managed for his family by Mr. C. N. Lakdawalla, who has been connected with it for many years. Through the firm's establishment in the thoroughfare mentioned are received and despatched large quantities of provisions, especially flour, in which the firm's trade runs into about 6,000 bags of 196 lbs. each per month. The front section is in the form of a general store, and at the back is excellent warehouse accommodation for the materials in which the firm deal.

There is a branch of the business, entitled " Pettah Commercial Stores," in Dam Street, where all kinds of groceries, provisions, oilmen's stores, and general household requirements are kept in extensive variety. The firm's telegraphic address is " Anchor," Colombo.

THE CEYLON BAKERY, Chatham Street.

It is certainly very remarkable that amongst all peoples bread, the staff of life, never becomes a surfeit to the palate like most other foods. Nevertheless, there are many kinds of bread—good, bad, or indifferent, and good bread is probably the most commendable of all human productions. The Ceylon Bakery apparently think so judging by the care they take in the quality of their output—light, wholesome, palatable and beautifully browned loaves perfectly baked, of which they turn out about 1,500 lbs. daily, besides all manner of delicious cakes and pastries. They also make to order rich and ornate cakes for birthdays, weddings, and other festive occasions, in a large variety of very charming designs. The firm are army contractors and suppliers to naval contractors.

The business, established since 1885, is the largest of its kind in Colombo, and gives employment to about 70 persons. In Chatham Street the firm have popular tea rooms where their cakes and imported chocolates are obtainable. Their bakery premises are situated in Pettah and Slave Island. The present company was formed in 1925, and the general manager is Mr. C. M. Nilgiria.

J. B. PINTO and SONS, Druggists and Dispensing Chemists, 30 Chatham Street.

All business undertakings represent varying degrees of utility and importance. None, however, is more necessary than that of the druggist and dispensing chemist, on whose service and supplies hang frequently the issues of life and death. Amongst Colombo's representative firms in that connection mention must be made of Messrs. J. B. Pinto and Sons, who endeavour to exemplify the care and efficiency so indispensable in the pharmaceutical trade, especially in the making up of doctors' prescriptions, when the slightest inattention or forgetfulness may lead to irremediable and lamentable consequences. In a climate like that of Colombo it is imperative that pharmaceutical goods should be as fresh and pure as possible. Accordingly, Messrs. J. B. Pinto and Sons regulate their stock so that, while sufficient to meet the demands of their trade, it is not too bulky but just of the right quantity to ensure its perfection. They obtain their importations direct from the leading sources of manufacture in England, where the firm are held in due regard.

Messrs. J. P. Pinto and Sons commenced business in 1896 at 43, Chatham Street, and removed in 1914 into their present more commodious and attractive establishment. The firm's telegraphic address is " Pintosons," Colombo.

BRITISH-CEYLON TRADING CO., Merchants and Manufacturers' Representatives, 17, Baillie Street.

The British-Ceylon Trading Co. was established in 1922, and was reconstructed in 1924. The company operate as general merchants and importers of hardware, cement, cutlery, oilmen's stores, flour, glassware, enamelware, electro-plated goods, rugs, carpets, etc. As exporters they handle all classes of Ceylon produce, but especially ebony, satin, and teak woods. There are branches of the business at Kandy, Galle, and Jaffna. The partners are Messrs. M. Benjamin and C. P. Chelladurai. The company's cable address is " Bensdor," and the codes used are Bentley's and the A B C 5th edition. They are sole agents in Ceylon for the following:

A. Boake Roberts & Co., Ltd., London.
F. A. C. Van der Linden & Co., Hamburg.
Mesmaekers Freres, Belgium.
Rotterdam Cheese Co., Holland.
George Beruhardt, Leipzig.
Gustav Engel, Berlin.
D. R. Simpson & Co., Bombay.
The Noble Dairy, Bombay.

The British-Ceylon Trading Co. own and operate **THE COLOMBO SHIP-CHANDLERY CO.**, Stevedores and Dubashes, which was established in 1924.

A. V. R. A. ADYCAPPA CHETTY, General Merchant, 15-22, Seat Street, Pettah

One of the most prominent and influential names in the busy and interesting Pettah district of Colombo is that of A. V. R. A. Adycappa Chetty, whose business, established by him in 1887, is familiarly referred to as the " A. V. R. A.," and is concerned chiefly with wholesale trade in perfumes, oilmen's stores, haberdashery, condiments, preserved foods, etc. He is agent for Dr. George Dralle's soaps and perfumes, The Indo-Petroleum Co.'s candles, etc., and sub-agent for Lever Bros.' " Sunlight " soap, etc. In the title of the business the A. indicates grandfather, the letters V. R. his son, and A. the son of the latter. The son of Mr. A. V. R. A. Adycappa Chetty, Mr. A. Veerappa Chetty, has travelled extensively throughout Europe for the purpose of studying business methods and conditions, and is now in charge of the concern. The firm's telegraphic address is " Avra," and the codes used are the A B C 5th and 6th editions, Bentley's, and private.

WIJAYARATNA and CO., Newsagents and Booksellers, Manning Mansions, Slave Island.

Bookselling is usually only a department of the concerns by which it is carried on in the Orient; but Messrs. Wijayaratna and Co. are devoted to it entirely, and are the only firm in Ceylon with that distinction. It may, therefore, be assumed, and rightly, that their stock is thoroughly comprehensive and representative of modern literature in its most popular phases. Their establishment in Manning Mansions has a glass frontage of about 50 feet, and in its commodious interior may be found reading matter to suit all tastes grave and gay—books to be treasured after perusal, and others, cheap editions, not meant to endure but to while away hours of recreation and rest, together with all the well-known magazines and illustrated periodicals.

The firm have been for about ten years Ceylon Government Railway bookstall contractors, and acted similarly for a previous period of fifteen years. The business was established in 1887 by Mr. M. Z. Wijayaratna, but was taken over in 1909 by his nephew, Mr. V. D. de Fonseka, the present proprietor, who left the original name unchanged. That gentleman is a specialist in rare books on Ceylon, of which he has a magnificent collection, some of them being about 200 years old. The firm's telegraphic address is " Wijita," Colombo.

PERERA and SON,

Bakers and Confectioners, Steuart Place, Colpetty, and Bristol Hotel Building, Fort.

THERE is nothing more common than a loaf of bread; there are few things cheaper; but there is nothing more intrinsically valuable; nothing more continually used and yet less considered. Behind the golden crust is a more precious equivalent than can be extracted from the gold mine; and behind the silken texture of the snowy crumb is something more beautiful than the hangings of kings' palaces. People doubtless do not have such thoughts about the bread made by Messrs. Perera and Son, but that is the fault of the people, not of the bread. Light delicious bread made by them, when regarded as emblematic of the staff of the Commonwealth, is of more importance than the gold standards of nations.

Messrs. Perera and Son supply much of the bread consumed in the homes of the principal European and other local residents. They are also popular for their many varieties of confectionery and cakes, including beautiful and artistic examples of all kinds for weddings. birthdays, and festive occasions.

The firm's bakery at Colpetty gives employment to 50 persons, and at the time of writing arrangements are being made for its complete remodelling and equipment with the latest machinery pertaining to the trade, as the result of the visit of its proprietor, Mr. K. A. Albert Perera, to Great Britain and Germany for the purpose of studying the best baking plants in that connection there.

The business was started in 1907 by Mr. Charles Perera, who retired in 1921, leaving it under the sole control of his son, Mr. K. A. A. Perera already referred to. The firm's telegraphic address is " Pastry," Colombo.

NEW CENTRAL BOOT WORKS, 16, Baillie Street.

ALL the operations in the production of boots and shoes are performed by machinery in the great factories in America and Europe devoted to that branch of industry, and to-day it is seldom that one comes across a firm maintaining the ideals and traditions of the shoe-makers' craft as it used to be conducted entirely by hand. Such a firm, however, is found in the one carrying on business under the name of the New Central Boot Works. That undertaking is an interesting contrast to the ordinary stores where footwear is obtainable *en masse*, and not according to order. Shoes made to fit the exact measurements of one's feet are naturally much more likely to prove comfortable than those made on standard scale. Furthermore, the hand-made article has always been regarded as much better and more reliable in every way than the product of mass production by machinery.

But, be that as it may, the New Central Boot Works of Colombo is serving an excellent role, and is deserving of every encouragement. Boots and shoes are made there to suit every requirement, and the materials in which they can be produced offer a wide selection to customers, who may, if they so desire, provide their own. Many factory-made boots and shoes are of very inferior substance, which is not detected until they are subjected to wet and hard wear. The high quality leather supplied by the New Central Boot Works is well calculated to withstand the roughest usage. The firm are also leather merchants and importers of everything associated with gentlemen's outfitting, haberdashery, etc.

The business has been established since 1912, and the managing partner is Mr. W. S. Silva.

H. M. GUNASEKARA,

Broker, Auctioneer, Valuer and Commission Agent, Marlborough House, Union Place, Slave Island.

MARLBOROUGH HOUSE, Union Place, Slave Island, is an address historically suggestive and reminiscent, but it is much more interesting than anything that can be inferred from its nomenclature, for is it not the place where Colombo's regular weekly auction sales are held—auction sales that solve many an economic problem and bring profit and pleasure to many persons. The goods assembled there week after week are as varied as human necessity, and eloquent of the mutability of human affairs—things of beauty and utility for ordinary circumstances or uncommon purposes, articles of every material, cloth and leather, wood and steel, silver and gold, glass and china, books and pictures, articles common and unique, familiar and mysterious. Nowhere in Colombo is a better resort for the seeker of curios and valuable objects of art, for Mr. H. M. Gunasekara, proprietor of the business, was for thirteen years an official of the Colombo Museum and Library, and is a greatly experienced connoisseur in odds and ends of old china, jewellery, and the infinity of articles for the curio cabinet and the places of distinctive display. Mr. Gunasekara's auctioneering services are highly appreciated when houses have to be given up and their contents disposed of. He has very many testimonials in that connection, including a large number from prominent people thanking him for the able and satisfactory manner in which their goods and chattels had been sold, and the unexpectedly high prices which he had obtained for them.

Mr. Gunasekara is the only person in Colombo who sells stamps by auction. He has been established since 1912, and operates also as a broker, valuer, and commission agent.

M. B. UDUMAN, Proprietor of Travellers' Mart Pharmacy, Travellers' Mart, Travellers' Motor Touring Co., York House, York Street.

At the head of York Street is the Travellers' Mart Pharmacy, which is well named in view of the comprehensive assortment of necessary things provided there for the traveller by sea or land. No goods are more imperative than those pertaining to the prevention and remedying of pain and illness and the enhancement of physical welfare, and it is in such things that the Travellers' Mart Pharmacy caters with thorough understanding of the pharmaceutical trade. The great development which has taken place in patent medicines, for instance, is exemplified in the establishment in question by the many famous specifics included in its stock, together with all kinds of toilet articles, perfumery, etc. The making up of doctors' prescriptions is an important department of the business, and is in charge of a qualified expert.

YORK HOUSE AND TRAVELLERS' MART PHARMACY.

The business was founded many years ago under the name of Fort Cash Chemists, and used to be located at No. 1b, Chatham Street. In 1926 it was taken over by Mr. M. B. Uduman, who is a very successful merchant, and has many interests in Colombo, including a good deal of land and house property.

Mr. Uduman is owner of the business carried on under the name of the Travellers' Mart, also at the head of York Street, where a very comprehensive assortment of tobacco, cigars, and cigarettes meets all requirements in that connection and justifies the popularity of the concern amongst smokers. The Travellers' Mart is also noteworthy as printer and publisher of Ceylon picture postcards, of which it has one of the largest and best selections in the island.

Mr. Uduman likewise owns and operates the Travellers' Motor Touring Co., which has an excellent fleet of the latest seven-seater cars in charge of experienced and careful drivers.

Mr. Uduman's telegraphic address is "Enver," and the codes used by him are the 4th and 5th editions of Bentley's, and private.

S. W. WALLES and CO., Livery Stable-Keepers, Veterinarians and Shoeing Smiths, Importers of Horses; Carriage-builders, Undertakers, and Commission Agents, 79, Union Place.

At the beginning of the present century the horse still retained its indispensability to human requirements, and was the chief medium for the conveyance of goods and people on country road and city street. Although the coming of the motor vehicle has relegated it to the limbo of the obsolete, the noble animal that has served humanity throughout the ages in peace and war is still in evidence in Colombo, as in other centres of population, and the principal concern there in association with horses is that of Messrs. S. W. Walles and Co., which, established in 1878, is reminiscent of the times when the livery stablekeeper's facilities and resources contributed very much to the daily routine of business and pleasure. In pre-motoring days Messrs. S. W. Walles and Co.'s operations in the importation of horses were on an extensive scale. Their trade in that connection is now, of course, very much smaller, although in the importation of racehorses and estate hacks they still operate fairly well considering the changed times. The firm devote special attention to the reception, care, and despatch of horses to any part of the world.

In former days, too, Messrs. S. W. Walles and Co. were the principal coach and carriage builders and saddle and harness makers in Colombo. They also still continue these branches of trade, and exercise great care in endeavouring to exemplify the skilled workmanship with which they have always been associated. This is well demonstrated by their activities as manufacturers of boots and shoes, all of which are made by hand on the old-fashioned principles, when the shoemaker's craft and its traditions had not been ousted by machinery.

Messrs. S. W. Walles and Co. have likewise been prominent as funeral furnishers and undertakers. To them have been entrusted the funerals of Governors and many prominent people; and in the firm's office may be seen a testimonial regarding the very efficient manner in which they embalmed and despatched to Europe the body of one of the Governors of Indo-China.

The proprietor of the business is Mr. S. D. Walles, grandson of the original founder.

A. C. SUMPS and SON, Manufacturers of Rattan, Bamboo, Coir and Khus-Khus Goods, 24, Union Place.

A visit to the premises of Messrs. A. C. Sumps and Son affords an interesting insight into the manufacture of cane furniture, especially of the best quality. This firm have been established since 1859, and the great variety of their artistic designs in chairs and settees, cradles, baskets, and everything that can be made of the materials handled, is well worth inspection by visitors to the port. Behind the office and showroom is the factory, where the highly-skilled workers are engaged in their respective occupations, each of them specialising in various branches of the trade. Particularly noteworthy is the firm's cane matting, which is practically indestructible, and is made to order in any measurements. It is excellently adapted for covering the floors of dining-rooms, drawing-rooms, bedrooms, bathrooms, etc. It requires no tacks nor nails to hold it in position, for its own weight does that, and it can be folded up instantly for cleaning or storage. The cane used by Messrs. A. C. Sumps and Son is the best quality of Singapore cane, which is very much better for manufacture into furniture than the cane grown in Ceylon.

At the Wembley Exhibition Messrs. A. C. Sumps and Son were awarded a gold medal for the high-class character of their productions, a fact that speaks more eloquently than columns of printed eulogy. As already mentioned, their business was established in 1859, and was taken over in 1921 by the present proprietor, Mr. Edwin Pate.

P. D. SIEBEL, Horticulturist, Turret Road and Flower Road, Cinnamon Gardens.

In the beautiful district of the Cinnamon Gardens are situated the extensive gardens which, founded by the late Mr. P. D. Siebel, render to the people of Colombo a service that is very highly appreciated. That service places before them practically the entire floral resources for which the island is famous. The horticulturist's trade in Great Britain is greatly hampered by seasonal limitations and the long winter when floral decorations are restricted to evergreens and hothouse productions. In Ceylon it is summer all the year round; and so in the delightful Siebel gardens is concentrated everything that can be utilised in plant, tree, and flower for the expression of joy or sorrow or the pleasure of daily routine in home decoration. The Siebel gardens are in two sections of several acres each. One is exactly opposite Victoria Park, and the other not far away in Flower Road. The flora of Ceylon is very rich, comprising upwards of 3,000 flowering plants and ferns, or three times as many as in the British Isles. It can, therefore, be well understood how great are the Siebel resources in the supply of everything pertaining to horticulture. An example of this was afforded at the Colombo Motor Exhibition of 1927, to which the Siebel gardens supplied more than 1,500 plants for decorative purposes. From these gardens are obtainable all kinds of plants and trees on hire at very moderate rates. Particularly noteworthy is the versatility manifested there in the supply of funeral wreaths, which are made up in exquisite designs to suit every requirement.

It is interesting to note that at the Colombo Agri-Horticulturist Exhibition in 1899 Mr. Siebel received a gold medal for his plants and flowers, the only one ever given in that connection in the island. A branch of the business is established at Kandy.

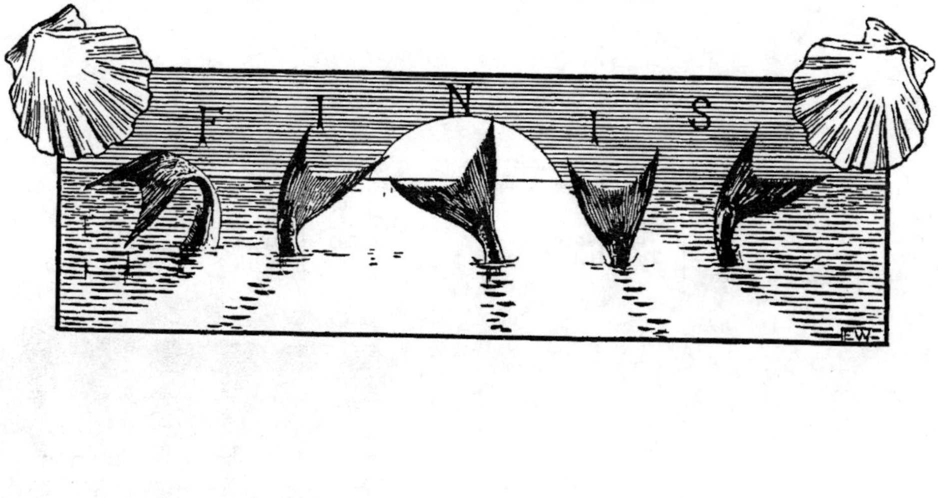

INDEX.

CEYLON AND COLOMBO.

HISTORICAL AND DESCRIPTIVE—Pages 397-431.

CEYLON AND COLOMBO—*continued.*

INDEX.

COMMERCIAL COLOMBO.